African Development in the 21st Century

African Development in the 21st Century: Adebayo Adedeji's Theories and Contributions

===========❖===========

Edited by:
Amos Sawyer
Afeikhena Jerome
Ejeviome Eloho Otobo

AFRICA WORLD PRESS
TRENTON | LONDON | CAPE TOWN | NAIROBI | ADDIS ABABA | ASMARA | IBADAN

AFRICA WORLD PRESS
541 West Ingham Avenue | Suite B
Trenton, New Jersey 08638

Copyright © 2015 Amos Sawyer, Afeikhena Jerome and Ejeviome Eloho Otobo

All rights reserved. No part of this publication may be reproduced, stored in a retrieval system or transmitted in any form or by any means electronic, mechanical, photocopying, recording or otherwise without the prior written permission of the publisher.

Cover design: Courtesy of Wits University Press

Library of Congress Cataloging-in-Publication Data

African development in the 21st century : reflections on Adebayo Adedeji's theories and contributions / edited by Amos Sawyer, Afeikhena Jerome and Ejeviome Eloho Otobo.
   page cm
  Foreword by Joaquim Alberto Chissano.
  Includes bibliographical references and index.
  ISBN 978-1-59221-976-6 (hard cover) -- ISBN 978-1-59221-977-3 (pbk.) 1. Adedeji, Adebayo--Influence. 2. Africa--Economic policy. 3. Economic development--Africa. 4. Africa--Economic conditions--21st century. 5. Structural adjustment (Economic policy)--Africa. I. Sawyer, Amos, editor of compilation. II. Jerome, Afeikhena, editor of compilation, author. III. Otobo, Ejeviome Eloho, editor of compilation, author. IV. Adedeji, Adebayo, honouree.
  HC800.A5654 2014
  338.96--dc23
                                    2013045213

TABLE OF CONTENTS

List of Tables and Figures VII

Acknowledgements IX

Abbreviations and Acronyms XI

Foreword XIII
Joaquim Alberto Chissano

Introduction 1
Amos Sawyer, Afeikhena Jerome and Ejeviome Eloho Otobo

Part 1. Reflections On Policies And Strategies For Africa's Development 15

Chapter 1. Contemporary Perspectives on The Lagos Plan of Action and Structural Adjustment in the 1980s 17
Richard Jolly

Chapter 2. The Rediscovery of the African Alternative Framework to Structural Adjustment Programmes 29
Ali Abdel Gadir Ali

Chapter 3. Stabilization, Structural Adjustment and Sustainable Development of Sub-Saharan Africa 53
Ademola Ariyo And Babajide Fowowe

Part 2. Regional Integration and Cooperation 75

Chapter 4. A Tale of Two Prophets: Jean Monnet and Adebayo Adedeji 77
Adekeye Adebajo

Chapter 5. African Integration and Development 91
Yousif A. Suliman

Part 3. Building Institutions and Finances towards the Development of Africa 115

Chapter 6. African Countries: Three Deficits and Three Futures 117
Ejeviome Eloho Otobo

Chapter 7. Institution Building for Development in Africa 139
Hesphina Rukato

Chapter 8. Africa's Development Agenda after the Global Economic and Financial Crisis of 2008-2009 159
Afeikhena Jerome, Oluyele Akinkugbe and Francis Chigunta

Part 4. Conflict, Democracy and Development in Africa 189

Chapter 9. Causes of Conflict and the Dynamics of Conflict Activation 191
James Katorobo

Contributors 207

Index 209

LIST OF TABLES AND FIGURES

List of tables

Table 3.1: Average macroeconomic variables for selected countries before and after SAP 59
Table 3.2: Test for differences between pre- and post-SAP data 60
Table 5.1 RECs' objectives, status and overlaps 100
Table 5.2: Sectoral goals of RECs 102
Table 6.1: Factors of production as sources of economic growth in historical perspective 129
Table 6.2: Commodity dependency and diversification of selected African economies, 2011-2012 133
Table 7.1: The eight RECs recognized by the AU and the other six integration blocs 147
Table 7.2 RECs and their objectives 148

List of figures

Figure 3.1: Real GDP growth rate: aggregate and per capita 61
Figure 3.2: Agriculture value added as a ratio to GDP 63
Figure 3.3: Prices of agricultural products 65

Figure 3.4: Sub-Saharan Africa (SSA) and OECD human development indicators (HDI), 1980–2000 66
Figure 5.1 African development and interdependence 93
Figure 7.1: Objectives of the African Union 144
Figure 8.1: Growth performance of different regions of the world, 1960–2010 167
Figure 9.1 Potential fault lines that result in the breakdown of peace 195

ACKNOWLEDGEMENTS

This book, written in honor of Adebayo Adedeji, is a collaborative work; and as such, each individual contributor is indebted to friends and professional colleagues. We sincerely appreciate contributors' patience and dedication in revising their chapters, as well as their commitment to academic rigor and quality. However, our greatest appreciation goes to the contributors who have been close associates of Adebayo Adedeji in the course of his illustrious career at national and international levels.

Many others have enriched the book by providing their valuable critiques. We would like to express our gratitude, in particular, to Omotunde Johnson, Olu Ajakaiye, Bayo Olukoshi, Said Adejumobi, Laura Nyirinkinde, Abdulazeez Jalloh and Emmanuel Nnadozie who were kind enough to peer review various chapters. Patrick Edebor and Alex Gboyega also provided invaluable editorial assistance.

The co-editors would also like to thank Roshan Cader, commissioning editor at Witwatersrand University Press, and her colleagues for their unflinching support and professionalism. We are extremely grateful to the two anonymous reviewers from the University of Witwatersrand, Johannesburg for helping to focus and reshape the book.

Finally, we would like to express our gratitude to our families and friends for their understanding and consistent support as we navigated through various phases of the project.

Amos Sawyer,
Afeikhena Jerome
and
Ejeviome Eloho Otobo

ABBREVIATIONS AND ACRONYMS

AAF-SAP	African Alternative Framework to Structural Adjustment Programs for Socio-Economic Recovery and Transformation
ACDESS	African Centre for Development and Strategic Studies
AEC	African Economic Community (Abuja Treaty)
AfDB	African Development Bank
APRM	African Peer Review Mechanism
AU	African Union (Formerly, OAU)
BWI	Bretton Wood Institutions
CDF	Comprehensive Development Framework
CEMAC	Central African Monetary and Economic Community
CENSAD	Community of Sahel-Saharan States
CEPGL	Economic Community of the Great Lakes Countries
CODESRIA	Council for the Development of Social Science Research in Africa
COMESA	Common Market for Eastern and Southern Africa
EAC	East African Community
ECCAS	Economic Community of Central African States
ECOWAS	Economic Community of West African States
ECSC	European Coal and Steel Community
IGAD	Intergovernmental Authority on Development
IMF	International Monetary Fund
IOC	Indian Ocean Commission
LPA	Lagos Plan of Action
MDGs	Millennium Development Goals

MRU	Mano River Union
NEPAD	New Partnership for Africa's Development
NIEO	New International Economic Order
OAU	Organization of African Unity (now AU)
OPEC	Organization of Petroleum Exporting Countries
PTA	Preferential Trade Area for Eastern and Southern Africa
RECs	Regional Economic Communities
SACU	Southern African Customs Union
SADC	Southern African Development Community
UEMOA	West African Economic and Monetary Union
UN	United Nations
UNECA	United Nations Economic Commission for Africa
UNPAAERD	United Nations Program of Action for African Economic Recovery and Development

FOREWORD

Africa is stepping onto a new and higher growth and development trajectory. After a brief spurt of post-independence growth and the disappointing and widely acknowledged dismal performance of the 1980s, which Adebayo Adedeji referred to as ‚the lost decade' in Africa, the development community entered the 1990s with an emerging new consensus on African development. At the beginning of the last decade, a new crop of African leaders took the lead in charting the continent's revival. They launched the African Union in 2002, effectively replacing the Organization of African Unity which had been the premier continental organization in Africa and elaborated an economic vision under the New Partnership for African Development, emphasizing sound economic policies, good governance and accountability.

Many African countries are today making tangible progress towards democratization, a reduction in the number of conflicts and the promotion of broad-based citizen participation in both the economic and political spheres of their countries. Over the past one-and-a-half decades, several African countries have held multi-party elections, sometimes for the first time. While elections have not always been flawless, the direction is clear: Africa is witnessing a real movement towards better governance, a prerequisite for development. Macroeconomic policies are much improved across the continent and efforts are underway to strengthen corporate governance.

Despite this progress, it is nevertheless obvious that Africa still has a long road to travel with regard to sustainable development.

Africa entered the 21st century with a surfeit of deficits, such as poverty, rapid urbanization, gender inequality, and food insecurity. There is growing recognition that, if African countries are to be launched on a path of sustained growth and economic transformation, they must dedicate more efforts to building economic and political institutions that are pro-development, strengthen the rule of law and ensure the efficient delivery of social services. Too much of Africa's growth is coming from the export of natural resources and commodities with very little value addition. Indeed, manufacturing continues to account for low share of the Gross Domestic Product – contributing less than 10 per cent of GDP – in many of the larger economies of the region. In part, this is attributable to a reflection of the dominance of agriculture and in part to the persisting weaknesses in adapting science and technological innovations to the agricultural and industrial production in the region.

This book, written to honor Adebayo Adedeji, the intellectual leader of Africa's quest for home-grown approaches to development and good governance, sheds new light on many of the difficult policy challenges that Adedeji tackled during his career. His capacity and commitment to speak for Africa and on African issues remains unmatched, especially when he was Executive Secretary of the United Nations Economic Community for Africa (UNECA). He has been a brilliant, confident and tenacious proponent of African development. Moreover, Adebayo Adedeji is also a highly respected African statesman and one of Africa's most astute practitioners of public policy.

Adebayo Adedeji's contributions to Africa's development, especially during his tenure as Executive Secretary of UNECA, are wide ranging. They spanned regional cooperation and integration: Adedeji spearheaded the formation of the Economic Community of West African States, the Preferential Trading Area Common Market of Eastern and Southern Africa and the Economic Community of Central African States; he articulated the *African Alternative Framework to Structural Adjustment Programme in Africa* (1988–1989) which first led to "adjustment with a human face", and ultimately led to the focus on poverty reduction. As an economic thinker, he is the original designer of the conceptual framework of sub-regional integration in West Africa, and the Lagos Plan of Action for Africa (1980–2000).

FOREWORD

The contributions in this book focus on Adebayo Adedeji's theories and contributions to Africa's development during his long and distinguished career at the national, continental and international levels. They honor a very deserving servant of Africa who has left a legacy of disciplined scholarship, bold and creative thinking and a deep and abiding faith in Africa and its enormous potential and possibilities for transformation. With this legacy attesting to his true worth, it is not at all surprising that Adebayo Adedeji has been named by Routledge among the fifty most influential thinkers of the 20th century and the early 21st century.

This book, therefore, is a fitting tribute to a man of grand stature and a role model for many yet to come. It is also a landmark contribution to unraveling Africa's development trajectory since independence and a major reference source and compendium for all those interested in the past, present and future of Africa's development process.

H. E. Joaquim Alberto Chissano
Former President of Mozambique

INTRODUCTION

Amos Sawyer, Afeikhena Jerome and Ejeviome Eloho Otobo

Africa's "lost decade" and Adedeji's influence

Generally acknowledged as a "lost decade" for Africa's development, the 1980s were marked by dismal economic performance, reflected in low economic growth and even stagnation, high external indebtedness, weak commodity prices and – worst of all – the beginning of de-industrialization from an already weak industrial base. The decade was also characterized by the last vestiges of Africa's anti-colonial struggles and political instability, resulting in frequent coups d'état that led to a high prevalence of military regimes across the region and in civil wars. During the "lost decade", Africa's current trajectory of rapid growth and the generally positive outlook portrayed in the *Financial Times* (11–16 March 2013) and in *The Economist* ("A Hopeful Continent", 2–8 March 2013) looked unlikely and distant. In an ironic twist of history, Europe is now the region undergoing economic crisis. However, as will be shown later in this book, the brighter prospects that have indeed materialized since the mid1990s were envisioned in "the willed future" that United Nations Economic Commission for Africa (UNECA) articulated while under the leadership of Adebayo Adedeji, a distinguished scholar and committed public servant.

During this period, when poor economic performance twinned with political instability in Africa, three developments emerged that would shape the continent's prospects. First, the 1980s coincided with the structural adjustment programs that the Bretton Woods Institutions – the International Monetary Fund and the World Bank – imposed on many African countries to promote reforms of their economies. Second, as the negative effects of the structural adjustment programs began to be felt in Africa and elsewhere, fierce policy debate ensued between protagonists and critics. Third, the coincidence of dismal economic performance with political instability led to the realization that poor governance resulted in weak institutions and a lack of political inclusion and that widespread corruption was a major cause of Africa's lack of development. This was the context in which Adedeji worked during his stewardship of UNECA from 1975–1991.

Born in 1930 in Ijebu-Ode, Ogun State, Nigeria, Adedeji received his bachelor's degree in Economics from the University College, Leicester and went on to earn a master's degree in Public Administration from Harvard University and a doctorate in Economics from the University of London in 1967. He has been awarded honorary degrees from eight universities across the world, the latest being the University of Johannesburg, South Africa, in March 2008.

After his tenure as professor of Public Administration and director of the Institute of Administration at the University of Ife (now Obafemi Awolowo University), in Ife-Ife, Nigeria, Adedeji served as Nigeria's Federal Commissioner (Minister) for Economic Development and Reconstruction from 1971–1975. From there, Adedeji went on to have a successful and distinguished career, assuming the position of Under Under-Secretary-General and, Executive Secretary of UNECA.

Adedeji's professional engagement as both scholar and practitioner focused intensely on developing a paradigm for African development that was African-driven, reliant upon indigenous factor inputs and that promoted African regional integration. After independence, when the French and British sought to maintain strong ties with their former colonies through the Organization internationale de la Francophonie and the British Commonwealth – thereby creating a bigger challenge for those who advocated a regional approach to the development of post-independence Africa – it was Adedeji who came up with a design for the establishment of the Economic Community of West African States (ECOWAS). After he joined UNECA in 1975, he led the efforts to create the

INTRODUCTION

Preferential Trading Area (PTA) which was replaced by the Common Market for Eastern and Southern Africa (COMESA), and Economic Community of Central African States (ECCAS). Indeed, given his interest in and contribution to pan-African integration, he has been compared to Jean Monnet, the French political economist widely regarded as the "father" of European integration because of the lead positions that he occupied in the formative institution of the High Authority of the European Coal and Steel Community (ECSC) – the precursor to the European Economic Community.

Adedeji's prominence in international circles was mainly the result of his stewardship of UNECA from 1975–1991. His contributions to Africa's development during his tenure as Executive Secretary were wide-ranging and profound, especially in three areas: establishing a database for quantitative and qualitative social and economic research, so that policy research could be grounded in empirical reality; strengthening Africa's human capacity for policy research and implementation; and constructing African-centered development frameworks and strategies, as distinct from and opposed to reliance upon models of development formulated to promote a conception of development that did not situate the people of Africa at its core. Under Adedeji's leadership, UNECA established or inspired the establishment of institutions for economic management and technical cooperation; deepened the undertaking of economic analysis and forecasting; accelerated regional cooperation and integration and sharpened the articulation of policies and strategies for Africa's development.

Adedeji was insistent on the development and implementation of African-centered development policies and programs at a time when the Washington Consensus, as developed by the Bretton Woods Institutions and adopted by the powerful western nations, was the dominant paradigm for development imposed on developing countries. Through rigorous analyses and extensive continent-wide consultations undertaken in the late 1970s, UNECA, under Adedeji's leadership, articulated the *Monrovia Strategy for the Economic, Social and Cultural Development of Africa* (1979) which was transmuted into the *Lagos Plan of Action for the Economic Development of Africa, 1980–2000* (Organization of African Unity, 1981) which broke with the Washington Consensus. This did not go down well with the Bretton Woods Institutions and those countries that controlled them. The World Bank immediately countered with its *Accelerated Development in*

3

sub-Saharan Africa: An Agenda for Action (1981). While the Monrovia Strategy and the Lagos Plan of Action (LPA) focused on a self-reliant, self-sustaining and regional approach to Africa's development, the World Bank's 'Accelerated Development in sub-Saharan Africa' emphasized the acceleration of raw-material exportation and the reinforcement of colonial economic ties. As Adedeji put it himself, "battles" were waged "for the African mind".[1]

Adedeji's combined work on advocacy for and prognostications on economic policy for Africa suggests comparisons with Raul Prebisch, the Argentinian economist, who also used his stewardship of the United Nations Economic Commission for Latin America and Caribbean (1950–1963) to challenge the prevailing orthodoxy in development circles. Adedeji used African political structures, such as the organs of the Organization of African Unity, as the owners and purveyors of African-centered development strategies and, in so doing, rallied Africa behind his ideas. In April 1982, African ministers responsible for economic development and planning adopted the Declaration on the World Bank's *Accelerated Development in sub-Saharan Africa: An Agenda for Action* opposing the recommendations in that document and calling for the full implementation of the LPA[2]. This was a coup for Adedeji and a setback for the World Bank and its President, Barber Conable, who opposed Adedeji's African-centered approach to African development.

Under Adedeji's leadership, UNECA stoutly opposed the structural adjustment programs that were designed by the Bretton Woods Institutions as a solution to the crisis – which, in fact, had been partly caused by failed policies that had been dictated from abroad. UNECA's policy document, *African Alternative Framework to Structural Adjustment Programmes for Socio-Economic Recovery and Transformation* (AAF-SAP), was vigorously promoted by African countries and in 1989 adopted by the General Assembly of the

---

1 See Adebayo Adedeji, "The ECA: Forging a Future for Africa" in Berthelot, Y (ed.) 2004. *Unity and Diversity in Development Ideas: Perspectives from the UN Regional Commissions*. Bloomington: Indiana University Press (UN Intellectual History Project Series).

2 The full title of the World Bank's report of October 1981 is *Accelerated Development in sub-Saharan: An Agenda for Action*. The Declaration referred to was adopted in 1982 by the United Nations Economic Commission for Africa (ECA) Ministers against the World Bank's *Agenda for Action* and in support of the *Lagos of Plan of Action*.

United Nations with the United States being the only major western power opposed to it. This, indeed, was another triumph for Adedeji. In *The Power of UN Ideas: Lessons from the First 60 Years* (2005), Richard Jolly, Louis Emmerji and Tomas Weiss have noted that, "economic adjustment policies in sub-Saharan Africa and Latin America are now widely acknowledged to have been too narrow, too restrictive or too rushed. UNICEF, the Economic Commission for Africa and the International Labor Organization (ILO) argued for a broader approach from the mid-1980s". Indeed, AAF-SAP was the culmination of a long-running debate on appropriate economic policies for Africa, between UNECA, under Adedeji, and the Bretton Woods Institutions, that stretched back to 1976.

Adedeji believed development and democracy are two sides of the same coin and that one cannot be advanced without the other. Therefore, he championed efforts to deepen and make more inclusive the institutions of democratic governance in Africa. In pursuit of this belief, he pushed for the "International Conference on Popular Participation in the Recovery and Transformation Process in Africa" to be held in Arusha, Tanzania in 1990. The conference adopted the African Charter for popular participation in development and transformation, which, among other things, committed African governments, civil society organizations and sub-regional bodies to pursue inclusive participatory processes of governance and deepen their commitment to constitutional rule and electoral democracy.

Efforts to deepen democracy in African countries have since gained momentum and, as of February 2014, have been buttressed, most notably by the process of the African Peer Review Mechanism (APRM) to which 34 countries have voluntarily subscribed. Adedeji, himself served as a member of the APRM Review Panel from 2003–2010 and as its chair from July 2007 to July 2010. Moreover, civil society organizations and, in particular, women's organizations, are playing a greater role across the region.

In recognition of his meritorious service at various levels and his commitment to development in Africa, Adedeji received the International Gold Mercury Award in 1982 as well as the Arthur Houghton Star Crystal Award of the African-American Institute in 1991. In 2008, he received the Gordon Draper Award, a prize instituted by the Commonwealth Association for Public Administration and Management; again for commitment to excellence and visionary leadership. In 2006, David Simon identified Adebayo Adedeji as one of the fifty most influential development thinkers of the twentieth century[3]. He is also one of the 71 personalities who influenced the policy formulation and development paradigms of the United Nations System of Organizations.

The need to examine Adedeji's diverse contributions to Africa's development has informed the topics in this book. Written by scholars, policy-makers, policy advisers, political leaders, former and current senior United Nations officials, independent consultants and leaders of civil society organizations and think-tanks, the book covers a wide range of policy issues. It has two themes: Adedeji's contributions during his long and distinguished career at national, continental and international levels; and Africa's past challenges, present trends and future prospects. What emerges is that, not only was Adedeji a major player in helping Africa to cope with economic and political challenges in the 1980s, but some of the solutions that he proffered and that seemed controversial at the time have become part of conventional wisdom. No one expected that the journey from controversy to orthodoxy and consensus would be easy. Equally, no one should expect that African countries will find it easy to build its own institutions; to train its people to acquire managerial, scientific and technological skills to run their countries; and – for that matter – to assert their voice on regional and international affairs. Through Adedeji's firm commitment to alternative economic development practices for Africa and his defiance of orthodox beliefs, he has presented African leaders with alternative prospects, policies and strategies to consider in realizing Africa's growth and development. As these leaders confront a myriad of future challenges, it up is to them to implement the political will for these policies and strategies to enable sustainable development.

Structure of Prospects for African Development

African Development in the 21st Century is organized into four parts; with each one considering a major theme in African development. Part I presents reflections on the policies and strategies for Africa's

---

[3] See David Simon (ed) 2006. *Fifty Key Thinkers on Development*. Oxford and New York: Routledge.

development since 1976. Part 2 focuses on regional integration and cooperation. Part 3 examines some of the prognostications on, and institutional props for, Africa's development. Part 4 rounds off the discourse by presenting in-depth analyses of conflicts and development in Africa. The content and issues are shared across the parts and chapters, and these naturally overlap and interact. All the chapters have been written to contextualize, illustrate and illuminate the rich contributions to African economic development that Adedeji has made in the course of his regional and international public service.

Part 1: Reflections on policies and strategies for Africa's development

The three chapters in Part I examine different aspects of the policies and strategies on Africa's development dating back to 1976, a year after Adedeji assumed office as Executive Secretary of UNECA.

In Chapter 1, Richard Jolly, drawing from his personal experience of working closely with Adedeji, provides an insightful historical analysis of the battles he fought with the Bretton Woods Institutions over the appropriate economic and social policies for Africa's development. He notes that these battles were fought in three stages. The first salvo was fired by Adedeji in 1976 when the UNECA Secretariat produced the *Revised Framework of Principles for the Implementation of the New International Economic Order in Africa*. This framework for development was built on three pillars: promotion of an increasing measure of self-reliance; acceleration of growth and diversification, linked to local capacity; and progressive reduction of unemployment and mass poverty.

The second stage began with the publication of the *Lagos Plan of Action for the Economic Development of Africa, 1980–2000*, prepared for and adopted by UNECA Conference of Ministers and later endorsed at the meeting of Heads of State and Government held in Lagos in 1980. The publication of the *African Alternative Framework to Structural Adjustment Programmes for Socio-Economic Recovery and Transformation* (AAF-SAP) in 1989 was the third stage of the battle.

Following AAF-SAP, the World Bank published *Sub-Saharan Africa – From Crisis to Economic Growth: A Long-Term Perspective Study* (1989). Its tone and content were more sobering than previous World Bank reports on Africa. However, by this time the chorus of criticisms of structural adjustment had become so widespread and persistent that the president of the World Bank convened a meeting with the United Nations agencies and African regional organizations in May 1989 to reach a common understanding. Jolly concludes that "it is little consolation today that the alternatives presented at the time by UNECA were given so little attention and support by the main donor countries or by the World Bank and the IMF".

In Chapter 2, Ali Abdel Gadir Ali observes that, after the acknowledged failure of structural adjustment programs to achieve their growth objectives, most of the current ideas on promoting development in Africa involve the rediscovery of ideas that had been previously articulated by African policy makers and scholars; foremost among which is Adedeji. Ali's primary focus of analysis and comparison is the AAF-SAP published in 1989 under the leadership of Adedeji. Ali notes that it did not take long for the failure of structural adjustment programs to become evident to all: in 1999 – ten years after AAF-SAP was articulated – the tide of research evidence, policy advocacy and economic actions began to turn against Structural Adjustment Programs. Ali concludes that the policies of the democratically elected government of Malawi represent a final unraveling of structural adjustment and a validation of AAF-SAP.

In Chapter 3, Ademola Ariyo and Babajide Fowowe examine the features of the stabilization and structural adjustment programs imposed on African countries by the Bretton Woods Institutions and of *AAF-SAP*. The authors offer research findings on the impact of structural adjustment programs on African economic performance from 1970 to 2000; a timeframe enabling them to capture performance trends during the period before and after the structural adjustment programs. The authors provide statistical analysis to show the gap between the promise and performance of the Structural Adjustment Programs proposed by the World Bank.

Ariyo and Fowowe conclude Chapter 3 by posing the question: Why did the Bretton Woods Institutions continue to press on with the implementation of Structural Adjustment Programs, in view of the overwhelming evidence and criticism that they were not meeting the development needs they set out to address? They argue that the main motive for continuing was the need to lend more money; in addition, the uncritical acceptance of offers of external loan support to implement structural adjustment was facilitated by self-serving leadership in Africa that both lacked accountability and felt a sense of helplessness in the absence of financial support from the Bretton Woods Institutions.

Part 2: Regional integration and cooperation

In Chapter 4, Adekeye Adebajo assesses the role, vision and impact of two political gladiators from France and Nigeria respectively – Jean Monnet and Adebayo Adedeji – regarded as the fathers of regional integration in Europe and Africa. He draws a number of interesting parallels between the two men, despite their different backgrounds: they both assisted in reconstructing their respective economies after destructive civil wars (the Second World War, 1939–1945, for Monnet and the Nigerian Civil War, 1967–1970, for Adedeji); they both had distinguished careers in the international civil service; and they both devoted considerable energy to regional integration and were ultimately frustrated in their quests to unite Europe and Africa, respectively.

Adebajo notes further that Adedeji is widely regarded as being instrumental in the formation of ECOWAS, which he "midwifed" through using shuttle diplomacy while serving as Nigeria's Minister of Economic Planning. As an astute practitioner of public policy and an artful statesman, Adedeji exerted his influence on the design of ECOWAS and successfully navigated it through the policy-making labyrinths of the 16 West African countries. In addition to his formative role of ECOWAS, Adedeji's 17-year tenure at UNECA was eventful, as he converted the institution into a pan-African platform for forging regional integration and south-south cooperation.

In Chapter 5, Yousif Suliman documents the major contributions that Adedeji, under the authority of UNECA, made in promoting regional integration in Africa. Suliman ranks regional cooperation and integration as Africa's greatest challenge, and as Adedeji's most significant contribution to Africa's development. Some of Adedeji's achievements include the establishment of Regional Economic Communities (REC); the formation and strengthening of ECOWAS; the establishment of the Preferential Trade Area(PTA) for Eastern and Southern Africa – now the Common Market for Eastern and Southern Africa (COMESA) – as well as the Economic Community of Central African States (ECCAS); and the establishment of thirty UNECA-sponsored institutions all over the African continent, covering such diverse areas as development planning, cartography, aerospace surveys, engineering design and finance, among others.

Suliman concludes by arguing for a developmental approach to regional integration in Africa and proffers an agenda for regional integration on the continent, which he terms an "agenda for a willed future". The key elements of such an approach would include taking charge of Africa's destiny; building education and knowledge capacities in the context of regional integration; expanding sub-regional infrastructure networks; modernizing and expanding production sectors for diversification and competitiveness; creating conditions for the flow and retention of cross-border foreign investment; rationalizing Regional Economic Communities and empowering their supranational authority to enforce common community decisions.

Part 3: Building institutions and finances towards the development of Africa

In Chapter 6, Ejeviome Eloho Otobo calls attention to and builds on Adedeji's work on gauging Africa's future. He begins by noting that in 1983 UNECA, under the leadership of Adedeji, published a little-noticed but highly significant report, *ECA and Africa's Development 1983–2008: A Preliminary Perspective Study'*, which charted two possible scenarios – either pessimistic or optimistic – for Africa's development prospects over a 25-year period. The report referred to these scenarios as the historical trends scenario or "a horrendous future" (pessimistic) and the normative development scenario or "a willed future" (optimistic).

The predictions of the pessimistic scenario were two-fold: first, African countries would witness growing dependency on foreign imports and support; and second, they would witness a possible deterioration in their political, economic and social conditions. Otobo argues that, while there has been marked improvement in economic performance in the past decade, it is important to recognize the structural constraints that have impeded Africa's development in the past and still cast shadows over its long-term prospects. He refers to these structural constraints as deficits and identifies three of them: the stability deficit, the organizational deficit and the scientific deficit.

INTRODUCTION

Otobo concludes that the abilities of individual African countries to overcome the three deficits will determine what the future holds for each of them. The countries that make the most progress in addressing or overcoming the three deficits will emerge politically stable, socially cohesive and economically vibrant. In those country contexts, the good news about the region will endure and will comprehensively undermine the uniformly bleak portrayal of Africa that frequently dominates some foreign commentaries about the continent.

In Chapter 7, Hesphina Rukato reviews current approaches to institution building and makes the case for new approaches that are responsive to the development agenda of Africa. Rukato argues that institutions should reflect the people's development aspirations and their national values and should be based on their historical experiences. Drawing on President Obama's speech to the Ghanaian parliament in 2009, where he said that "Africa needs strong institutions as opposed to strong men", she concludes that the only way to advance the process of regional integration agreements is for African countries to provide adequate funding towards continental organization (*vis-a-vis* to the African Union) and to the Regional Economic Communities. For Rukato, it is inconceivable that a strategic objective such as regional integration should be left to the whims of financial support by Africa's foreign partners.

In Chapter 8, Afeikhena Jerome, Oluyele Akinkugbe and Francis Chigunta examine the problem of rethinking Africa's development agenda in the aftermath of the global economic and financial crisis of 2008 to 2009. They note that, while it was at first widely thought that Africa would not be affected because of its limited financial integration with the rest of the world, the continent – particularly the middle-income and resource-rich countries – was hard hit by the crisis, mainly through its secondary effects, notably due to loss of export earnings, reduced service earnings from tourism and remittances and less inflow of aid and other development assistance. The crisis also had discernible impacts on the social sectors and other human development indicators, threatening to further impede Africa's progress in the attainment of the Millennium Development Goals. The authors argue that, paradoxically, the crisis has provided a unique opportunity for Africa to rethink its development agenda as the dominant neo-liberal economic paradigm, the Washington Consensus, has fallen into disrepute. Taking a cue from the experience of Asia, Africa needs to reclaim the debate on its development and to follow Adedeji's approach of relying less on imported ideas, which have proven to be unworkable.

The authors observe that the recent growth in Africa has not been accompanied by significant structural transformation of their economies Indeed, economic structures of several African countries, especially in resource-rich countries such as Angola, DRC and Nigeria, which have become more dependent on exporting primary commodities (such as oil, gas, minerals and metal ores) to mostly developed countries thus making them very vulnerable to external shocks such as the global financial crisis of 2008. They conclude that a new economic paradigm that focuses on structural transformation of African economies will find more fruitful ideas in the development strategies proposed by Adedeji while at UNECA.

Part 4: Conflict, democracy and development in Africa

In Chapter 9, James Katorobo considers Adedeji's contribution to the understanding and management of conflicts in Africa. He examines causes of conflicts and the dynamics of conflict activation in Africa, using Adedeji's, *Comprehending and Mastering Conflicts in Africa* (1999). Adedeji's analytic assumptions are that, without a comprehensive understanding of the roots of conflict in Africa, the conflicts cannot be controlled. This approach allows for the recognition of the many interconnected causes and complexities of the entire conflict phenomenon. In conclusion, Katorobo posits that, while the framework and the methodology proposed by Adedeji are still germane, they need to be updated and built upon to be applied effectively.

References

Adedeji, A. (ed) 1999. *Comprehending and Mastering African Conflicts*. London: Zed Books.

Cline-Cole, R. 2006. "Adebayo Adedeji" in D Simon (ed) *Fifty Key Thinkers on Development*. Oxford and New York: Routledge.

Jolly, R, Emmerji, L and Weiss, T. 2005. *The Power of UN Ideas: Lessons from the First 60 Years.* London: Grundy & Northedge.

Organization of African Unity (OAU). 1981. *Lagos Plan of Action for the Economic Development of Africa, 1980–2000.* Addis Ababa:

OAU.
UNECA. 1983. *ECA and Africa's Development 1983-2008: A Preliminary Perspective Study*. Addis Ababa: UNECA.
UNECA. 1989. *African Alternative Framework to Structural Adjustment Programmes for Socio-Economic Recovery and Transformation* (AAF-SAP). Available at: www.uneca.org.
World Bank. 1981. *Accelerated Development in sub-Saharan Africa: An Agenda for Action*. Washington, D.C: World Bank.
World Bank. 1989. *Sub-Saharan Africa: From Crisis to Economic Growth: A Long Term Perspective Study*. Washington DC: IBRD/World Bank.

PART 1.
REFLECTIONS ON POLICIES AND STRATEGIES FOR AFRICA'S DEVELOPMENT

CHAPTER 1. CONTEMPORARY PERSPECTIVES ON THE LAGOS PLAN OF ACTION AND STRUCTURAL ADJUSTMENT IN THE 1980s

Richard Jolly

Introduction[1]

When Adebayo Adedeji took up leadership of the United Nations Economic Commission for Africa (UNECA) in 1975, 43 out of the 54 African countries were independent – including all the large countries except Angola, Mozambique, Zimbabwe and Namibia. A host of African multilateral institutions had been established and economic growth from 1961–1970, the United Nation (UN)'s first Development Decade, had accelerated to 4.5 per cent in sub-Saharan Africa and 11 per cent in North Africa.

Nonetheless, economic development during the 1960s was judged inadequate, not only in Africa but worldwide. The search was on for new approaches. The United States had unilaterally abandoned the Bretton Woods system in 1971. The United Nations (UN) in 1972 held the first global conference on Environment and Development and preparations were soon underway for others – on

---

1   Much of the story is documented in articles, books and official documents. In this piece, I also draw on my personal experiences and interactions with "Prof" as Adebayo Adedeji was affectionately called by his friends when he was Executive Secretary of UNECA and I was Deputy Executive Secretary of UNICEF.

population and on world food problems. Oil prices in 1973–1974 increased three or four fold, resulting in a transfer of some 2 per cent of global gross national product (GNP) to the oil-exporting Organization of Petroleum Exporting Countries (OPEC) from the oil-importing countries (the so-called "NOPEC" countries). Leaders from developing countries in all parts of the world began calling for a New International Economic Order (NIEO).

Although a NIEO is usually dismissed as absurdly unrealistic, it is arguable that with bold international leadership, the vision of a NIEO might have been achieved and would have led to a more balanced and equitable global economy than emerged over the 1980s and 1990s. All countries, including the developed countries, could have gained from better global arrangements, just as all had done better economically during the two and a half decades after 1945, when the Bretton Woods system operated in its earlier form. But after nearly two years of negotiations, frustration and stalemate, it became clear that those with power, the industrial countries and the OPEC group, preferred business as usual in international economic relations to fundamental change.

For most of Africa, this set the stage for two decades of debt, recession and economic setbacks, combined with a forced march of economic stabilization and structural adjustment, led by the Bretton Woods Institutions and the political imperatives of the Washington Consensus.

Faced with the economic challenges of Africa's most difficult period – from the mid-1970s to the early 1990s – Adebayo Adedeji was subject to almost continuous political battering and economic attacks by the World Bank and the International Monetary Fund (IMF) and by many of the developed countries. But he withstood all these, stood up for Africa and presented an authentic African vision of independent economic advancement. Although he did not succeed in many of these battles, over time some of the priorities for which he argued have been accepted.

Adedeji presided over UNECA during these momentous years of challenge. Politically, some progress was made. All the remaining countries in Africa became independent, with South Africa moving to majority rule and re-joining UNECA in 1994. But economically, the 1980s and much of the 1990s became a lost decade for development. Adedeji recognized the challenge – and led the fight against this. This chapter chronicles Adedeji's battles with the international financial institutions.

The Lagos Plan of Action (LPA)

Step one was in 1976, soon after Adedeji had assumed office. The UNECA Secretariat produced the *Revised Framework of Principles for the Implementation of the New International Economic Order in Africa*. This national and regional development strategy framework was built on three pillars: promotion of an increasing measure of self-reliance; an acceleration of growth and diversification, linked to geography and local capacity; and a progressive reduction of unemployment and mass poverty, including a fairer distribution of the benefits of economic development and income. This strategy implied driving growth and self-reliance domestically, looking inwards rather than outwards, and driving regional development by African, and not foreign interests.

Step two came three years later, after a good deal of further work and consultation by the UNECA Secretariat. This led to *The Lagos Plan of Action for the Economic Development of Africa, 1980–2000*, prepared for and by the UNECA Conference of Ministers and later endorsed by the Heads of State and Government meeting held in Lagos in 1980.

Step three was not a single measure but a succession of conflicting initiatives, which Adedeji has described as "the Battle for the African Mind'" (Adedeji 2004). These extended over the whole of the 1980s and beyond, when Adedeji threw his energies into defending the principles and content of the LPA against the mainstream of World Bank and IMF orthodoxy and policy and the severe conditionalities of structural adjustment.

The Berg Report and structural adjustment

The grounds for this battle were laid within a year of the publication of the LPA, when the World Bank issued its own report in 1981, *Accelerated Development in Sub-Saharan Africa: An Agenda for Action*, popularly known as the Berg Report, and named after the document's main author. According to the Bank's own history, the Berg Report received "unexpectedly negative" receptions in a remarkably diverse variety of places, including a meeting of donors (the Development Assistance Committee), an Arab-OPEC meeting, the European Economic Community, the United Nations

Development Program and a conference of the United Nations Children's Fund (UNICEF) (Kapur, Lewis and Webb, 1997: 717–718). Criticisms of the Berg Report were many and diverse. World Bank historians said its "emphasis on policy reflected a mono-dimensional view" of Africa's problems, which they saw as a foil to the LPA and the leading edge of a neo-liberal agenda. President Nyerere of Tanzania commented that it was met by "a scream of frustration" in a meeting of UNECA Development Ministers) (Kapur, Lewis and Webb, 1997: 718).

Notwithstanding this reception, the World Bank used the Berg Report to set much of its frame for policy and actions over the subsequent decade. It also increasingly used the Report for the coordination of donor policy and actions. Its neo-liberal approach was soon extended into the conditionalities which governed IMF loans as part of structural adjustment. Although by the end of the 1980s this viewpoint had taken on a new name (the "Washington Consensus"), it was not so much a turning away from the Berg ideas as an embodiment of many of its perspectives and policy recommendations in a wider and more explicit range of policies and ideology driven by external concerns.

In challenging these perspectives, Adedeji was at his best and his most loyal to Africa – even though largely unsuccessful. The battles lasted over the whole of the 1980s and indeed to the end of Adedeji's term of office. Though the LPA remained his touchstone, Adedeji adapted its priorities and policies to the urgent necessities of coping with recession, increasing shortages of foreign exchange and rising debt.

By the mid-1980s, with Africa in economic crisis and following famine in 26 countries, the UN organized an 18-month emergency program of support. This was followed by a major international conference which led to the unveiling of the UN Program of Action for African Economic Recovery and Development (UNPAAERD). Adedeji was appointed chair of a meeting to coordinate the UN response.[2] Most of the UN agencies involved in coping with the

---

2 As vice-chair, I had a good chance to witness Adedeji at his best. Adedeji never allowed the meeting to become simply acrimonious or over-personal. I remember the laughter, the serious but light-hearted interchanges, the passion tempered with vision and expounding the practicalities of alternatives. Certain individuals stand out for their contributions – notably Ambassador Stephen Lewis, who was the

policies of structural adjustment attended. The World Bank and the IMF were also there. The agenda was detailed and the discussion and debates were specific and frank; mostly very critical of the form which adjustment was taking and critical of the World Bank and the IMF for not taking more serious account of UN concerns and the mounting evidence of the economic and human consequences of the adjustment policies, which were required of countries as conditions for obtaining loans or grants.

By the late 1980s, and following the publication in 1989 of UNECA's *African Alternative Framework to Structural Adjustment Programs for Economic Recovery and Transformation*, the World Bank came out with a much more responsive study, presented in draft form to the UNPAAERD coordinating committee. Known as the *Long Term Perspective Study* (World Bank, 1989), in tone and content it was markedly different from anything previously produced by the World Bank. The UNPAAERD committee responded positively and asked how it came to be produced. The key author, Ram Agarwal, a World Bank staff-member, related how he had spent 18 months visiting many countries in Africa to obtain background material for the study. He described how this had totally changed his perspectives and understanding from what was typical in the World Bank in Washington. It was a key moment – though in the event, the World Bank decided that the study should be finalized by someone else, though still retaining many of the earlier elements. [3]

By the end of the 1980s, criticism of structural adjustment had become widespread – and news of disagreements in the UN was hitting the press. President Conable of the World Bank wrote to the heads of the main UN Development Funds, expressing that – while he was confident that there was underlying agreement on the main policies of adjustment – he was concerned that African countries were getting confused at the mixed messages they were receiving on structural adjustment, and inviting agency heads to a small, high-level meeting in Washington to sort out the confusions. The meeting was held in May 1989 – in the World Bank, with Edward Jaycox, the World Bank's Vice-President for Africa in the chair.[4] Adedeji came in a deliberate few minutes late. Nothing could seriously take place

---

Secretary General's representative for UNPAAERD, Sadig Rasheed of UNECA and Adedeji himself.
3   Ram Agarwal himself was, however, transferred to China!
4   The author was among those who attended.

before his arrival and he wanted, by his delay, to make this clear. Most of the representatives from the UN were supportive of Adedeji. The World Bank was desperate to show unity and get agreement on a joint statement – so desperate, that my UNICEF colleague who was acting as one of the go-betweens told me that anything we wanted in a joint statement would be accepted, and it was.[5]

This might give a somewhat lighthearted impression of debates on structural adjustment and its consequences in the 1980s. It should not. The ideological conflicts described by Adedeji as "battles for the African mind" were anything but lighthearted or inconsequential. On the one side was the dogma of structural adjustment guided by the Berg Report and later the Washington Consensus; essentially policies for opening African economies to free trade and free markets, as desired by the industrial countries. On the other side, supported by most UN agencies, were ideas and priorities for African development given by the LPA and related human concerns. The battles raged over most of the 1980s and beyond. Though the World Bank gradually became more flexible, the battles were essentially won by the Bretton Woods Institutions, operating overwhelmingly in the interests of the main industrial countries, backed up by their economic and voting power.

Evaluation with hindsight

Now, over two decades later, the disastrous consequences of structural adjustment are known with brutal clarity. Sub-Saharan Africa's economies declined with widespread cutbacks in education, health and the public services. The twenty-year change of GNP per capita in sub-Saharan Africa from 1980 to 2000 was in a decline of minus 15 per cent, compared with positive growth of plus 36 per cent achieved from 1960 to 1980 (Weisbrot, Naiman and Kim, 2001). This not only had immediate, devastating economic consequences; it held back investments in economic and human infrastructure and the transformations, nationally and regionally, required for African advance in the 21st century. Put simply and directly, it blocked the vision for broad-based African advance set out in the LPA.

The appalling consequences of structural adjustment are still not fully or widely realized, let alone acknowledged by the dominant developed countries or mainstream economists. The weakness of

---

5   The final declaration can be found in Adedeji, 2004.

governance in many African countries today is taken as proof that a shift to market approaches was necessary, rather than as the result – at least in part – of two decades of cutbacks in public services and salaries. The more positive growth rates achieved for a few years in the early 2000s, at least for some countries, are taken as evidence that after some delay, the long-run results of structural adjustment have begun to work – even though set back by the global recession of 2008–2009. Some see the two decades of the 1980s and 1990s as demonstrating the old adage, "no long-term gain, without short-term pain". And some even add that the "good results" might have come earlier if the policies of adjustment had been more carefully and consistently followed.[6]

Fortunately, data is now available to test the validity of these views and time has permitted more rigorous economic assessment.[7] In a recent review of a wide range of econometric research on structural adjustment from 1978 onwards, Vreeland, in his book on the IMF, considers explicitly the effectiveness of structural adjustment. He poses the question, "How effective has the IMF been at promoting economic growth?" His answer is: "Not very. Not only is evidence of growth promotion weak, recent studies even show that IMF programs have a significant *negative* effect on economic growth" (Vreeland, 2007: 73–94). Vreeland bases these conclusions on a careful review of a range of econometric studies which over time have become increasingly more sophisticated, measuring not only "before and after results", but also such matters as the degree of compliance, short- and long-term impacts (after the results of the structural adjustment have taken effect) and whether countries successfully completed IMF programs or not. Taking account of this full range of studies, Vreeland concluded in 2007 that "the newly emerging consensus is that IMF programs hurt economic growth."

This is a damning conclusion to reach about the operations of the IMF, the world's major international financial institution. The last

---

6   Advances in the early 2000s were largely based on increases in mineral production and other exports, rather than on increases in agricultural and other production for local consumption.

7   In addition to an almost endless series of reports by the World Bank, a number of studies were made by independent researchers. These are summarized in Kapur, Lewis and Webb, 1997: 790–799. (But note that this and most other studies were completed in the1990s. Longer term data sets and more sophisticated research are now available.)

two decades of the twentieth century were dominated economically by policies formulated by the World Bank and the IMF, with African voices from African institutions marginalized. The results for Africa and its peoples are now only too clear: a lost decade or two, with most of sub-Saharan Africa and its people left poorer in 2000 than they were in 1980.

As a matter of historical record, the role of Adedeji and UNECA during this period needs to be recognized and acknowledged. Consistently, from 1975 to 1991, Adedeji and UNECA presented an alternative vision and alternative policies to achieve it. This vision and almost all these policies received support in a succession of meetings of African governments and often of other parts of the UN – but to no avail. It is little consolation today that the alternatives presented at the time by UNECA were given so little attention and support by the main donor countries or by the World Bank and the IMF.

There is a further irony. By the end of the 1980s, when structural adjustment programs were often seen as not working, a major explanation was the failure of many African countries "to take ownership" of the structural adjustment programs. This explanation was repeated many times, without any questioning of the fact that African ministers had on many occasions endorsed African alternatives to orthodox adjustment programs – but these had never been taken seriously by the international financial institutions. These alternatives had been dismissed almost without investigation – even when the evidence was emerging that the orthodox programs had serious weaknesses and were not working to restore economic growth.

But would the LPA, if implemented, have been any better? Certainly, the LPA would have had more legitimacy from African governments. Many of its elements of domestically driven priorities and growth mirror those followed in Asia – with spectacular results. Is Africa so different? If the LPA had received support from the international financial institutions and donors, it surely would have led to a more dynamic period for African development. It is also arguable that greater African dynamism would also have benefited industrial countries – through more trade and investment opportunities, through rising African incomes and arguably through more political stability in African countries.

These counterfactual points deserve deeper and fuller

investigation at country and regional levels. Hopefully some researchers, especially from Africa, will take up this challenge. A good starting point is that today the World Bank and the IMF have become more doubtful of their earlier orthodoxy and more flexible in the conditions which they formulate for developing countries.

Conclusions

It is not too early to draw some conclusions for the future, especially for the role of international agencies, both the World Bank and the IMF, and the UN agencies.

- The positive roles of the UN regional commissions need to be given greater recognition, along with the Regional Development Banks. These institutions are closer to the ground, more in touch with professional thinking in the region and usually command greater respect and confidence than institutions based in Washington or New York. They also have the capacity to take account of the specific characteristics and needs of individual countries. This has been recognized in Asia – especially after the 1998–2000 financial crisis – and to a lesser extent in Latin America. It should be recognized in Africa.
- There is need for the World Bank and the IMF to recognize the contributions of other parts of the UN and work more closely with them, including with the regional commissions as well as the Regional Development Banks. Much closer links with the UN were intended when the international financial institutions were created but this has never been accepted, except in the thinnest form of formalities.
- The historical record shows that the UN agencies have often been "ahead of the curve"[8] in development thinking and policies in comparison with the Bretton Woods Institutions. A more balanced two-way exchange of information and research between the international financial institutions and the UN could increase the effectiveness of all the institutions concerned. The approaches of the

---

8   This was the title of the first volume of the UN Intellectual History Project: Emmerij,L; Jolly, R; and Weiss, TG 2001. Ahead of the Curve: UN Ideas and Global Challenges. Bloomington: Indiana University Press. The final volume has been published: Emmerij,L; Jolly, R; and Weiss, TG, 2009. UN Ideas That Changed the World Bloomington: Indiana University Press. Details can be found on the UN History Website: www.unhistory.org

international financial institutions are basically economic and those of the UN are typically multi-disciplinary. The international financial institutions predominantly reflect the interests of the developed countries; the UN predominantly reflects a diversity of third world interests. This, in principle, shows some potential for gains from comparative advantage. But, in addition, the UN always has commanded greater confidence and greater political legitimacy among most developing countries. There is much, therefore, to build on.

- Within the international community, there is need to revisit the era of structural adjustment and learn its full lessons. The World Bank history makes clear the initial and widespread doubts about the Berg Report – yet it was adopted by the Bank with "an intrepid flourish". Even as the years rolled by and evidence increasingly emerged to show that structural adjustment was not working as planned, the Bank and the IMF pressed ahead. Structural adjustment was indeed having devastating economic and social effects. Opposition grew, failures piled on failures and the Bank itself began to lose confidence.[9] But it took more than a decade before the Bank became more flexible and open to major change. Even then, it was reluctant to turn to UNECA – and preferred economists and ministers who shared its views and ideology, rather than those with closer experience of Africa.

This experience needs to be probed afresh. How can global economic and financial institutions avoid repetition of this economic tragedy which held most of a continent ransom for two decades? In the records of the twentieth century this should be treated like the Great Recession of the 1930s as a human-caused disaster that should never have happened.

---

9   "The journey to seek out the source of Africa's problems began with an intrepid flourish. But as the years rolled by, behind its public confidence were substantial doubts fed by a mixture of frustration and bafflement as expectations were repeatedly thwarted. Disappointment turned into irritation at the seeming recalcitrance of the clients to partake of its wisdom. This view, which was increasingly shared by other donors, gradually led the Bank to adopt a burgeoning conditionality agenda, from economic to social and political issues, and within economic issues to ever more detailed micro-level conditionality." (Kapur, Lewis and Webb, 1997: 720)

References

Adedeji, A. 2004. "The ECA: Forging a future for Africa" in Y. Berthelot (ed.) *Unity and Diversity in Development Ideas: Perspectives From the UN Regional Commissions.* Bloomington: Indiana University Press).

Jolly, R, Emmerij, L and Weiss TG. 2009. *UN Ideas That Changed the World.* Bloomington: Indiana University Press.

Kapur, D, Lewis, JP and Webb, R. 1997. *The World Bank: Its First Half Century*, Volume 1. Washington D.C: The Brookings Institution.

UNECA. 1980. *Lagos Plan of Action for the Economic Development of Africa, 1980–2000.* Organization of African Unity, republished by the United Nations Economic Commission for Africa.

UNECA. 1989. *African Alternative Framework for Structural Adjustment Programmes for Socio Economic Recovery and Transformation (AAF-SAP)*, ECA Resolution 676 (XXIV) 7 April 1989, (ECOSOC document E/ECA/CM.15/48.

Vreeland, JR. 2007. *The International Monetary Fund: Politics of Conditional Lending.* Oxford: Routledge.

Weisbrot, M, Naiman, R and Kim, J. 2001. *The Emperor Has No Growth: Declining Growth in the Era of Globalization.* Washington D.C: Center for Economic and Policy Research.

World Bank. 1981. *Accelerated Development in Sub-Saharan Africa, an Agenda for Action*: Washington D.C: World Bank.

World Bank. 1989. *Sub-Saharan Africa – From Crisis to Economic Growth: A Long Term Perspective Study.* Washington D.C: IBRD/World Bank.

CHAPTER 2. THE REDISCOVERY OF THE AFRICAN ALTERNATIVE FRAMEWORK TO STRUCTURAL ADJUSTMENT PROGRAMMES

Ali Abdel Gadir Ali

Introduction

A recently published official history of the United Nations Economic Commission for Africa (UNECA) tells us that the Nigerian professor of Public Administration, Adebayo Adedeji, was the third Executive Secretary of UNECA, serving from 1975 to 1991 (UNECA, 2009). Under his watch, and in collaboration with the Organization of African Unity (OAU – now African Union), UNECA and African intellectuals under the platform of the Council for the Development of Social Science Research in Africa (CODESRIA) fought a number of intellectual battles that revolved around the nature of the development challenges facing Africa. The first such battle was fought in defense of the Lagos Plan of Action (LPA) adopted by the OAU Assembly of Heads of State and Government in April 1980. Not surprisingly, given the content of development thought at the time and the continental mandate of UNECA, the LPA was written in the tradition of the first generation of development economists of the 1940s and 1950s (up to the 1970s).[1]

---

1 The classification of development economists into two generations derives from Meier (2001).

Such a tradition formulated grand and visionary models of development strategy that aimed at effecting structural transformation with a central role assigned to the government in planning and programing development. The policy content of these models was informed by the observation that "a less-developed economy was characterized by pervasive market failures. To correct or avoid market failure, they advocated central coordination and allocation of resources. The newly expanding subject of welfare economics also provided considerable rationale for government action to correct market failure" (Meier, 2001: 14). In addition to pervasive market failures, the role of the government was justified in the belief that the supply of entrepreneurs was limited in these countries, and that major structural changes, rather than marginal adjustments, were needed to achieve development. Thus, the "government of a developmental state was to promote capital accumulation, utilise reserves of surplus labour, undertake policies of deliberate industrialisation, relax the foreign exchange constraint through import substitution, and coordinate the allocation of resources through programming and planning" (Meier, 2001: 14–5).[2]

No sooner was the LPA adopted by the OAU than the World Bank, representing the interests of the advanced countries and masquerading as Africa's development partner, came up with a competing strategy for the continent in a report that was to become famous by the name of its chief author: the Berg Report. It is now firmly established that the Berg Report provided the theoretical justification for the Structural Adjustment Programs (SAPs) that were to be imposed on Africa, and especially sub-Saharan Africa, from the mid-1980s to the end of the 1990s.[3]

---

2   Classical examples of visionary models of development include Nurkse's (1953) "vicious circle of poverty", Rosenstein-Rodan's (1943) "big push", Leibenstein's (1957) "critical minimum effort" and "low-level equilibrium trap", Lewis' "dual economy model", Rostow's "take-off stage", and Chenery's "two-gap model". The ideas expressed in these early contributions to development economics are called the "high development theory" by Krugman (1997). Lewis' (1954) dual economy model is one of the most quoted papers in the development economics literature.

3   For an interesting account of the institutional perspective, World Bank and other events that eventually gave rise to SAPs, see, for example, Stein (2008).

It is also well known that, in writing the World Bank-commissioned report, Berg was influenced by what Meier classifies as the second generation of development economists (1975 up to the present). This second generation is seen as having been "almost moralistic, dedicated to a sombre realism grounded on fundamental principles of neo-classical economics" (Meier, 2001: 17). Neo-classical economics is seen by this generation as being good for the governments of the developing countries. "Governments were admonished not only to remove price distortions but also to 'get all policies right'. Not differences in initial conditions but differences in policies were now thought to explain the disparate performances of developing countries. A country was not poor because of the vicious circle of poverty but because of poor policies. Markets, prices and incentives should be of central concern in policy making" (Meier, 2001: 17).

The focus of development analysis moved from grand visionary models of the process of development to the investigation of particular features of underdevelopment using studies at the micro level, facilitated by the greater availability of micro-level data. According to the second generation of development economists the "correct policies were to move from inward-looking strategies toward liberalisation of foreign trade regime and export promotion; to submit to stabilisation programmes; to privatise state-owned enterprises; and to follow the dictates of the market price system. Through its guidance toward the correct policies, neo-classical economics was believed to be the safeguard against policy induced distortions and nonmarket failures" (Meier, 2001: 19).

SAPs were the second battle ground fought by UNECA under Adedeji's watch. In 1989 UNECA published its report titled the *African Alternative Framework to Structural Adjustment Programmes for Socio-Economic Recovery and Transformation* (AAF-SAP). In his foreword to the AAF-SAP, Adedeji succinctly summarized the irrelevance of the SAPs to the structural development problems of the continent: from "an economic point of view, the orthodox adjustment programmes, by their very design, assume that the classical instruments of control of money supply, credit squeeze, exchange rate and interest rate adjustments, trade liberalisation, etc. which may be valid in well-structured economies, could bring about positive results in African economies characterised by weak and disarticulate structures" (UNECA, 1989: i). He went on to explain why an AAF-

SAP was needed at the time by noting that the "overall assessment of orthodox adjustment programmes has led to the conclusion that although these programmes aim at restoring growth, generally through the achievement of fiscal and external balances and the free play of market forces, these objectives cannot be achieved without addressing the fundamental structural bottlenecks of African economies" (UNECA 1989: ii).

Though long, the official title of the AAF-SAP document carried the development concerns of the continent: an African alternative framework to SAPs for socio-economic recovery and transformation. Part of the title that does not appear in its abbreviated form (AAF-SAP) crucially reflects the true development orientation of the document: that the true concern of the continent is "socio-economic recovery and transformation". In his foreword, Adedeji explains the holistic nature of the proposed African framework thus: under AAF-SAP "the macro-economic framework, the policy directions and measures, and the implementation strategies take into account the dynamic relationships existing among all major elements related to adjustment with transformation" (UNECA, 1989: iii). By long-term development in AAF-SAP is meant sustainable development, at the center of which is the human dimension: "the recognition that it is only through the motivation and the empowerment of people as well as the ensuring of the equitable distribution of income that development can take place on a sustainable basis" (UNECA, 1989: iii).

In a typical UN diplomatic fashion, Adedeji expressed the hope that AAF-SAP would "constitute a basis for constructive dialogue between African countries and their development partners in the implementation and financing of country programmes. It is hoped that on the basis of such mutual understanding, the resources provided by the international community will lead to sustainable development through adjustment with transformation thus ensuring that the 1990s will witness the socio-economic revival of Africa". Despite these nicely worded hopes, the 1980s and the 1990s came to be known as the lost decades of development.[4]

With this brief review of the content of AAF-SAP as a starting point, the objectives of this chapter are to present AAF-SAP in

---

4   The term the "lost decades" of development was coined by William Easterly.

historical perspective and to remind the reader of two major issues: (i) that the development challenges facing Africa, and especially sub-Sahara Africa, remain the same as they were under Adedeji's leadership of UNECA, despite the passage of time; and (ii) following the acknowledged failure of SAPs to achieve their growth objective, most current ideas about what is needed to effect development in the region constitute a rediscovery of pre-existing ideas floated by African writers, policy makers, and thinkers.

The chapter deals with the African perspectives on the development of sub-Saharan Africa, thus addressing issue (i) above, and gives examples of pre-existing African ideas currently being discussed by Africa's development partners as new, or novel, ways for effecting development in the region including the need for a holistic development framework; the overarching objective of development and issues of equity; and the relevant development policies.

African perspectives on development

In a fundamental sense, AAF-SAP represented the way Africa appraised the theoretical or, better still, the ideological foundations of SAPs. Ten years after the publication of the AAF-SAP document, its analysis and conclusions were reconfirmed by a set of thirty studies commissioned by CODESRIA.[5] Out of these, twenty-five studies were by African economists; the rest by African non-economists. The results of the studies were synthesized in *Our Continent, Our Future: African Perspectives on Structural Adjustment* (Mkandawire and Soludo, 1999) and an edited selection of thirteen studies was published in *African Voices on Structural Adjustment: A Companion to Our Continent, Our Future* (edited by Mkandawire and Soludo, 2003). "The issues covered in the selected papers include: critical evaluation of the model and methodologies for performance evaluation under SAP; comparative development experiences; trade liberalisation and regional integration; SAP, technology and industrialisation in Africa; poverty under adjustment; reforms, external and domestic factors,

---

5   The Council for the Development of Social Science Research in Africa (CODESRIA) was established in 1973, with its headquarters in Dakar, Senegal. It is an independent Pan-African research organization. According to its website (www.codesria.org) "it is recognised as the pioneer centre of social knowledge production on the continent".

and implications for agriculture and rural development; and financial sector reforms and resource mobilisation" (Mkandawire and Soludo 2003: viii).

Not surprisingly, the synthesized volume starts off by looking at the initial conditions of the region subscribing to the idea that "path dependence" is one of the most important features of the process of social and economic changes.[6] Included in the initial conditions are: physical conditions (such as ecology, size of countries, geographical location, infrastructure, and resource endowments); human capital; past economic performance (that is, pre-SAPs); extreme dependence on the external economic environment; physical capital; industrialization experience; performance of agriculture; technical and scientific capacity; social differentiation; overall political-economic structure; and political transformation.

After reviewing the evidence on initial conditions, Mkandawire and Soludo concluded that by the "mid-1970s, many countries could point to significant progress in initiating processes of economic and social development. Some level of industrialisation had been initiated, levels of school enrolment had increased, new roads had been constructed, the indigenisation of the civil service had advanced and so forth. However, it was also clear that the economies were still woefully underdeveloped and vulnerable to global economic change, without the wherewithal for rapid adjustment" (1999: 20). Needless to say, this evaluation of the initial conditions and their implications for development in general, as well as the adjustment events, thereof is almost identical with that of the first chapter in the AAF-SAP document.

In their volume, Mkandawire and Soludo (1999) discussed the nature of the African development crisis that preceded the adjustment decades, tracing its origin to the 1973 and 1979 oil price increases which precipitated, among other external factors, recession in the developed countries, declining demand for raw materials, and high interest rates. While it is recognized that such a changing external economic environment necessitated the need for some form of "adjustment" by African countries, the SAP was not the only option available. The central message of the SAP imposed on Africa

---

6   The authors explain that by path dependence is meant that "what eventually happens to an economy depends greatly on the point of departure".

was to "get the prices right, unleash the markets and rein in the state". The principal components of this policy program, as reviewed by Mkandawire and Soludo (1999), included: an anti-industrial policy stance; the liberalization of agricultural markets; financial liberalization; the opening-up of economies and the liberalization of trade regimes; the allocation of budget resources to education on the basis of the rate of return; and administrative reforms to enable technocrats to initiate and implement market-based economic reforms.

As expected, a critical review of the empirical evidence on the effect of SAPs was undertaken; noting in the process the major methodological difficulties involved in assessing the ultimate effects. The review of the empirical evidence included the effects of SAPs on economic growth, agriculture, industrial performance, technology, trade, financial resource mobilization, mobilization of foreign capital, human resources, poverty, social programs, state capacity and privatization. The overall conclusion of the critical review of the evidence on the impact of SAPs in sub-Saharan Africa is that every "reasonable analysis of the adjustment process in Africa so far returns the same verdict: it has not succeeded in laying the foundations for sustainable growth and development" (Mkandawire and Soludo, 1999: 87). This assertion reaffirms Adedeji's conclusion on AAF-SAP ten years earlier.

The final chapter of the synthesized volume of studies offers "development fundamentals" that are relevant to sub-Saharan African and that go beyond the SAPs' "stabilisation fundamentals". Such development fundamentals "simultaneously address the following issues: equity, economic growth, economic stability and political legitimacy" (Mkandawire and Soludo 1999: 89). A careful review of the details of these development fundamentals shows that their policy content is consistent with what UNECA listed, albeit in tabular form, as a "summary of proposed policy instruments and measures under AAF-SAP" (1989: 38-43).

A close reading of the CODESRIA books and AAF-SAP document shows that the African perspectives on development are more consistent with a broader understanding of the development process than those embodied in the orthodox SAPs. Such an understanding is provided by Sen who convincingly argues that "development can be seen as a process of expanding the real freedoms that people enjoy" (1999: 3). Without getting deeply involved in the philosophical foundations of this approach, it is important to note that it requires judging the welfare of individuals not in terms of the utility of goods and services, or in terms of primary goods, but rather in terms of "substantive capabilities to choose a life one has reason to value"(1999: 74). Capability is thus the substantive freedom to achieve alternative functioning combinations or, less formally put, the freedom to achieve various lifestyles such as the ability to live to old age, engage in economic transactions, or participate in political activities.

This is a much broader approach to understanding what is meant by development, compared to other approaches that identify development only with increases in per capita incomes, industrialization, technological advance or social modernization. In presenting empirical evidence in the context of this broader approach to development, Sen identified five instrumental freedoms that have immediate policy relevance: *political freedom*, including "the political entitlements associated with democracies in the broadest sense"; *economic facilities*, in the sense of the "opportunities that individuals respectively enjoy to utilise economic resources for the purpose of consumption, or production, or exchange"; *social opportunities* in the sense of "the arrangements that society makes for education, health care and so on"; *transparency guarantees* in the sense of "the freedom to deal with one another under guarantees of disclosure and lucidity"; and *protective security* in the sense of the provision of a "social safety net for preventing the (vulnerable sections of society) from being reduced to abject misery, and in some cases even starvation and death" (1999: 38–40). Sen notes that in essence, these five "instrumental freedoms tend to the general capability of a person to live more freely, but they also serve to complement one another" (1999: 38).

It is important to note one of the most important conclusions of Mkandawire and Soludo and its implications for Africa's self-appraisal of its economic problems. According to them, what "is not often appreciated is that most of what appears today as new insights about the imperatives of poverty reduction, investment in infrastructure and education, the requirements for rapid industrialisation, and the structural and institutional bottlenecks of Africa's underdevelopment are nothing but the rehearsal of old but disparaged ideas of African scholars and policy makers" (1999:139).

The need for a holistic development framework

As noted earlier, Adedeji emphasized the holistic nature of the AAF-SAP for Socio-Economic Recovery and Transformation in 1989. Ten years later, the World Bank seems to have discovered the need for such a development framework to conduct its development finance business. In 1999 the then president of the World Bank, James Wolfensohn, came up with an initiative called the Comprehensive Development Framework (CDF). The CDF aims to enhance the effectiveness of development partners in bringing about desired development outcomes in developing countries. It is "an approach by which countries can achieve more effective poverty reduction. It emphasises the interdependence of all elements of development social, structural, human, governance, environmental, economic and financial" (CDF Secretariat, 2000). The framework is articulated around four major principles: a long-term, holistic development framework; country ownership of development programs and policies; country-led partnership among various stakeholders; and results orientation.[7]

The advent of the CDF can be taken as signifying a return to the application of the basic concepts of development economics, as distinct from the application of narrow neo-classical economic theory propositions to developing countries. More relevant to our current emphasis is the understanding that the CDF initiative could be taken as a rediscovery of AAF-SAP.

In December of 1999 (the same year of the CDF) the World Bank and the IMF "introduced a new approach to their relations with low-income countries, centred around the development and implementation of poverty reduction strategies (PRS) by countries as a precondition for access to debt relief and concessional financing from both institutions" (International Monetary Fund and the World Bank Development Committee, 2005: 1). A Poverty Reduction Strategy Paper (PRSP) was to be prepared, in collaboration with external partners should the need arise, and owned by countries. The core elements of the PRSP included:

---

7 In formulating the CDF Wolfensohn was intellectually influenced by Amartya Sen and Joseph Stiglitz.

i. A documentation of the participatory process invoked by the country to solidify the ownership of the development program;
ii. A detailed diagnosis of the state of poverty in the country including money and metric dimensions, broader capability, deprivation dimensions and dimensions gleaned from participatory poverty assessments;
iii. A rigorous identification and setting of medium- and long-term goals for poverty reduction with relevant and realistic indicators of progress, inclusive of annual and medium-term targets; and,
iv. A clear specification of appropriate and feasible priorities for public actions.[8]

In a real sense, the PRSP process could be taken as a recognition, albeit grudgingly and belatedly, of the failure to market SAPs as appropriate development strategies for developing countries in general, and countries in Africa in particular, as a special laboratory for testing the pet models of the second-generation development economists residing in the World Bank.[9] Despite this recognition, however, central to the PRSP process are the stability of the macroeconomic framework; the appropriate choice of fiscal policies and the adequacy and credibility of the financing plan of the development program; the suitability of the structural and sectoral policies and policies for social inclusion and equity; and the directions of improvements in governance and public sector management. Thus, despite the rediscovery of the need for development strategies that have at their core the overarching objective of development as poverty reduction, the World Bank and the IMF, by insisting on the SAP-type policies as a PRSP core component, did not seem to have learnt from experience.

On the basis of this rediscovery of the need for broader frameworks to effect development transformation, and of poverty reduction as an objective of development – as embodied in the PRSP process – the World Bank announced in August 2004 that it was replacing its "adjustment lending" instrument with a "development policy lending" instrument.[10] A careful reading of the World Bank

---

8   See, for example, IMF and IDA (2001). Currently, 49 countries have prepared national PRSPs, half of them in sub-Saharan Africa.
9   The pet models of the IMF and the World Bank are competently and critically reviewed by Tarp (1993) and Soludo (2003).
10 At the time, policy-based lending in support of a country's policy programme accounted for about one third of the Bank's annual lending.

document, *Operational Policies: Development Policy Lending* (2004) reveals that this change is informed by the CDF.

Recalling that SAPs were originally perceived as growth enhancing, irrespective of their development implications, the World Bank persevered in its attempts to learn more about the nature of economic growth processes, especially those that took place during the adjustment decades. The result is a World Bank report entitled *Economic Growth in the 1990s: Learning from a Decade of Reform*. A summary of the report is provided in Zagha, Nankani and Gill (2006). According to the summary, the following six lessons have been learnt:

i. expectations about the impact of reforms on growth were unrealistic;
ii. reforms should promote growth, not just efficiency;
iii. necessary conditions for economic growth can be created in numerous ways – not all of them equally conducive to growth. Any sustained growth process is based on accumulation of capital, efficient use of resources, technological progress, and a socially acceptable distribution of income;
iv. stabilization and macroeconomic management need to be growth-oriented;
v. governments need to be made accountable, not bypassed; and
vi. governments should abandon formulaic policymaking in which 'any reform goes' and concentrate on supporting growth. To do so, they must identify the binding constraints to growth, which, in turn, necessitates recognizing country-specific characteristics and undertaking more economic analysis and rigor than a formulaic approach would call for.

Despite the above lessons, the World Bank felt that more learning about growth was needed. In April 2006, the Bank inaugurated a 21-member Commission on Growth and Development which produced a report in 2008 entitled *The Growth Report: Strategies for Sustainable Growth and Inclusive Development*.[11] The report looked at

---

The announcement, posted on 10 August 2004, was made by James Adams, Vice-President and Head of the Operations Policy and Country Services Network.

11 The composition of the commission was such that 15 members came from developing countries, three from advanced countries (Sweden, UK and USA), two academics (R. Solow and Michael Spence, who chaired the Commission), and one from the World Bank. Both Solow and

the experience of high-growth economies since 1950: a sample of 13 countries that had achieved an average annual GDP growth rate of 7 per cent or more for 25 years or longer.[12] The report identified four common features of the growth processes that gave rise to such success: (i) strategic integration with the world economy; (ii) mobility of resources, particularly labor; (iii) high savings and investment rates; and, (iv) capable governments committed to growth.[13]

Almost ten years after the CDF, and twenty years after AAF-SAP, on 2 June 2009, the new senior vice-president and chief economist of the World Bank, Justin Y. Lin, came up with a framework for rethinking development, based on the above-noted common features of successful growth identified in the Growth Report, and described as belonging to the "new structural economics".[14] To the above-noted common features – called by Lin "stylised facts of modern economic growth" – macroeconomic stability is added as a fifth stylized fact; the "mobility of resources, particularly labour" is interpreted as meaning "market allocation of resources".

The new structural economic framework is neo-classical, emphasizing that the development of countries depends on their comparative advantage along a continuum of development from a low-income agrarian economy to a high-income industrialized economy. Along this continuum an economy's structure of factor endowments evolves, requiring a corresponding infrastructure to facilitate its operations and transactions. The evolution of the economic structure, in turn, depends on what is termed "industrial up-grading". In this development evolution, the market is seen as the basic mechanism for effective resource allocation; but, since

---

Spence are Noble Laureates in Economics; and, of course, Solow is the father of neoclassical economic growth theory.

12 The 13 successful, high growth economies included Botswana from sub-Saharan Africa, Oman from the Middle East, Brazil from Latin America, and Malta from Europe. The rest are from Asia, including Japan and China.

13 For details see Commission on Growth and Development (2008: 17-31).

14 For the details of the framework and its relationship to the Growth Report, see Lin (2010), Lin and Monga (2010); and Ju, Lin and Wang (2009) for the mathematical formulation of a model that represents the framework.

industrial upgrading entails large externalities to firms' costs and returns to capital investment, there is a need for the government to play an active role in facilitating industrial upgrading and improvement in infrastructure.

The overarching objective of development and issues of equity

In its articulation of Africa's development objectives the AAF-SAP document clearly stated that the "ultimate goal of development in Africa is to ensure the overall well-being of the people through a sustained improvement in their living standards. It is this quintessential human aspect of development that underlies all other objectives that Africa will have to pursue, be they economic, social, cultural or political" (UNECA, 1989: 10).

In September 2000, poverty reduction was belatedly recognized as the overarching objective of development in developing countries. That wide recognition is embodied in the Millennium Development Goals, adopted by the Millennium Summit of the United Nations in September 2000. The Millennium Development Goals are based on the International Development Goals of the Organization for Economic Cooperation and Development. With the exception of the eighth goal on global partnership for development, the remaining seven goals are poverty related.[15] The first Millennium Development Goal is to reduce poverty measured in 1990 by half by the year 2015, whereby poverty is meant the
headcount ratio and where an international poverty line of US$1 per person per day, at 1985 purchasing power parity, is used. The headcount ratio is the ratio of the number of people falling below this poverty line to total population.[16]
Though there was little information in 1989 to conduct conventional poverty analysis, the AAF-SAP document noted that "regrettably, the realisation of the objective of raising the welfare of the people has

---

15 For an official statement of the Millennium Development Goals see United Nations (2001). The websites of the UNDP, World Bank and the IMF have summary versions for the goals and the associated indicators.

16 In technical terms, the head count ratio, denoted as H or P0, is defined as $H=P0= q/n$, where q is the number of the poor and n is total population.

proved elusive. Instead, there has been increased immiseration and suffering for the majority of the population, with an increase in the numbers of people in absolute poverty and those who are perpetually vulnerable and threatened by the adversities of nature as well as the malaise of socio-economic disruptions" (UNECA, 1989: 10). Since 1989, empirical research on the state and behavior of poverty over time has accumulated to support the assertions of AAF-SAP.

Estimates of poverty by world regions are reported in Chen and Ravallion (2008). Drawing on a sample of 6,754 national sample surveys from 116 countries, poverty results are reported for two African sub-regions: sub-Saharan Africa (with 41 countries and 1,120 surveys) and North Africa (as part of the Middle East and North Africa region of the World Bank, with five out of seven countries and 16 surveys).[17] The results are reported for an international poverty line of US$1.25 per person, per day at 2005 purchasing power parity.

According to these results (Chen and Ravallion, 2008: 32, table 7), in the early 1980s sub-Saharan Africa, with a headcount ratio of about 0.51, had the third highest poverty incidence among all the developing world regions; with East Asia and the Pacific (with a headcount ratio of about 0.79) and South Asia (with a headcount ratio of about 0.59) respectively ranking as the highest and second highest. By 1990, sub-Saharan Africa had the second highest poverty incidence (with a head-count ratio of about 0.55 compared to 0.56 for East Asia and the Pacific) and by 1993 it became the highest poverty incidence region, maintaining that position up to 2005.

In terms of time trends, the results show that for all regions except sub-Saharan Africa, Eastern Europe and Central Asia, poverty incidence declined over time. The reduction in the incidence of poverty was most dramatic for East Asia which saw its headcount ratio declining by about 61 per cent from about 0.79 to about 0.18; and the decline was systematic over the time period with a very clear trend. At the other extreme the increase in the incidence of poverty

---

17 Sub-Saharan African countries in the sample are: Botswana (2 surveys); Burkina Faso (2), Burundi (2), Cameron (1), Central African Republic (1), Cote d'Ivoire (4), Ethiopia (3), Gambia (2), Ghana (3), Kenya (3), Lesotho (3), Madagascar (3), Mali (2), Malawi (1) Mauritania (4), Mozambique (1), Namibia (1), Niger (2), Nigeria (3), Rwanda (1), Senegal (2), Sierra Leone (1), South Africa (3), Swaziland (1), Tanzania (1), Uganda (4), Zambia (4), and Zimbabwe (2).

was most pronounced in Eastern Europe and Central Asia, albeit starting from low incidence and remaining low at the end of the period with a headcount ratio of only 0.05 in 2005. The incidence of poverty in sub-Saharan Africa increased by about 7 per cent between 1981 and 1996, and then declined by the same percentage by 2005, returning to its 1981 level. But, by 2005 sub-Saharan Africa was by far the poorest region among developing world regions, with about 50 per cent of its total population living below a poverty line of US$1.25 per person per day in 2005 purchasing power parity. Thus, the current incidence of poverty in sub-Saharan Africa is about 11 times that of the lowest incidence region in the developing world (i.e. Middle East and North Africa with a headcount ratio of only 0.05).

In the context of the above results it is known that any money-metric measure of poverty, such as the headcount ratio of the first Millennium Development Goal, can be expressed as depending on per capita consumption expenditure and the degree of inequality in the distribution of consumption expenditure in society. An increase in per capita consumption expenditure, with unchanged distribution, is expected to lead to a reduction in poverty; while an increase in the degree of inequality in the distribution of consumption expenditure with unchanged per capita consumption is expected to increase poverty. Thus, changes in poverty over time, especially during the process of development, would depend not only on economic growth (that is, increase in per capita consumption expenditure) as emphasized in conventional SAPs, but also on changes in the degree of inequality in the distribution of consumption expenditure (that is, the equity dimension of development); a dimension which was missing in SAPs.

Equity in the African development process was the central issue in AAF-SAP. As Adedeji rightly said in 1989, "at the centre of the alternative framework is the human dimension – the recognition that it is only through the motivation and the empowerment of people as well as the ensuring of the equitable distribution of income that development can take place on a sustainable basis" (UNECA, 1989: iii).

After denying the importance of equity in the development process for about 16 years since the publication of AAF-SAP, the World Bank's *World Development Report* (2005a) finally came round to addressing the issue in a direct fashion. The main message of the report is that "equity is complementary, in some fundamental respects, to the pursuit of long-term prosperity.... Greater equity is thus doubly good for poverty reduction: through potential beneficial effects on aggregate long-run development and through greater opportunities for poorer groups within any society" (World Bank 2005a: 2). The complementarity between equity and prosperity is explained in terms of the pervasive market failures in developing economies (for example, markets for credit, insurance, land, and human capital), and the fact "that high levels of economic and political inequality tend to lead to economic institutions and social arrangements that systematically favour the interests of those with more influence" (World Bank 2005a: 2).

The report notes that an "equity lens adds three new – or at least, often neglected –perspectives to development policy-making: first, the best policies for poverty reduction could involve redistribution of influence, advantage, or subsidies away from dominant groups; second, while such equity-enhancing redistributions can often be efficiency-increasing, possible tradeoffs are to be assessed in the design of policy; and third, the dichotomy between policies for growth and policies specifically aimed at equity is false" (World Bank 2005a: 10).

For Africa, the World Bank's (2005b) action plan is a strategy for "creating shared growth in Africa" as per the title of the public lecture by Nankani (2005).[18] By shared growth is meant "growth that creates benefits throughout society, including the poor, including those living in more remote rural areas, including women and youth. This is not an automatic process of 'trickle down'. It is not enough simply to assume that everyone will eventually gain if the economy continues to grow" (Nankani, 2005: 2).[19]

The shared growth strategy for Africa is inspired by the East Asian experience. The World Bank has still much to learn from their experience. In East Asia, according to Page, "highly visible wealth sharing mechanisms – such as universal primary education, land reform, and free basic health care – were put in place to induce non-

---

18 Nankani was Vice-President of the World Bank for the Africa Region.
19 The last sentence in the quotation could be understood as refuting an earlier result by two World Bank economists purporting to show that per capita GDP growth increases the incomes of the poor and the rich by the same percentage rate. See Ali (2001) for a methodological critique of this result

elites to support the growth process. Unlike simple redistributive mechanisms, such as food or fuel subsidies or public employment in productive activities, these mechanisms signalled to the population that all parties would share in the benefits of growth through increased capacity to participate in and benefit from the process of economic change" (2005: 16).[20] Paradoxically, Asian wealth sharing mechanisms, especially education and health, were in place in Africa in its immediate post-independence period but were curtailed since the mid-1970s and the 1980s under SAPs.

Relevant development policies

As is well known, in the early years of the development experience (from 1960 until the middle of the 1970s), development policy in the developing countries revolved around social equity mechanisms, including public expenditure on health and education, food price subsidies, agricultural input price subsidies, other social transfers and public employment. From the middle of the 1970s until the end of 1990s, under SAPs, such policies came to be labeled as "bad economic policies".

A careful reading of the "proposed policy instruments and measures under AAF-SAP" shows that the core of the "perceived bad economic policies" of the 1960s and 1970s constituted the relevant development policies proposed for the region. UNECA lists the policy instruments and measures required for socio-economic recovery and transformation under four broad headings (UNECA, 1989: 38–40; table 5.2):

i. *measures and instruments for strengthening and diversifying production capacity*: with ten measures that included land reforms, purposive allocation of government expenditure and public investment, sectoral allocation of credit, and rationalized exchange rate and interest rate policies;
ii. *measures and instruments for improving the level of income and the pattern of its distribution*: with five measures that included enhanced mobilization of domestic revenue, reduction of expenditure on defense, rationalization of deficit financing, and relevant food pricing policies;
iii. *measures and instruments for the pattern of expenditure for the satisfaction of needs*: with eight measures that included increased government expenditure on the social sectors, supply-increasing pricing policies,

---

20 John Page was the Chief Economist of the Africa Region of the World Bank.

      selective use of trade policy, and relevant debt service policy; and,
iv. *measures and instruments for institutional support*: with five measures that included the creation of adequately funded rural food production credit systems, strengthening agricultural research, and the creation of rural institutions.

After wasting two decades on experimentation with SAP policies, the donor community is rediscovering that what they dubbed as "bad economic policies" do, after all, constitute relevant development policies in the context of sub-Saharan Africa. One rediscovery was made by the Commission for Africa. In a remarkable and almost heretical fashion, the report of the Commission noted that the "decades in which Asia was investing, the 1970s and 1980s, were the years of crisis when African governments were slashing the budgets of both clinics and schools at the behest of the International Monetary Fund. Evidence shows that IMF and World Bank economic policy in the 1980s and early 1990s took little account of how these policies would potentially impact on the poor in Africa" (Commission for Africa, 2005: 30).[21]

More important from a development policy perspective, the Commission for Africa recommended, among other things, that "primary school fees to be abolished throughout Africa" (39); that donor "countries and international financial institutions must change their policies to allow recurrent expenditure – including teachers' salaries – to be paid for from aid" (40); that salaries of health workers "should be increased to ensure staff are not wooed from their jobs" (40); that "rich nations should support the removal of fees for basic healthcare ... and basic healthcare should be free for poor people" (41); and that African governments "must take measures to give poor people, particularly women, access to land and secure

---

21 The Commission for Africa was established by the British Prime Minister, Tony Blair, in 2004. Blair chaired the Commission, the members of which included 16 people invited in their "individual and personal capacities" with a majority of Africans. "The task we were set was this: to define the challenges facing Africa, and to provide clear recommendations on how to support the changes needed to reduce poverty" (Commission for Africa 2005: 2). It is perhaps interesting to note that the title of the report of the Commission seems to have been coined as a response to the title of the book by Mkandawire and Soludo (1999): "Our Continent, Our Future: African Perspectives on Structural Adjustment".

property rights" (46.).

Another rediscovery was made by the World Bank. The report identifies three areas of public policy intervention from an equity focus: (i) investment in human capacity (early childhood development, schooling, health, safety nets, and taxes for equity); (ii) expanding access to justice, land, and infrastructure (building equitable justice systems, greater equity in access to land, equitable provision of infrastructure); and (iii) promoting fairness in markets (financial, labor, and products) (World Bank, 2005a). Despite this belated recognition of AAF-SAP-identified measures and instruments for socio-economic recovery and transformation, when discussing "greater equity in access to land" the report was quick to note that broader "access to land does not necessarily have to come through ownership", expressing a preference for working through the land market (World Bank, 2005a 13). Similarly, for the equitable provision of infrastructure, it is admitted that while "the public sector will in many cases remain the main source of funds for infrastructure investments aimed at broadening opportunities for those who have the fewest, the efficiency of the private sector can also be harnessed". (World Bank, 2005a 14).

A more telling and highly ironic example of the rediscovery of the relevance of AAF-SAP interventionist policies, dubbed "bad policies" by Africa's development partners in the 1980s and 1990s, is the praise heaped by these partners on the 2005 Malawi subsidy policy for fertilizer and high-yielding seeds. The story, as told by Fleshman, unfolds as follows: in "2005 the government of President Bingu wa Mutharika began subsidising fertilisers and high yielding seeds for Malawi's smallholders. The action cut fertiliser prices by 80 per cent and slashed the cost of hybrid maize seeds from 600 kwasha per bag to 30. The impact was dramatic. The following year Malawi's maize harvest more than doubled, to 2.7 million tonnes. It rose again in 2007 to 3.4 mn tonnes – enough to feed the nation and sell 400,000 tonnes to the UN's World Food Programme and hundreds of thousands of tonnes to neighbouring countries, generating US$120 million in sales" (Fleshman, 2008: 3). In technical terms, the subsidy scheme showed that, other things remaining the same, a reduction in the price of the fertilizer input of 80 per cent gave rise to an increase in output of more than 100 per cent, meaning an elasticity of about 1.3 in one year – an impressive achievement by all standards.

In 1999 the government of Malawi had introduced "a modest programme of free starter packs of fertiliser and seeds for family farmers in an effort to boost production". The results were impressive, but the subsidies ran afoul of the pro-market policies of the World Bank and the International Monetary Fund (IMF), which argued that subsidies were "crowding out commercial sales and constituted undue government interference in the economy. Under considerable pressure from these financing institutions, the programme was phased out. The IMF insisted that Malawi sell much of its national grain reserve to pay off the debts of the state-owned maize marketing agency". By contrast, in 2005, the government of Malawi "defied the donors and launched the subsidy scheme on its own funds... and the next year the donors supported it" (Fleshman, 2008: 3).

Conclusion

It is perhaps fitting to note that AAF-SAP was cognizant of the fact that the achievements of the objectives of socio-economic recovery and transformation "will call for wide-ranging changes in the democratisation of society within the social and economic framework as well as in development strategies and policies. The political systems will need to evolve to allow for full participation by all sectors of society" (UNECA 1989: 15).

Such a recognition of the crucial importance of governance issues caused Tarp to commend UNECA, under the leadership of Adedeji, for being "remarkably blunt about the need for increased democratisation and greater mass participation in decision-making. It is acknowledged that basic human rights and individual freedom are often lacking in sub-Saharan Africa. The UNECA is also aware that the pervasive lack of democracy makes mobilisation of domestic support, indispensable for reforms to succeed, exceedingly difficult"(1993: 146).[22]

---

22 We hasten to note that Tarp was negative overall regarding AAF-SAP's contribution to the adjustment debate; he found it sufficiently disappointing to remark that "nothing new in terms of analytical insights emerge" (1993: 149). This overall negative assessment should be appropriately appreciated by noting that Tarp's book was devoted to a critical review of the "pet" adjustment models of the IMF and the World Bank. He seems to have forgotten that AAF-SAP was not a

Unfortunately, this earlier call for democratization of the region, by its own sons and daughters, was subsequently incorporated into the conditionality of access to concessional foreign assistance from donor countries. The conditionality incorporating aspects of the AAF-SAP's call for democratization of society was understood by the donor community to mean the full embrace of the western model of liberal democracy, with an obvious preference for the American presidential model.

The democratization process which engulfed the region since 1989, though commendable, was celebrated in the specialized literature, not from the perspective of socio-economic recovery and transformation, but rather from the perspective of implementing pure economic reform packages of the SAP variety. Thus, for example, Bates (2006: 27) celebrates the democratization wave in the 1990s by noting that "local champions of political reform joined with international financial institutions to seek political change in low income countries. In no place was this truer than in Africa, where political change came quickly between 1985 and 1995.The percentage of countries with multiparty systems rose dramatically, and the percentage of military governments declined".

But was this the political change envisaged by AAF-SAP? Certainly not. Under AAF-SAP are specific requirements of "the democratization of society within *the social and economic framework as well as in development strategies and policies*", as earlier noted. Moreover, according to Mkandawire (2006: 1), the answer is in the negative, given the "predominance of economic policies that hamper democracies from addressing issues of equity and poverty". Empirical evidence to show that the new democracies are implementing orthodox SAP policies, and have tended to be even more orthodox in their policies than consolidated democracies, is provided for Africa, Asia and Latin America. "Unlike Latin America, none of the new democracies in Africa have experimented with heterodox policies. They went straight to orthodox policies" (Mkandawire, 2006: 10).

A major aspect of the political economy of development of the continent that needs to be seriously debated is that conventional SAPs had their African supporters despite the overall shared African

---

model, but a framework which could be formalized in various types of structural models.

conviction of the structural nature of the development crisis. As noted in the introduction and the section on the African perspective on development, such a development vision was articulated in the Lagos Plan of Action and the AAF-SAP, among other sources. "Most African governments signed the documents, and, none of these governments has publicly dissociated itself from the ideas espoused in them. But the World Bank virulently attacked these documents, and every African government that wished to have successful debt rescheduling or aid negotiations distanced itself from the principles in them" (Mkandawire and Soludo, 1999:139).

President Bingu wa Mutharika was, indeed, one of Adedeji's colleagues and collaborators in the UNECA Secretariat for more than a decade. And, sixteen years after the publication of the AAF-SAP document by UNECA when it was under the capable leadership of Adedeji, Malawi taught us that, after all, democratically elected African governments can call the bluff of the so-called Africa's development partners.

References

Ali, AAG. 2001. "Growth is good for the poor: Policy messaging in the small and in the large", *AERC Research News* 6: 6–8.

Bates, R. 2006. "Beyond the ballot box: Political reform and policy reform in contemporary Africa", *Finance and Development* 43: 4. Available at: http://www.imf.org/external/pubs/ft/fan-dd/2006/12/bates.htm.

CDF Secretariat. 2000. *Overview and Background of the Comprehensive Development Framework*. Available at: www.worldbank.org/cdf (currently in archives).

Chen, S, and Ravallion, M. 2008. "The developing world is poorer than we thought, but no less successful in the fight against poverty", *WPS* 4703. Available at: www.worldbank.org.

Commission for Africa. 2005. *Our Common Interest: An Argument*. London: Penguin Books.

Fleshman, M. 2008. "A harvest of hope for African farmers: Malawi subsidies stimulate a bumper crop", *Africa Renewal*, October 2008. Available at: http://www.un.org/africarenewal/magazine/october-2008/harvest-hope-african-farmers.

International Monetary Fund and the World Bank Development Committee. 2005. *2005 Review of the Poverty Reduction Strategy Approach: Balancing Accountabilities and Scaling Up Results.*

Available at: http://www.imf.org/external/np/pp/eng/2005/091905p.pdf.

International Monetary Fund and the World Bank. 2001. *Poverty Reduction Strategy Papers: Progress in Implementation*, Available at: http://www.imf.org/external/np/prsp/2001/042001.htm.

Ju, J, Lin, JY and Wang, Y. 2009. *Endowment Structures, Industrial Dynamics, and Economic Growth*. Policy Research Working Paper Series 5055, World Bank.

Leibenstein, H. 1957. *Economic Backwardness and Economic Growth*. New York: Wiley.

Lewis, WA. 1954. "Economic development with unlimited supplies of labour", *The Manchester School* 22: 139–191.

Lin, JY and Monga C. 2010. *The Growth Report and New Structural Economics*, Policy Research Working Paper No. 5336, the World Bank, www.worldbank.org.

Lin, JY. 2010. "New structural economics: A framework for rethinking development", *WPS* 5197. Available at: www.worldbank.org.

Meier, G. 2001. "The old generation of development economists and the new", in G Meier, and J Stiglitz (eds). *Frontiers of Development Economics: The Future in Perspective*. Oxford: Oxford University Press.

Mkandawire, T and Soludo, C (eds). 2003. *African Voices on Structural Adjustment: A Companion to "Our Continent, Our Future: African Perspectives on Structural Adjustment"*. Dakar: CODESRIA.

Mkandawire, T. 2006, Disempowering New Democracies and the Persistence of Poverty. Geneva: UNRISD, Democracy, Governance and Human Rights-paper No. 21

Mkandawire, T and Soludo, C. 1999. *Our Continent, Our Future: African Perspectives on Structural Adjustment*. Dakar: CODESRIA.

Nankani, G. 2005. *Creating Shared Growth in Africa*. Public Lecture on 6 December 2004. World Bank, Washington, D.C. Available at: www.worldbank.org.

Nurkse, R. 1953. *Problems of Capital Formation in Underdeveloped Countries*. Oxford: Oxford University Press.

Page, J. 2005. *Strategies for Pro-Poor Growth: Pro-Poor, Pro-Growth or Both?* Available at: http://web.worldbank.org/archive/website-01010/ WEB/IMAGES/STRATEGI.PDF

Rosenstein-Rodan, PN. 1943. "Problems of industrialization in Eastern and Southern Europe", *Economic Journal*, 53.:202- 211

Sen, AK. 1999. *Development as Freedom.* Oxford: Oxford University Press.
Soludo, C. 2003. "In search of alternative analytical and methodological frameworks for an African economic development model", in C. Soludo and T. Mkandawire (eds). *African Voices on Structural Adjustment.* New Jersey: Africa World Press.
Stein, H. 2008. *Beyond the World Bank Agenda: An Institutional Approach to Development.* Chicago: University of Chicago Press.
Tarp, F. 1993. *Stabilization and Structural Adjustment: Macroeconomic Frameworks for Analyzing the Crisis in Sub-Saharan Africa.* London: Routledge.
UNECA. 1989. *African Alternative Framework to Structural Adjustment Programmes for Socio-Economic Recovery and Transformation (AAF-SAP).* Available at: www.uneca.org.
UNECA. 2009. *ECA and Africa: Fifty Years of Partnership.* Ethiopia: Addis Ababa.
World Bank. 2004. *Operational Policies: Development Policy Lending.* Available at: www.worldbank.org.
World Bank. 2005a. *World Development Report 2006: Equity and Development.* Available at: www.worldbank.org.
World Bank. 2005b. *Meeting the Challenge of Africa's Development: A World Bank Group Action Plan.* Available at: www.worldbank.org.
Zagha, R, Nankani, G, and Gill, I. 2006. "Rethinking growth", *Finance and Development* 43(1). Available at http://www.imf.org/external/pubs/ft/fandd/2006/03/zagha.htm.

CHAPTER 3. STABILIZATION, STRUCTURAL ADJUSTMENT AND SUSTAINABLE DEVELOPMENT OF SUB-SAHARAN AFRICA

Ademola Ariyo and Babajide Fowowe

Introduction

Sub-Saharan Africa is arguably the richest sub-continent in the world in terms of resource endowment. However, it is also acknowledged to be the poorest part of the world. This paradox has been attributed to several factors; the rallying one being the endemic poor macroeconomic management by successive governments in respective sub-Saharan Africa countries. However, the region continues to enjoy sustained patronage from the international community, presumably towards ensuring prudent management of its abundant resources. It has, therefore, been a recipient of several "donated" economic reform programs over the years.

The stabilization and Structural Adjustment Program (SAP) packaged by the Bretton Woods Institutions was the most comprehensive of these "donated" programs. Its introduction was greeted with skepticism and concern about its long-term net effect on the sub-Saharan Africa, given the non-sustainable positive effect of its predecessors. In fact, the United Nations system also raised some concerns about the initiative based on the negative consequences of its initial implementation by some sub-Saharan Africa countries. The United Nations Economic Commission for Africa (UNECA), under the leadership of Adebayo Adedeji, eventually proposed an *African Alternative Framework to Structural Adjustment Programmes* (AAF-SAP), which it believed would better help the real transformation and sustainable development of sub-Saharan Africa. Nevertheless, implementation of SAP continued, with financial support from the Bretton Woods Institutions. The effect of its implementation has gone through its full cycle, and the time is ripe to evaluate its net effect on sub-Saharan Africa.

This is the main objective of this chapter, which attempts to explain the behavior of key economic indicators before and after SAP intervention, with a view to assessing its differential impact on sub-Saharan Africa. It will also help relate the findings to the contesting arguments provided by SAP versus AAF-SAP schools of thought. While counter-factual evidence based on AAF-SAP might not be feasible, the appraisal will nevertheless enhance an informed judgment of the validity of the contesting positions of the two schools and other stakeholder groups. The lessons will help guide the conceptualization, design and implementation of similar initiatives in the future.

The remainder of the chapter is arranged as follows. The next section articulates the main thrust, key components and the financing of SAP, as well as the major postulations of AAF-SAP. This allows an articulation of the areas of similarities and differences between the contesting initiatives. Next, we discuss the methodology employed, followed by data analysis and discussion of the study's findings, using a decision-theoretic framework to explain that the position of the Bretton Woods Institutions – informed largely by the desire to maximize its utility – led to massive lending for SAP implementation, regardless of its net effect on the affected countries and their citizens. This is followed by a discussion of some necessary conditions for ensuring sub-Saharan Africa's sustainable development in the aftermath of SAP, while the final section contains the concluding remarks.

Stabilization and structural adjustment

Overview

The word "adjustment" refers to bridging the gap between what exists and what is required (Hussain and Faruqee, 1994). Bridging this gap usually requires institutional reforms and series of policies, programs and activities. There are two components of this program. The first is *stabilization*, which seeks to halt the process precipitating the slide in a nation's economic performance. It encompasses short-term measures for instant or quick relief. The other component is *structural adjustment*, aimed at evolving a more effective and efficient operating system towards enhanced quality of macroeconomic management of each target economy.

SAP generally focuses on four major policy areas. First, a common starting point is the adjustment in the area of foreign exchange management, beginning with currency devaluation in order to deal with overvaluation of national currencies. This leads to an automatic increase in the price of imports, and ultimately of domestic prices, especially of import-dependent economies, with the consequent inflationary trends.

Second, drastic cuts in government spending are used to reduce deficits in the public sector and also to shift resources and economic activities from the public to the private sector. It also seeks to effect a decrease in aggregate demand in order to stem inflation. The cuts often lead to elimination or significant reduction in subsidies and some government services. These include education, health and other sectors that contribute to social welfare, particularly of low income and vulnerable groups. The privatization of state-owned enterprises is also a major tool employed to reduce the size of the public sector. It has the potential for reducing public sector deficit and wasteful expenditure. However, it has also played a significant role in promoting exclusive emphasis on the market, to the neglect of the welfare promotion and human development roles of the state.

Third, SAP has been used to stimulate major and irreversible economic restructuring through market deregulation, including labor and capital markets. This, in turn, creates strong pressures to restructure production, necessitating the introduction of new technologies and reorganization of labor-intensive processes, and placing emphasis on efficiency and modernization.

Finally, this process was reinforced by trade liberalization and the easing of rules regulating foreign investment, increasing the degree of globalization of the economy, and shifting emphasis towards production of tradables over non-tradables. This reinforces the need for higher productivity to enhance the competitiveness of exports.

It will be recalled that the Bretton Woods Institutions readily provided massive loans for the implementation of SAP in every sub-

Saharan Africa country. Several conditionalities attached to such loans virtually made the lenders the effective managers of the SAP-implementing economies.

Concerns of AAF-SAP

SAP came under heavy criticism following the first round of its implementation by some African countries. These criticisms stemmed from the fact that the economies of implementing countries actually deteriorated rather than improved, especially in the short run. This fuelled the fear and arguments that SAP would not be able to adequately address the problems of African economies. In addition, most United Nations agencies criticized SAP for its neglect of human issues in its design and implementation. Such views were actively debated in 1986 at the extra-ordinary session of the United Nations General Assembly, which evolved a strategy encapsulated in its United Nations Program of Action for African Economic Recovery and Development (UNPAAERD). The central tenet of UNPAAERD was that adjustment, though necessary for economic recovery of African countries, should not be conceived and implemented in the "narrow" manner as proposed by the Bretton Woods Institutions and that, rather, policies should be focused on sustainable (human-centered) development. The most detailed analysis of the major flaws of SAP was contained in the AAF-SAP released by UNECA.

The AAF-SAP identified the neglect of the structural features and problems of African countries as a major flaw of SAP. These include predominance of subsistence and commercial activities, narrow production base, neglect of the informal sector, environmental degradation, and lopsided development. Others include fragmentation of the African economy, heavy external dependence and weak institutional capabilities. AAF-SAP admitted that the focus of SAP was to achieve fiscal and external balances and ensure that markets operated freely, which was laudable. It, however, noted that these alone would not help achieve the much-desired economic transformation, which it considered a *sine qua non* for accelerated growth and sustainable development. It also argued that SAP's exclusive reliance on presumed competitive domestic and external markets was nothing short of self-delusion, given that African economies are basically characterized by imperfect and distorted markets, price rigidities, fragile production structures and weak institutions.

One of the notable features of AAF-SAP was its emphasis on the social dimension of development, which was ignored by SAP. These include issues such as generation of gainful employment for the citizenry and equitable income distribution. Deriving from this neglect of socio-economic issues, SAP tended to offer only a short-term solution to improvements in macroeconomic aggregates, in a manner that could result in the deterioration of socio-economic variables over time, such as employment and poverty alleviation.

The major thrust of AAF-SAP, therefore, was that, though desirable and even inevitable, structural adjustment must be accompanied with policies and programs that ensure structural transformation that will help overcome the deficiencies and peculiarities of the economies of sub-Saharan Africa. Towards this end, AAF-SAP prepared three themes on which the structural adjustment for sub-Saharan Africa must be anchored. These are:

i. A more human-centered development process that will also ensure diversification from primary production to the manufacturing of local raw materials;
ii. A really inclusive policy and development process that will enhance the quality of economic governance, which is a necessary condition for balanced and sustainable development, including continual improvement in human welfare; and
iii. Promotion and sustenance of a high level of investment towards achieving the desired level of growth coupled with high quality public service delivery, to be achieved through strong and efficient public institutions.

AAF-SAP emphasized that without these, SAP may not effectively address the fundamental development obstacles confronting sub-Saharan Africa.

Methodology

As noted earlier, this chapter seeks to provide research evidence bearing on the differential effects of SAP on Africa's socio-economic performance. Such evidence should be related to its underlying objectives of stabilizing the economy and the ensuing structural adjustment expected to enhance, among other things, the international sustainable development of sub-Saharan Africa. We will also provide evidence on the extent to which SAP has impacted on other desirable outcomes enunciated in the AAF-SAP document. These considerations have informed the components of the methodology employed for this chapter.

Research design

To capture as accurately as possible the differential impact of SAP, we adopted a pre- and post-SAP research design. Hence, we have selected the period from 1970 to 2000 as the study period, as it allows us to have sufficient trend data for the pre- and post-SAP analysis. The modal year for the commencement of implementation of SAP across sub-Saharan Africa was 1986, and this was adopted as the cut-off year for the pre- and post-analytical design. Similarly, we did not go beyond 2000 when SAP had run its full-cycle, and new initiatives were being introduced to chart a new course for each African country.

Relevant indicators

The socio-economic variables targeted by both SAP and AAF-SAP constituted the element indicator for our analysis. These include the trend and volatility in economic output in aggregate and per capita terms; sub-Saharan Africa's share in world trade; agricultural value-added, external debt; and real trends in human development indicators. Time series data covering the study period were collected in respect of selected variables. A simple t-test for differences in means of pre- and post-SAP time-series data was considered appropriate for providing the required research evidence. In addition, simple line graphs were provided to facilitate better appreciation of the pre- and post-SAP behavior of selected variables.

Data analysis

Summary data analysis

Table 3.1 presents a country-level overview of average values of selected macroeconomic indicators across sub-Saharan Africa. For example, while post-SAP GDP growth rate was higher for Burkina Faso and Ghana, it was lower in Cameroun, Kenya and Malawi. All the countries however recorded significant increases in external debt flows. The last row summarizes the average for sub-Saharan Africa as a whole, with observations similar to those for individual countries therein.

Table 3.1: Average macroeconomic variables for selected countries before and after SAP

Country	Period	GDP Gr	PC GDP Grow	Agric	Debt	Inv
Benin	pre-SAP	2.98	-0.01	33.38	37.38	15.51
	post-SAP	3.98	0.58	36.12	77.66	16.12
Burkina Faso	pre-SAP	3.57	1.07	29.36	18.89	18.59
	post-SAP	4.96	1.94	32.22	52.31	22.38
Cameroon	pre-SAP	5.64	2.64	28.21	32.45	22.58
	post-SAP	0.76	-1.85	24.07	94.02	14.94
Gambia	pre-SAP	4.48	1.04	34.55	55.12	15.47
	post-SAP	3.53	-0.22	30.01	120.20	19.42
Ghana	pre-SAP	1.32	-1.35	51.84	35.88	8.64
	post-SAP	4.39	1.68	40.69	80.71	19.07
Kenya	pre-SAP	7.02	3.17	35.35	38.34	23.33
	post-SAP	2.98	-0.32	31.57	71.39	20.17
Malawi	pre-SAP	4.81	1.59	42.78	54.27	26.23
	post-SAP	3.42	0.23	40.54	109.71	17.99
Mali	pre-SAP	2.42	0.15	52.84	67.80	16.07
	post-SAP	4.23	1.53	46.33	120.16	22.62
Nigeria	pre-SAP	3.70	0.88	33.03	26.79	20.09
	post-SAP	3.75	0.85	31.86	119.15	19.31
Senegal	pre-SAP	2.67	-0.26	25.41	25.33	16.50
	post-SAP	2.76	-0.10	20.75	77.50	14.15
Togo	pre-SAP	2.45	-0.52	29.55	64.29	26.81
	post-SAP	2.90	-0.40	35.82	103.67	16.55
Zambia	pre-SAP	1.34	-1.93	15.00	111.08	25.21
	post-SAP	1.09	-1.56	20.32	220.67	14.11
Sub-Saharan Africa	Pre-SAP	3.09	0.19	20.79	25.67	23.03
	Post-SAP	2.43	-0.33	19.34	66.71	17.75

Source: World Bank, 2008

Notes: GDP= GDP (constant US$ million), GDPGR= GDP Growth (%), PC GDP Grow= per capita GDP growth (%), Agric= Agriculture, value added (% of GDP), Debt= External debt (% of GNI), Inv=Investment (% of GDP)

Table 3.2, on the other hand, presents the results of the t-test for differences in pre- and post-SAP means for selected variables. The results suggest insignificant pre- and post-SAP differences with respect to aggregate and per capita real GDP growth, at the 5 per cent significance level. Significant differences were however reported with respect to agricultural value-added, external debt and investment ratio. These form the basis for more detailed analysis and the discussion of these summary findings.

Table 3.2: Test for differences between pre- and post-SAP data

	GDP Gr	PC GDP Grow	Agric	Debt	Inv
Pre-SAP	3.09	0.19	20.79	25.67	23.03
Post-SAP	2.43	-0.33	19.34	66.71	17.75
T-Test	0.17 [0.8674]	-0.08 [0.9373]	4.47* [0.0006]	-10.89* [0.0000]	6.27* [0.0000]

Source: World Bank. 2008
Notes: See Table 3.1 for definitions of variables
The null hypothesis of the t-test is that the difference between the pre-SAP and post-SAP mean values is zero. * indicates that the t-test is statistically significant at the 5% level.

Discussion of results

Real GDP growth rate

The results showed no significant difference in the real GDP growth rate both in aggregate and per capita terms between the pre- and post-SAP era, suggesting the absence of its differential impact on the aggregate output of sub-Saharan Africa, in spite of the comprehensive stabilization and structural adjustment programs across the continent. This also implies SAP's inability to transform the structure of the economy and productive systems of sub-Saharan Africa. A comparison of the trends of aggregate and per capita GDP growth rates reported in Figure 3.1 shows that the latter was generally lower than the former. This suggests that the rate of growth of real GDP was, on average, less than the growth rate of the population.

Moreover, it appears SAP could not adequately protect African economies against the vagaries of the international economic environment in 1992, when both growth rates nosedived into the negative before reverting to the positive thereafter. Of further concern was the persistence of the general episodic fluctuations in the real growth rates even after SAP. This was another evidence of the absence of a transformation of the productive systems, which could have significantly insulated the economies of sub-Saharan Africa against the vagaries of the international trading environment.

Figure 3.1: Real GDP growth rate: aggregate and per capita

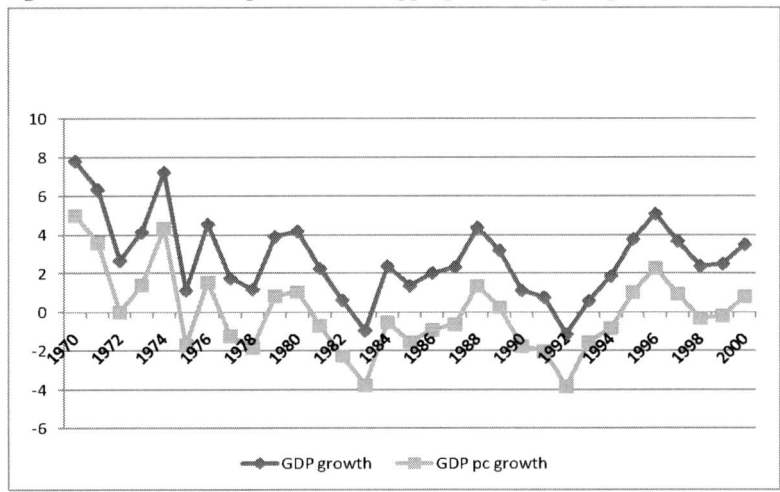

Source: World Bank, 2008

Real commodity prices

One of the major goals of SAP was to encourage increased production and export of agricultural commodities in a liberalized economy. This precipitated the scrapping of commodity boards which hitherto ensured right quality of exportable agricultural products, and also guaranteed agreed minimum price to farmers. Hence, individual farmers became exposed to the vagaries of international commodity markets, while the quality of their exports could not be guaranteed. In the process, real commodity prices declined gradually but steadily after SAP, thus aggravating the operating and financial risks to which farmers became exposed. The resultant sharp decline in agricultural output threw many farmers into involuntary unemployment. Hence, the legacy which SAP endowed to farmers was their displacement from their normal means of livelihood without providing viable alternatives for them. This was the beginning of large scale-abject poverty, which still stares a large majority of citizens of sub-Saharan Africa countries in the face.

Agricultural value-added

Agriculture was the mainstay of most economies in sub-Saharan Africa before SAP was introduced during the 1980s. Yet, public sector agencies in charge of the agricultural sector were one of the first targets to be eliminated under the institutional reforms of SAP, culminating in the scrapping of commodity boards and associated structures. The aim was to enhance the level of liberalization of the commodity trade sector, which would in turn significantly increase the contribution of the sector to national output, employment generation and food security. Incidentally, there were no reliable data on agricultural production in sub-Saharan Africa to evaluate the realization of these anticipated benefits. However, we had access to data on agricultural value-added as a proportion of GDP, which is even more germane to the focus of this study.

The findings reported in Table 3.2 showed that the pre-SAP values were significantly higher than the post-SAP era, while Figure 3.2 also provides an insight into the nature of fluctuations in this indicator. Noteworthy were the higher fluctuations therein as from 1984, when farmers in many sub-Saharan African countries became exposed directly to the vagaries of the international commodity markets, with the scrapping of commodity boards. It is also important to recognize the sharp decline in this indicator as from 1998, when the cumulative effects of SAP on the agricultural sector seem to have matured. The trend generally suggests a negative long-term effect of SAP on this indicator.

Figure 3.2: Agriculture value added as a ratio to GDP

Agriculture value added as a ratio to GDP (%)

[Line graph showing values declining from about 22.5% in 1970 to about 17.5% in 2000, with fluctuations including dips around 1980, 1992, and recoveries in between.]

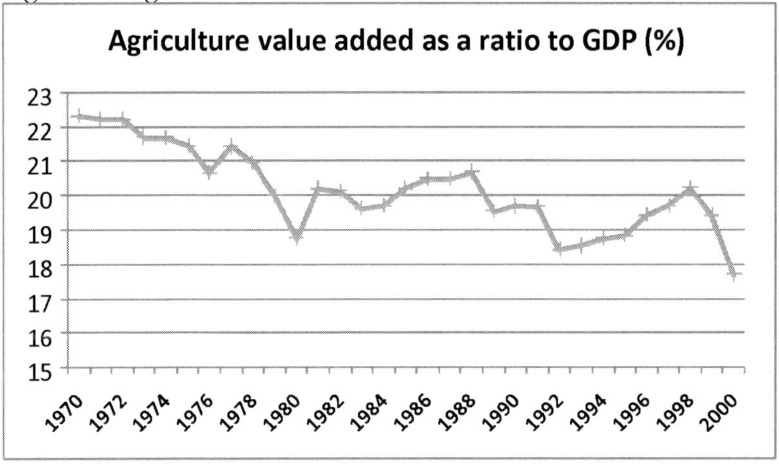

Source: World Bank, 2008

Gross domestic investment ratio

A post-SAP deregulated and liberalized sub-Saharan Africa is supposed to attract significant increase in investment inflows to propel the realization of the much-needed growth. Towards this end, we evaluated the response of domestic investment to SAP. Table 3.2 shows that the post-SAP domestic investment ratio (gross domestic investment as a production of GDP) in sub-Saharan Africa was significantly lower than its pre-SAP level. This infers that the causes and sources of any improvement in aggregate national output were driven by external factors, thus aggravating the level of dependence of the economies of sub-Saharan Africa.

External debt profile

A lot of resource inflows were required for the implementation of SAP. Potential sources of these inflows include national savings, domestic investments, and debt-denominated or non-debt capital flows. At the commencement of implementation of SAP, most of these non-debt sources were not viable in sub-Saharan Africa. The only reliable source available for funding SAP therefore was external loans, where massive flows for SAP implementation precipitated persistent serious fiscal sustainability problems for sub-Saharan Africa.

There was another notable dimension to these loan-support

flows. One of the cardinal objectives of SAP was to evolve a deregulated economic system in which the market would play a dominant role in the allocation of national resources, with the private sector expected to become the engine of growth. The realization of this objective was dependent on the level of support available to the private sector. However, perhaps ironically, most of the resource flows went to the public sector, with a corresponding decrease in resource flows to the private sector (Ariyo, 1996a). There was, therefore, an inherent contradiction between the aims of SAP and prioritization of resource flows to the private sector as targeted agents of envisaged sustainable improvements in the economy of sub-Saharan Africa, on one hand, and the massive debt-creating flows to the public sector, on the other hand.

Africa's share of world trade

Trade is the engine of international economic relations and largely determines the welfare of every nation participating therein. Hence, an important benchmark for assessing the worth of SAP is the extent to which it affects the share of sub-Saharan Africa in world trade. More importantly, in consonance with the export-led growth philosophy, there should be a sustained appreciable increase in the exports of any liberalizing sub-Saharan Africa country to the world, while its importation of final consumer goods should reduce significantly, over time. In addition, the boost in domestic industrial goods anchored on local content policy should reflect in a significant reduction in the importation of other categories of goods and services.

The findings reported in Figure 3.3 suggest the opposite for post-SAP sub-Saharan Africa, whereby the decline that started as from 1980 accelerated during the post-SAP era, and this trend continued until around 2000. These findings call into question the net benefit of SAP in enhancing sub-Saharan Africa's share in world trade. Incidentally, the proceeds of increased export were expected to finance the huge external loans used to finalize the implementation of SAP.

Figure 3.3: Prices of agricultural products

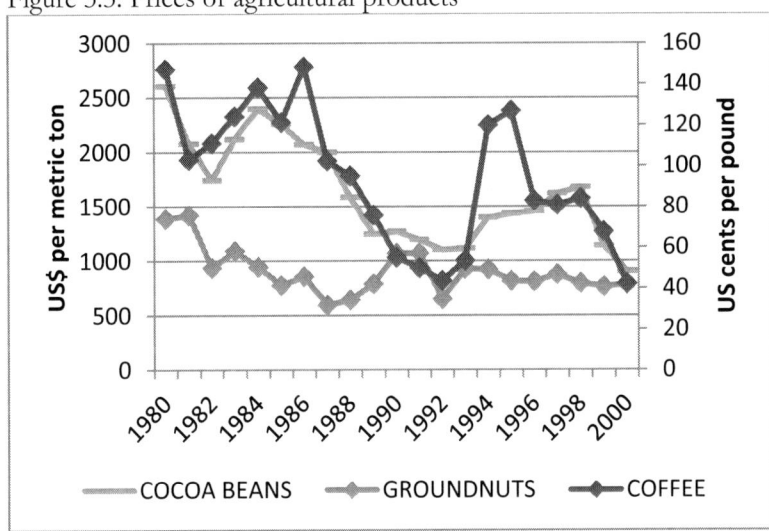

Source: International Monetary Fund, 2008

Human development indicators (HDI)

The net impact on human development is the ultimate measure of effective public policy program, SAP inclusive. This appears to inform the mainstreaming of this human dimension by AAF-SAP. Unfortunately, we had no access to reliable or adequate data on the changes in the level of and sovereignty of poverty, as a shadow indicator for change in human welfare.

Consequently, we utilized the limited five-yearly data on human development indicator (HDI) for sub-Saharan Africa that is published by both the United Nations Development Program and the World Bank. The observed trend reported in Figure 3.4 shows that the HDI increased from about 0.41 in 1980 to about 0.49 in year 2000. This increase translates to a near-zero annual growth rate over the 25-year period. This does not seem to justify the massive resources committed by sub-Saharan Africa and the enormous sacrifices made by its citizens. In fact, we can conclude that the risk-adjusted rate of increase in HDI was really negative. The figure also showed that there was no change in the relative status of sub-Saharan African HDI compared to that of the countries of the Organization of Economic Cooperation and Development (OECD) during the period. This depicts the neutrality of SAP intervention in improving the relative position of HDI for sub-Saharan Africa.

Figure 3.4: Sub-Saharan Africa (SSA) and OECD human development indicators (HDI), 1980–2000

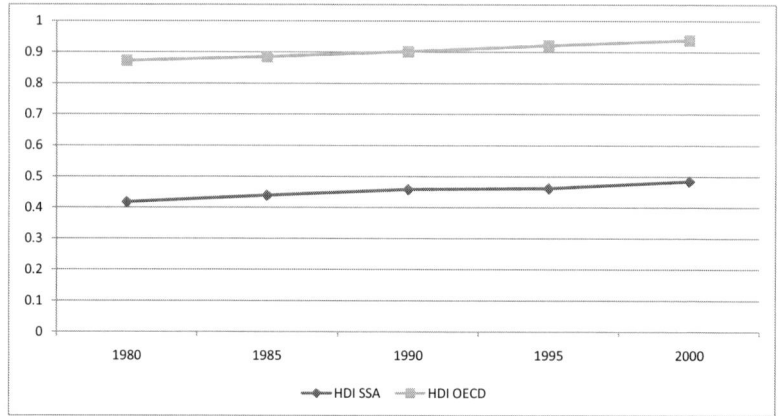

Source: United Nations Development Program, 2008

Utility considerations in lending support for SAP

One question that still bothers sub-Saharan Africa development experts and analysts is: Why did the Bretton Woods Institutions give full support to the implementation of SAP, in spite of credible signals that it would not address effectively the real development challenges of sub-Saharan Africa? This question remains potent, more so, when the predicted "failure" materialized. In our view, while there was consensus on its substance, there were divergences of views on the form of the initiative, especially with respect to the underlying assumptions, focus, scope and financing of SAP.

The literature on decision-making may provide some insight into the behavioral dimensions of this puzzle. In this regard, we elaborate the role of utility functions on the quality of decisions under conditions of uncertainty. Towards this, the literature has made a distinction between *predictions* versus *choice* in a task situation. For example, Howell and Burnett (1978) indicate that *prediction* involves all or non-specification of future event outcomes. Such prediction, the authors note, should reflect the event to which the judge ascribes the greatest likelihood at the moment. According to Benson and

Nichols (1982), *choice* requires the individual not only to predict the outcome of a future event or series of events, but to actually choose one alternative over the others and be prepared to accept the consequences. Hence, the only logical difference between prediction and choice is that the latter usually involves utility considerations.

This distinction is analogous to the one between *conclusions* versus *decisions* noted by Turkey (1960). He states that a *conclusion* is a statement which is to be accepted as applicable to the conditions of an experiment or observation unless and until unusually strong evidence to the contrary arises. These conclusions, he indicates, are established with careful regard to evidence, but without regard to consequence of specification in specific circumstances. *Decisions*, on the other hand, are based not only on an evaluation of available evidence, but also on the consequences of alternative courses of action open to the decision-maker. In other words, a decision entails the weighing of both the evidence concerning the relative merits of two (or more) alternative hypotheses and also the possible consequences of various actions. One then decides therefrom that a particular course of action is the most appropriate to take under the given circumstance, while the decision-maker takes responsibility for the consequences of such a decision.

The above review seems to help provide an explanation for the decision of the Bretton Woods Institutions to encourage implementation of SAP in spite of valid objections from several credible, eligible and informed sources. To put this in proper perspective, we highlight the features of the Bretton Woods Institutions lending operations. In the first instance, the Bretton Woods Institutions lend to needy countries without sharing the risk associated with the negative consequences of such decisions. Such framework enables these institutions to continually "push" their funds as loans to the vulnerable economies, whether they have a felt need for it or not. The profit from such lending helps to enlarge the pool of loanable funds. Secondly, through the numerous conditionalities attached to such loans, the Bretton Woods Institutions entrench themselves in a position to wield powers on the economic policy procedures and decisions of SAP-implementing countries.

Thirdly, the sustenance of this behavior is further enhanced by the fact that the Bretton Woods Institutions often initiate some of the programs for which they provide funding support. It is, therefore, not out of place to suspect that the Bretton Woods Institutions continually develop programs to guarantee lending outlets for their massive financial resources. This is the basis for the calculation of the "financing gap" by the Bretton Woods Institutions, which at the same time they are always ready to fill on their own terms and conditions.

A similar view applies to the self-serving leadership of many sub-Saharan Africa countries. In this regard, we recollect that SAP was implemented when many sub-Saharan African countries were under military regimes, which were not accountable to the citizenry. Hence, given their relatively low level of understanding of the technicalities inherent in SAP, they were easily persuaded to accept uncritically the offer of external loan support to implement SAP, without carrying the citizenry along. This culture has persisted ever since, even under the so-called democratic regimes in many sub-Saharan African countries. There was, therefore, a convergence of self-interest between the Bretton Woods Institutions and leaders of sub-Saharan Africa who are insulated from the consequences of their lending and borrowing decisions respectively. This free-riding framework is, no doubt, a major cause of the heavy indebtedness of sub-Saharan Africa to the international community. Available evidence indicates that this scenario has been, and remains, the main cause of mismanagement of sub-Saharan Africa economies (Ariyo, 1993).

A final observation relates to the heavy reliance on loans as the major source of development financing support for sub-Saharan Africa, perhaps due to the non-viability of non-debt sources. Unfortunately, these loans appear unable to foster the turn-around of sub-Saharan Africa, whereby they plunge into deeper indebtedness. It is also notable that the literature has argued that loans may never be the most desirable source of development financing for currently developing economics, especially if they were to attain the feat achieved by currently developed economies (Adesoye, 2008; Ariyo, 1999; Rostow, 1982). However, both the international lending institutions and the leadership of sub-Saharan Africa countries often act in contrast to these facts, mainly because of convergence of self-interest against the helpless citizens of sub-Saharan Africa countries. This dicey scenario calls for ingenuity in carving a new financial infrastructure conducive to the sustainable development of sub-Saharan Africa.

Evidence from the literature suggests that the failure of SAP could not have been a surprise. In fact, it represented another index in the list of failed initiatives similarly financed by the Bretton Woods Institutions, as the performance of the World Bank, over time, had been adjudged as dismal. Specifically, in one of its publications in the 1990s, the Bank admitted the high failure rates in its completed projects. For example, these soared to almost two-fifths of completed projects in 1991. Between 1981 and 1992, the failure rates were 15 per cent in 1981, 30.5 per cent in 1989 and 37.5 per cent in 1992 (Chatterjee, 1992).

Perhaps the SAP experience was a "breed apart" in two main respects. First, its comprehensiveness and the enormous resources committed to its implementation made it a high profile case. Secondly, perhaps unlike its predecessors, SAP was a failure foretold. It is therefore important to attempt to unravel the reasons for the implementation of SAP in spite of the well-grounded argument to the contrary, as well as prediction of its failure. The next section provides an insight from a decision-theoretic perspective.

The second major case relates to the operating procedures of the Bretton Woods Institutions. According to Adedeji (1995: 32) representatives of governments of affected African countries have attributed the dismal performance of the activities of the World Bank to some factors. These include the following:

i. Bank staff appear always to be driven more by pressure to lend than by a desire for successful project implementation;
ii. The Bank always insisted on the so-called international consultants with no local experience to prepare projects, resulting inevitably in poor quality. And where there is a condescension to use local talents, they are invariably the Bank's preferred experts; and
iii. Bank staff often make the potential recipients feel "psychologically pressured" to take the loan or leave it.

The third major cause was the attitude of African governments and their leaders which made sub-Saharan Africa appear to be helpless without support from the Bretton Woods Institutions. Such support is normally accompanied with tough measures which in effect erode their countries' sovereignty and power to determine and implement their own economic policies and programs. In support of this view point, Singer (1995:10) noted that "many people, including eminent scholars like Arthur Lewis, were sure that the proud and independent countries, poor as they might be, would refuse to accept such tough conditionality!" This prediction turned out to be an overrating of the ability to resist the Bank's neo-colonialism. As noted by Adedeji (1995: 31), "in the 1980s – Africa's lost decade, as I christened it – the strong influence of the Bretton Woods Institutions on African countries took unprecedented and unparalleled proportions".

Sub-Saharan Africas post-SAP turn-around: Some proposals

Many issues have been highlighted that need to be carefully considered to re-position post-SAP sub-Saharan Africa along the path of accelerated growth and sustainable development. To help put the issues in proper perspective, we have adopted a cause-and-effect framework for our discussion, so that we will not fall into the temptation of ignoring the substance, while chasing the shadows of the issues in focus.

In our view, Adedeji (2008) has articulated the major causes of the problems associated with SAP, and included other externally-driven reform programs or initiatives. According to him, SAP and its ilk were driven solely by ideological considerations reminiscent of the Cold War. Hence their formulation was neither guided by the requisite economic rationality nor the genuine concern about their real development potentials, especially for African countries. He identified the Bretton Woods Institutions as major agents for expanding and entrenching this ideological indoctrination across the globe, and as being, therefore, part of the problems of, rather than of the solutions to, the development challenges of developing countries.

The above provides a useful insight into the seemingly tractable ineffectiveness of externally driven economic reforms and development initiatives plaguing Africa. Hence, all subsequent efforts should prioritize the removal of these "termites", rather than focusing on their consequences. For example, there have been some loud agitations for the review of the mandate and activities of the Bretton Woods Institutions. There have, also been calls for the establishment of an African Monetary Fund to help address the peculiar problems of SAP. These types of initiatives should be revisited without further delay.

It is also important to start re-evaluating the desirability of debt-creating flows to finance the development of sub-Saharan Africa. There is widespread belief in sub-Saharan Africa and among development analysts that such support had not had, nor would it have, any enduring positive impact. The literature has also warned that developing economies should be very careful about loan financing if they are to achieve the feat attained by currently developed economies (Rostow, 1982). This is an important warning because it appears the servicing of any new loan becomes an additional burden and hence results in a net depletion of the lean resources of an already weak economy. This is why such an arrangement has been equated with the financing of underdevelopment (Ariyo, 2006). In fact the literature has shown that trade-based revenue, rather than loans or aid, is the most appropriate source of financing the development needs of developing economies (Adesoye, 2008; Ariyo, 1999).

A major issue relates to the sharing of responsibilities for the consequences of implementation of any international initiative. The problem appears to center on the financier having an upper hand in implementing SAP despite serious doubts about its benefit to sub-Saharan Africa. We also noted earlier that SAP was essentially a loan-push program, regardless of its outcomes, for reasons identified in the literature cited earlier. This practice of generating externalities for borrowing countries will continue unabated unless and until all parties are made to share the burden of the consequences of such lending or borrowing programs.

All these issues tie in closely with the five cardinal principles for development. These are: self-reliance, self-sustainment, socio-economic transformation, holistic human development, and democratization of the development process, which, according to Adedeji (2002), have been at the heart of every African-designed development initiative over time. These include the *Revised Framework of Principles of the Implementation of the New International Order in Africa* in 1976-1981-1986; the Monrovia Strategy in 1979; the Final Act of Lagos Plan of Action in 1980, and the AAF-SAP in 1988. Thus, even in cases where African governments have to obtain loans from the Bretton Woods Institutions or, as Adedeji (2002) called them, development merchant institutions, the best interests of the African people must be the ultimate objective. This requires that African governments and people must be the sole drivers of any projects that emanate from such loans or assistance.

Finally, it has been argued that reducing economic development to mere focus on capital accumulation and market-induced efficiency in resource allocation may perpetuate the backwardness of many poor countries (Jomo, 2008; Adedeji, 2008). These are fundamental issues that need to be addressed in future development initiatives which must be led by Africans themselves.

Conclusion

In this chapter, we have highlighted the contesting viewpoints regarding the relevance of stabilization and structural adjustment towards effectively addressing the development challenges of sub-Saharan Africa. These viewpoints were, on the one hand, those represented by the Bretton Woods Institutions and on the other hand, by AAF-SAP. We observe that while the two views endorsed the substance of stabilization and SAP, they differed on the underlying assumptions, scope and modalities of implementation, as well as the focus of impact assessment. Incidentally, the stylized facts presented suggest that SAP was a failure foretold by AAF-SAP. We have further noted that this was consistent with the high failure rates of similar Bretton Woods Institutions projects and programs over time.

We have also provided a seemingly novel perspective to explaining the Bretton Woods Institutions decision to go ahead with the implementation of its own version of SAP. For example, the decision-theoretic explanation suggests that the Bretton Woods Institutions may continue to operate as they do now as long as they are insulated from the consequences of their actions, while their "clients" fully bear the consequences thereof. Also highlighted was the undesirable attitude of African governments and their leaders, which has encouraged the perpetuation of the stance of the Bretton Woods Institutions as noted herewith. This seems to be a major discriminatory factor between the plight of sub-Saharan Africa and that of other peer countries of East Africa and Latin America, which deal with the Bretton Woods Institutions at arm's length.

The essence of this chapter is not to once again engage in buck-passing between the Bretton Woods Institutions and sub-Saharan Africa. Rather, it draws attention to key issues that need to be resolved once and for all by all parties concerned, in order to relieve sub-Saharan Africa from the cycle of lamentations about its plight under the new international economic order.

It is in view of this that we enjoin the Bretton Woods Institutions and sub-Saharan Africa to go back to the drawing board and chart a genuine new course of action towards making the desired difference. This calls for better understanding of the viewpoints of both parties, as well as the need to allow sub-Saharan Africa to have an effective voice in all issues affecting its future.

References

Adedeji, A. 1995. "An African perspective on Bretton Woods", in M ul Haq, R Jolly, P Streeten and K Haq (eds). *The UN and the Bretton Woods Institutions.* London: Macmillan.

Adedeji, A. 2002. "From the Lagos Plan of Action to the New Partnership for African Development and from the Final Act of Lagos to the Constitutive Act: Wither Africa?" Keynote Address presented at the African Forum for Envisioning Africa, Nairobi, Kenya, 26–29 April 2002.

Adedeji, A. 2008. "Neoclassicalism and all that: The mantra of marketisation, liberalisation, privatisation, globalisation and financialisation". Guest Lecture at the 2008 Ojetunji Aboyade Annual Memorial Lecture Series, University of Ibadan, Nigeria, 26 November.

Adesoye, B. 2008. "A portfolio selection approach to development financing in Nigeria". Unpublished PhD Thesis, University of Ibadan, Nigeria.

Ariyo, A. 1993. "Utility considerations in judgments under uncertainty: Evidence and some policy implications" in TA Oyejide and MI Obadan (eds) *Applied Economics and Economic Policy.* Ibadan: Ibadan University Press.

Ariyo, A. 1996a. "Economic reform, fiscal stance and the Nigerian private sector: Some reflections", in A. Ariyo (ed.) *Economic Reform and Macroeconomic Management in Nigeria.* Ibadan: Ibadan University Press.

Ariyo, A. 1996b. "Reliability of macroeconomic data: Evidence from Nigeria's debt data series", *African Development Review*, 7(1): 88–102.

Ariyo, A. 1999. "Appropriateness of development financing mix of sub-Saharan African countries: An evidence from Nigeria", *Nigerian Journal of Economic and Social Studies,* 41(1): 159–173.

Ariyo, A. 2006. "Development financing of underdevelopment". Inaugural Lecture, University of Ibadan, Nigeria, September 2006.

Benson, PG and Nichols, L. 1982. "An investigation of motivational

bias in subjective predictive probability distributions", *Decision Sciences* 13: 225–239.
Chatterjee, P. 1992. "World Bank failure soars to 37.5 per cent of completed projects in 1991", *Third World Economics* 55:2–3.
Haque, NU and Khan, MS. 1998. "Do IMF programmes work? A survey of the cross-country empirical evidence", *IMF Working Papers 98/169*, International Monetary Fund.
Howell, WC and Burnett, SA. 1978. Uncertainty measurement: A cognitive taxonomy. *Organisational Behavioural and Human Performance* 22:45–68.
Hussain, I and Faruqee, R (eds). 1994. *Adjustment in Africa: Lessons from Country Case Studies*. World Bank Regional and Sectoral Studies. Washington D.C: World Bank.
International Monetary Fund. 2008. *International Financial Statistics*. CD-ROM, Washington D.C: International Monetary Fund.
Rostow, WW. 1982. *Stages of Economic Development*. New York: Cambridge University Press.
Singer, HW. 1995. "An historical perspective", in M ul Haq, R Jolly, P Streeten and K Haq (eds). *The UN and the Bretton Woods Institutions*. London: Macmillan.
Turkey, JW. 1960. "Conclusions vs. decisions", *Technometrics* 2: 423–433.
UNECA. 1988. *African Alternative Framework to Structural Adjustment Programmes for Socio-Economic Recovery and Transformation (AAF-SAP)*. Addis-Ababa: ECA.
United Nations Development Program. 2008. *Human Development Indices*. New York: UNDP.
World Bank. 2008. *World Development Indicators* (CD-ROM). Washington D.C: World Bank.

PART 2.
REGIONAL INTEGRATION AND COOPERATION

CHAPTER 4. A TALE OF TWO PROPHETS: JEAN MONNET AND ADEBAYO ADEDEJI

Adekeye Adebajo

Introduction

This chapter[1] assesses the role, vision, and impact of two political prophets – Jean Monnet (France), and Adebayo Adedeji (Nigeria) – who are widely regarded to have been the fathers of regional integration in Europe and Africa respectively. Both Adedeji and Monnet came from small, provincial towns and attained global fame and recognition. Both were propelled into prominence and achieved professional success at an early age. Both were put in charge of reconstructing their countries after destructive conflicts: the Second World War (1939–1945) and the Nigerian Civil War (1967–1970). Both were men of vision and grand ideas who focused particularly on regional integration and peacemaking and who enjoyed the trust of powerful political actors on their respective continents. Both were pragmatists and realists who used the force of superior arguments and dynamic political maneuvering to promote their goals but who were, however, ultimately frustrated in their efforts to unite Europe

---

1 This chapter builds on earlier writings by Adebajo: "'African Cassandra' Adedeji comes full circle on NEPAD" (2006) and "Towers of Babel? The African Union and the European Union" (in Adebajo, 2010: 272–274).

and Africa respectively.

Jean Monnet

Jean Monnet is popularly regarded as the "father of European integration". This remarkable man, who grew up in the French brandy-producing town of Cognac, started out by working in his family's cognac business (The Society of Cognac Vine-growers). Monnet's travels to Europe, North America, Asia, and Africa provided him with an education on other cultures which he would later put at the service of international cooperation. His father had learned German in order to expand his business to the other side of the Rhine and beyond, traveling to Germany, Sweden, and Russia. As Monnet noted "we knew that our existence depended on the prosperity and the tastes of people all over the world" (1978: 40). A sense of *noblesse oblige* and a desire to contribute to the "public good" was inculcated in Jean by his father early in life.

Monnet did not like school much and what he described as "bookish knowledge", preferring the "school of life" which would enable him to "see the world". Sent by his father at the age of 16 to live with a wine merchant in London (after Jean abandoned his university entrance examinations), he learned English in order to be able to communicate with his clientele. At 18 years old, Monnet traveled to the United States, Sweden, Russia, Greece, and Egypt. As he later observed: "On my travels I had learned that economic forces were not blind and abstract, but could be measured and steered. Above all, I had come to realize that where there was organization there was real strength" (Monnet, 1978: 49).The cognac business thus forced Monnet to expand his horizons beyond the provincialism of his small French town to become a cosmopolitan citizen of the world.

During the First World War (1914–1918), through the Inter-Allied Maritime Commission, Monnet coordinated the supplies of merchant fleets, pushing them to charge the same freight rates to ensure more efficient delivery of priority supplies. During the Second World War, he also led Anglo-French supply programs. Though Monnet was keen to use international cooperation as a means of avoiding war, he also contributed to war efforts to achieve peace. He was always a pragmatic realist, rather than an idealistic pacifist. At the age of thirty, Monnet became Deputy Secretary-General of the League of Nations – the precursor to the United Nations (UN) – in

1919. He remained in the post until 1923, by which time he had become profoundly disillusioned with the bureaucratic squabbles and languid pace of decision-making. Monnet then managed the struggling family business after his father's death in 1923, before going into private banking in Eastern Europe, New York, San Francisco, and Shanghai, helping to reorganize the Chinese railway between 1934 and 1936. He was involved in efforts at creating an Anglo-French Union in 1940, and maintained contacts with American president, Franklin Roosevelt in Washington D.C. as a member of the British Supply Council between 1940 and 1943. Based on his experiences of playing a key role in fostering inter-Allied cooperation during Europe's two civil wars, one of Monnet's credos became the recognition that international cooperation could be used to overcome pernicious national rivalries.

Between 1947 and 1955, Monnet headed the *Commissariat du Plan*, the commission for France's post-war reconstruction. In the post, he devised the "Monnet plan" which modernized French agriculture and industry, using American aid from the Marshall plan of 1947. Monnet then became the chief architect of European integration, writing the Shuman plan of May 1950 (named after French foreign minister Robert Shuman). Later – between 1952 and 1955 – he served as president of the plan's main body: the High Authority of the Luxembourg-based European Coal and Steel Community (ECSC), which involved France, Germany, Italy, Belgium, the Netherlands and Luxembourg – the six founding members of the European Economic Community. The ECSC governments also created institutions such as the Common Assembly, the Special Council of Ministers and the Court of Justice: all forerunners of current European Union institutions.

Monnet pursued a gradualist approach to European integration and had an intuitive sense of what the political traffic could bear. He knew how hard to push his ideas, and understood the importance of giving other delegations from smaller countries – Belgium, the Netherlands, Luxembourg and Italy – time to digest concepts and allow these governments to contribute meaningfully to the process. As Monnet famously noted "Nothing is possible without men; nothing is lasting without institutions" (cited in Macklay, 1998: 28). He regarded the Shuman plan as chiefly a political means of dealing with economic problems, realizing that continued French efforts to control the German industrial areas of the Ruhr and Saar would only breed further antagonism between Paris and Bonn (Archer, 2008: 22). Thus, even though coal and steel were not the best industries to integrate economically – coal would soon decline as a source of energy in much of Europe – French coal and German steel had a potent symbolism, with steel widely viewed in France as a symbol of arms merchants and German military power. Cooperation in this area would thus send a powerful signal of Franco-German pacific intent. The ECSC eventually helped to avoid price discrimination and to promote healthy competition in these important sectors of Europe's economy.

Monnet's approach to negotiation of the Shuman plan was instructive: he always believed in preparing a draft text as a target for others to aim at, but was flexible enough for it to be amended while seeking to preserve its core. He pushed simple ideas consistently and patiently until they were accepted. He respected his opponents, and always sought to win them over through the consistent application of superior arguments rather than through condescension or confrontation. Monnet's patience and cosmopolitanism had been inculcated from his provincial upbringing in Cognac. As he noted: "I learned to listen and weigh my words. And I also was given a window on the world" (Monnet, 1978: 42). The weakness of the League of Nations, an organization that Monnet had served as Deputy Secretary-General for four years, convinced him of the need for a strong European executive. He, however, had the political wisdom to accept the need for a council of ministers, as well as parliamentary and judicial bodies to satisfy the demands of democratic states and European citizens (Pinder and Usherwood, 2007). During the ECSC negotiation process, Monnet coined the term "European Community" to describe the construction of his integration scheme (1978: 323).

After stepping down from the presidency of the ECSC High Authority in 1955, Monnet formed the Action Committee for the United States of Europe (ACUSE) as a pressure group for European integration that drew on political parties and trade unions across the six ECSC countries (Martin, 2006). At the 1955 European summit in Messina, Monnet pushed hard for a common market and European atomic agency, both of which were included in the Treaty of Rome that created the European Economic Community in 1957. Monnet worked closely with Walter Hallstein, a German former professor at Frankfurt University and strong advocate of European federalism, who went on to serve as the first president of the European Commission between 1958 and 1967.

In recognition of Monnet's enormous contributions to European integration, Roy Jenkins, the British president of the European Commission between 1977 and 1981, paid the Gallic visionary a glowing tribute in August 1977:

... after eighty-nine years of his life, Monnet remains, as he has been throughout, impregnably optimistic but not Utopian. He does not believe in miracles, and although he believes that crucial moments of opportunity must never be lost, he gives more importance to patience and direction than to speed and the construction of false timetables. His modesty and manner is underpinned by an unshakeable intellectual self-confidence. (1978: 12)

Barely 19 months after this tribute, Monnet died in March 1979 at the age of ninety, having devoted his life to promoting peace and regional integration in Europe.

Adebayo Adedeji

Our second political prophet, Nigerian scholar-diplomat, Adebayo Adedeji, is undoubtedly Africa's most renowned visionary of regional integration. Like Jean Monnet who grew up in the provincial French town of Cognac, Adedeji grew up in the south-western Nigerian town of Ijebu-Ode under British colonial rule. This experience left a fierce anti-colonial mark on Adedeji, impacting on his later professional exploits. His middle-class parents were farmers who worked on a cocoa and kola nut plantation and left him in the care of his disciplinarian grandmother "Mama Eleja": an enterprising, shrewd, and determined fish-seller and indomitable matriarch. Even though she was formally illiterate, Adedeji's grandmother pushed the young boy to study consistently, even arranging after-school tutorials for him. The precocious Adebayo was a child prodigy and outstanding student who responded well to the constant prodding. Adedeji's farmer-father was also an important influence on him as a young boy, encouraging him to study hard in order to gain admission to the country's top secondary school – King's College, Lagos – so that he could study medicine at university and become a doctor. (Adedeji instead attended Ijebu-Ode Grammar School as an early entrant). Adebayo's father also made his son work on his farm during school holidays, stressing to the young boy the importance of the "dignity of labor". Like Monnet's father, Adedeji's father encouraged him to travel and see the "outside world" (Sanmi-Ajiki, 2000).

After completing his primary and secondary education in Nigeria, Adedeji studied economics and public administration – rather than medicine – at the universities of Leicester, Harvard, and London, eventually obtaining a doctorate in economics. He had returned to Nigeria in 1958 – two years before the country's independence from British rule – to take up a senior post in the Western Region's Ministry of Economic Planning. Here, he put in long hours and was widely recognized as a rising star. In 1963, Adedeji – who had always described himself as a "reluctant civil servant" – left government service to take up an academic post at Nigeria's University of Ile-Ife (now Obafemi Awolowo University). Four years later at the age of 36, he had earned the title of Professor of Economics and Public Administration. He transformed the university's Institute of Administration into an effective training ground for both Nigerian and African public servants (Sanmi-Ajiki, 2000).

In 1971 at the age of 40, Adedeji was appointed Nigeria's Minister of Economic Reconstruction and Development by the military regime of General Yakubu Gowon. Adedeji would oversee the country's difficult post-war, peace-building efforts. Nigeria's civil war of 1967–1970 had resulted in one million deaths and led to much destruction of the country's infrastructure, particularly in the secessionist Eastern Region. The fortuitous discovery of large oil fields propelled Nigeria into becoming one of the world's largest oil exporters. Along with other cabinet colleagues and powerful mandarins, Adedeji crafted and implemented five-year national development plans that called for rapid industrialization and resulted in the building of dual carriageways, flyovers, and electricity pylons across the country.

Adedeji, as the "father of African integration", is also widely regarded as "the father of ECOWAS" (the Economic Community of West African States). He had outlined a vision for regional integration in West Africa in an academic article published in the *Journal of Modern African Studies* in 1970, before turning theory into practice by 1975 (Adedeji, 1970). While serving as Nigeria's Minister of Economic Development, Adedeji convinced 16 West African leaders to establish ECOWAS, following tireless "shuttle diplomacy" across the sub-region between 1972 and 1975. (Adedeji, 2004). He has since consistently argued that regional integration must be seen as an instrument for national survival and socio-economic transformation (Adedeji, 1993; Asante, 1991; Cline-Cole, 2006; Onimode, 2004; Onimode and Synge, 1995).

In 1975, Adedeji was head-hunted by the United Nations to lead its Addis Ababa-based Economic Commission for Africa. His 16-year tenure became the organization's longest and most dynamic: he converted the Economic Commission for Africa into a Pan-African platform to continue his efforts to promote economic integration, leading to the creation of the Common Market of Eastern and Southern Africa in 1981 and the Economic Community of Central African States in 1983 (Adedeji, 2009). The tireless Adedeji, who frequently worked 18-hour days, collaborated closely with successive Organization of African Unity Secretaries-General in Addis Ababa, and became a confidante and economic adviser to many African leaders whom he addressed at annual continental summits. Adedeji established a particularly close friendship with Julius Nyerere: after he had delivered a series of lectures in Tanzania in 1971, in which he had indiscreetly declared not having met any socialists in the country. Having advised the Namibian government for six years, Adedeji was bestowed an honorary citizenship of that country in 1997.

Adedeji established a reputation as a pragmatic economist more interested in solving problems than being constrained by ideological strait-jackets. He used the Economic Commission for Africa – assisted by a formidable team of largely African economists – to launch the most sustained assault on the structural adjustment programs implemented from the 1980s by the World Bank and the International Monetary Fund. Adedeji coined the widely used term "the lost decade" to describe Africa's rapid decline in the 1980s, and argued against what he saw as the Bretton Woods Institutions' approach of "growth without development" and export-led integration of African states into the world economy on massively unequal terms. He stressed instead the need for Africa to use its own resources to promote greater intra-African growth, prioritizing agriculture, and criticized the World Bank's desperate efforts to produce "structural adjustment program" success stories despite all evidence to the contrary.

Adedeji led the development of Africa's Alternative Framework to Structural Adjustment Programs for Socio-Economic Recovery and Transformation of 1989 and the African Charter for Popular Participation in Development and Transformation of 1990 (Adedeji, 2009). He has often challenged what he sees as Africa's "mindless imitation" of Western development models, and pushed instead for a human-centered view of development and integration which involved all of Africa's 800 million citizens. In addition to regional cooperation and integration, Adedeji championed the collective self-reliance and self-sustainability principles of his 1980 Lagos Plan of Action, which was adopted by the Organization of African Unity but left to gather dust on the shelves of African development ministries.

In *African Development: Adebayo Adedeji's Alternative Strategies*, S.K.B. Asante, the renowned Ghanaian political economist described him as an "African Cassandra": a visionary prophet who saw the future clearly, but whose prophesies often went unheeded until it was too late (Asante, 1991). In the end, the World Bank and the International Monetary Fund reversed the large cuts in education and health spending that had decimated Africa's socio-economic sector in the 1980s and 1990s. Debt relief also became fashionable over a decade after Adedeji had warned about the unsustainability of Africa's US$250 billion external debt in the 1980s. Consistent with this record, Adedeji has been a strong critic of aspects of the New Partnership for Africa's Development (NEPAD) of 2001, which was largely driven by then South African President, Thabo Mbeki (Adedeji, 2007). Some actually viewed Adedeji's elevation to the Panel of Eminent Persons of the African Peer Review Mechanism (APRM) in 2003 as a Machiavellian effort to co-opt one of NEPAD's most articulate critics.

However, Adedeji's integrity and fierce independence saw him continue to criticize the plan constructively. His main complaint was that NEPAD was ahistorical and too externally dependent in abandoning the self-reliant integration principles of the Lagos Plan of Action, and in naively ignoring the lessons in the failed African Alternative Framework of 1989 (which had stalled largely due to the failure of external donors to contribute substantive resources towards implementing the program) (Adedeji, 2007). After retiring from the Economic Commission for Africa in 1991, Adedeji continued his regional integration and peacemaking efforts in Africa: he served on a committee to review the ECOWAS treaty in 1992; he was on another body to transform the Organization of African Unity into the African Union in 2002; he was a mediator in Zimbabwe (with current South African Deputy President, Kgalema Motlanthe) in 2002; he headed the Commonwealth team to observe Kenya's election in 2002/2003; and in 2007, he chaired the committee which audited the five-year integration efforts of the African Union.

Following his retirement in 1991, Adedeji had also established the African Centre for Development and Strategic Studies as a policy think-tank in his hometown of Ijebu-Ode. Recognizing, like Monnet, that regional integration and development could not occur without resolving conflicts, Adedeji edited and published the widely cited *Comprehending and Mastering African Conflicts* in 1999 as a wide-ranging study of how to address the root causes of African conflicts based on detailed field research (Adedeji, 1999). Between 2005 and 2008, the African Centre for Development and Strategic Studies also published an annual review of African security challenges that included a conflict forecast.

By October 2010, thirty African countries had signed up for the APRM and 13 governments had gone through the process, which Adedeji chaired between July 2007 and July 2010. Under the APRM process, each country prepares a national program of action after undertaking a self-evaluation which involves government officials, civil society, and the private sector. The APRM Panel of Eminent Persons then submits a country review report to help African governments identify institutional, policy, and capacity weaknesses, before recommending remedies to these shortcomings. The peer review mechanism is intended to encourage countries to adopt sound policies, priorities, and standards for political, economic, development and sub-regional and continental integration through shared experiences (Adedeji, 2008). The mechanism was thus not crafted as a punitive process to sanction errant governments.

Adedeji was the lead panelist of the South African APRM country review process which took place between 2005 and 2007. The Country Review Report which was released in 2007, acknowledged the country's political and economic progress, but criticized the slow pace of socio-economic transformation and growing inequalities, and cautioned about the growing threat of xenophobic attacks in South Africa (African Peer Review Mechanism, 2007). Like the proverbial ostrich that buries its head in the sand, the notoriously thin-skinned government of Thabo Mbeki strongly objected to the report's criticisms, arrogantly and irresponsibly dismissing the xenophobic threat as "simply not true" (Bond, 2010: 26). Adedeji would once again prove to be a Cassandra: in May 2008, 62 foreigners were killed in South Africa and 100,000 people displaced in horrific attacks against foreigners.

In 1996 Adedeji edited *South Africa in Africa: Within or Apart?* which recognized South Africa's pivotal role in promoting regional integration on the continent. In 2007, he reviewed South Africa's political economy within the broader African context in a chapter titled "South Africa and Africa's Political Economy: Looking Inside from the Outside". Adedeji called for South Africans to "deconstruct" their colonially inherited political economy with the end of formal apartheid, and cautioned the country not to pursue the timid approach of other post-colonial African states that had failed to transform their colonial inheritance. He lamented the abandonment by the South African government (which was under pressure from external financial actors like the World Bank and International Monetary Fund as well as foreign investors) of the more socially activist Reconstruction and Development Program – implemented from 1994 – for the more conservative Growth, Employment and Redistribution macroeconomic strategy – adopted in 1996. He called, instead, for an effective and equitable developmental state in South Africa that would reduce social inequalities (Adedeji, 2007).

Adedeji was equally scathing in his criticisms of his own country, observing in relation to Nigeria's declining global standing in 2004 that: "No country that is confronted with a long period of political instability, economic stagnation, and regression, and is reputed to be one of the most corrupt societies in the world, has a moral basis to lead others. If it tries to, it will be resisted" (Adedeji, 2004: 24). In 1975 he had turned down the chance to become Nigeria's foreign minister, agreeing instead to chair a landmark review of his country's foreign policy (Adedeji, 2008). He also turned down the chance to head Nigeria's interim government after the annulment of democratic elections by the military in June 1993, but in 2005 he served as a member of Nigeria's National Political Reform Conference to chart the country's political future. Despite his distinguished, international status, Adedeji's attempt to secure the presidency of Nigeria after retiring from the Economic Commission for Africa in 1991 proved unsuccessful; in fact no Nigerian leader in 47 years had entered state house with a university education until Umaru Yar'Adua in May 2007.

The December 2007 report of the Audit of the African Union, which Adedeji chaired, called for an acceleration of regional integration on the continent, and made concrete recommendations for strengthening the African Union and Africa's Regional Economic

Communities (African Union, 2007). The report advocated strengthening national mechanisms to accelerate economic integration; incorporating decisions of regional bodies into national institutions; adhering to the African Union decision to recognize only eight Regional Economic Communities; focusing the Regional Economic Communities on activities to create an African Common Market and African Economic Community; and strengthening the African Union's internal mechanisms for more effective coordination and harmonization of the Regional Economic Communities. In the area of security, the document recommended that the research capacity of the African Union's 15-member Peace and Security Council be strengthened, and that the resources devoted to the African Union Peace Fund be massively increased (the fund was only six per cent of the regular African Union budget of US$142 million in 2007). The Audit report also urged the Peace and Security Council to seek greater participation by African civil society groups in its work (African Union, 2007).

In 2009, reflecting on the impact of the global financial crisis on African countries, which for three decades had obediently followed the often misguided economic advice of the two Bretton Woods Institutions, Adedeji noted sardonically, "the meltdown of the global financial architecture represents a judgment on the corrupt and evil world that has been overly concerned with the free market ideology at the expense of economic rationality" (Adedeji, 2009: 4–5). Adedeji highlighted the deleterious effects of financial deregulation across Africa on productivity-oriented entrepreneurs, decrying the rise of unscrupulous currency speculators. He further observed that, due to volatile macroeconomic conditions, banking and financial sectors in Africa had performed dismally in supporting productive investments that could have promoted domestic agriculture, manufacturing, and infrastructure development. He therefore called for the establishment of strong, independent institutions to monitor African central banks in order to ensure that "financialisation becomes a true instrument for development" (Adedeji, 2009: 4–5).

In July 2010, after over five decades of dedicated service to the continent, Adedeji effectively announced his retirement from public life at the African Union summit in Kampala, Uganda. The earlier tributes paid him by three African elder statesmen are worth recalling as they illustrate Adedeji's immense contributions to regional integration and development in Africa. Nigeria's General Yakubu

Gowon – in whose cabinet Adedeji had served for four years – described him as "a very practical and dynamic man who could hold his own in any place anywhere in the world"; Senegal's Abdou Diouf called Adedeji "a man who has played a considerable role in propagating an authentically African way of thinking about economic and social development"; while Zambia's Kenneth Kaunda noted that: "Africa will forever be grateful to him for the analytical and objective approach that he has adopted in his work" (Sanmi-Ajiki, 2000: v–vii). In a 2006 book, Adedeji was named among the world's fifty leading thinkers on development in a list that stretched back to such figures as Karl Marx (Cline-Cole, 2006).

Conclusion

It is often said that no prophet is honored in his own land. Adedeji was not given the opportunity to lead Nigeria, but his country and continent owe a great debt of gratitude to one of their most accomplished intellectual public servants, whose legacy is comparable to Europe's political visionary – Jean Monnet. Both led regional integration efforts on their respective continents. Both headed powerful international organizations – the United Nations ECA and the ECSC – through which they sought to promote their goals. Both enjoyed generating new ideas, but realized that they had to relate such concepts to practical action and muster political support to implement their visions. Both acted as technocrats operating skillfully behind the scenes in powerful bureaucracies. While Adedeji was a university professor, Monnet had no formal university education. However, both men shared an aversion to the operation of blind market forces, and regarded politics as inseparable from economics. Both saw regional integration as a means to promote peace and socio-economic development. Both were far-sighted visionaries who often saw the future more clearly than the leaders they sought to advice. In the end both men, however, proved to be Cassandras: Adedeji never saw his dream of an African common market fulfilled; while Monnet's dream of a European political union – the "United States of Europe" – has yet to be realized.

References

Adebajo, A. 2006. "'African Cassandra' Adedeji comes full circle on NEPAD". *Business Day*, 1 September.

Adebajo, A. 2010. *The Curse of Berlin: Africa after the Cold War.* Scottsville: University of Kwazulu-Natal Press; London: Hurst and Co.; New York: Columbia University Press.
Adedeji, A. (ed.) 1993. *Africa within the World: Beyond Dispossession and Dependence.* London: Zed Books.
Adedeji, A. (ed.) 1996. *South Africa in Africa: Within or Apart?* London: Zed Books.
Adedeji, A. (ed.) 1999. *Comprehending and Mastering African Conflicts.* London and New York: Zed Books.
Adedeji, A. 1970. "Prospects for regional economic cooperation in West Africa", *Journal of Modern African Studies* 8: 213–231.
Adedeji, A. 2004. "ECOWAS: A retrospective journey" in A Adebajo and I Rashid (eds) *West Africa's Security Challenges: Building Peace in a Troubled Region.* Boulder and London: Lynne Rienner: 21–49.
Adedeji, A. 2007. "South Africa and Africa's political economy: Looking inside from the outside" in A Adebajo, A Adedeji and C Landsberg (eds) *South Africa in Africa: The Post-Apartheid Era.* Scottsville: University of KwaZulu-Natal Press: 40–62.
Adedeji, A. 2008. "Foreword" in A Adebajo and R Mustapha (eds) *Gulliver's Troubles: Nigeria's Foreign Policy after the Cold War.* Scottsville: University of KwaZulu-Natal Press.
Adedeji, A. 2008. "NEPAD's African Peer Review Mechanism: Progress and prospects" in J Akokpari, A Ndinga-Muvumba, and T Murithi (eds) *The African Union and its Institutions.* Johannesburg: Jacana: 241–270.
Adedeji, A. 2009. "Africa and the crisis of global financial governance", *New Agenda* (First Quarter): 4.
Adedeji, A. 2009. "The Economic Commission for Africa" in A Adebajo (ed.) *From Global Apartheid to Global Village: Africa and the United Nations.* Scottsville: University of KwaZulu-Natal Press: 373–398.
African Centre for Development and Strategic Studies. 2005. *African Conflict, Peace and Governance Monitor.* Ibadan: Dokun Publishing House.
African Peer Review Mechanism (APRM). 2007. *Country Review Report of Republic of South Africa.* APRM Secretariat, Midrand, South Africa.

African Union. 2007. *Audit of the African Union: Towards A People-Centred Political and Socio-Economic Integration and Transformation of Africa*. Addis Ababa: African Union.
Archer, C. 2008. *The European Union*. London and New York: Routledge.
Asante, SKB. 1991. *African Development: Adebayo Adedeji's Alternative Strategies*. Ibadan: Spectrum.
Bond, P. 2010. "First class failure", *BBC Focus on Africa*, 21(4): 26.
Cline-Cole, R. 2006. "Adebayo Adedeji" in D Simon (ed.) *Fifty Key Thinkers on Development*. Oxford and New York: Routledge: 3–9.
Jenkins, R. 1978. "Foreword" in J Monnet, *Memoirs*. London and Johannesburg: William Collins Sons & Co.
Macklay, M. 1998. *The European Union*. Gloucestershire: Sutton Publishing Limited.
Martin, S. 2006. "Building on coal and steel: European integration in the 1950s and the 1960s" in D Dinan (ed.) *Origins and Evolution of the European Union*. Oxford, New York, Cape Town and Nairobi: Oxford University Press: 126–140.
Monnet, J. 1978. *Memoirs*. London and Johannesburg: William Collins Sons & Co.
Onimode, B and Synge, R. 1995. *Issues in African Development: Essays in Honour of Adebayo Adedeji at 65*. Ibadan: Heinemann.
Onimode, B. (ed.) 2004. *African Development and Governance Strategies in the 21st Century: Looking Back to Move Forward: Essays in Honour of Adebayo Adedeji at Seventy*. London and New York: Zed Books.
Pinder, J and Usherwood, S. 2007. *The European Union: A Very Short Introduction*. Oxford, New York, Cape Town and Nairobi: Oxford University Press.
Sanmi-Ajiki, T. 2000. *Adebayo Adedeji: A Rainbow in the Sky of Time*. Lagos: Newswatch Books.

CHAPTER 5. AFRICAN INTEGRATION AND DEVELOPMENT

Yousif A. Suliman

Introduction

Fast and balanced development has eluded post-independence Africa. The diagnostics depicts a continent in "bondage" with its colonial past, inheriting terms of unequal international exchange, and featuring lopsided development, a narrow production base, fragmented economies, excessive external openness and dependence, weak or inefficient institutions, poorly managed resources and a disengaged and highly complex and differentiated socio-political setting. As a continent, Africa has the largest number of low-income and poorly developed countries. These are no doubt characteristics of structural problems. Particularly in the 1980s, under the weight of "crisis management for economic survival", long-term development – of which regional integration is a fundamental component – had to be postponed, thereby intensifying the problem. The country-by-country approach to adjustment policies enforced by international financial institutions as a condition for support further militated against regional integration. Hence, the pursuit of an agenda for the creation of an Africa that was fully liberated, economically transformed and integrated, and a better place to live in and identify with became more urgent. Indeed, the development lag – particularly in comparison with other regions – compounded by international economic pressures, demanded new approaches to development and related policies. It became imperative that these policies should be suited to the continent's unique economic and socio-political setting. Only then would there be new truths about Africa. The search for the appropriate polices under Adedeji's leadership, particularly during his tenure as Executive Secretary of the United Nations Economic Commission for Africa (UNECA), emphasized the centrality of regional integration and popular participation in development. Indeed, these ideas still serve as major points of reference in Africa's development discourse. To this effect, this chapter proceeds to define what constitutes the development nexus and its interactions under this dispensation. The greater part, however, is devoted to regional integration, its constituents and status, closing with some suggestions for the way forward. The final part briefly revisits Adedeji's ideas and their relevance.

Vision and framework

Over the years, Adedeji advocated and ultimately formalized the core solutions to the intensifying socio-economic problems of the continent. The essential components of the way forward could be presented schematically as the vertices of a triangle, linked by the ultimate objective and glued through political will and capacity building (see Figure 5.1 below). Each of the elements is a necessary condition for African development. When they operate simultaneously, they satisfy the sufficiency criteria for the requisites of economic and social transformation. The elements are:

- alternative economic approach
- popular participation and good governance
- regional cooperation and integration
- long-term development.

Figure 5.1 African development and interdependence

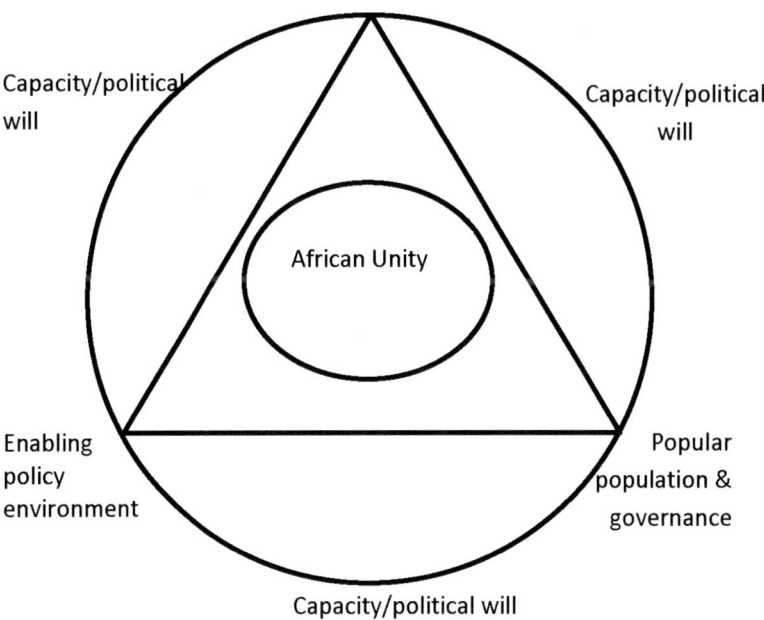

The alternative approach to economic policy, formalized in the celebrated *African Alternative Framework to Structural Adjustment Programmes for Socio-Economic Recovery and Transformation* (AAF-SAP), is the articulation of a body of adjustment policy components within the context of development (UNECA, 1989). This represented a departure from and challenge to the new orthodoxy advocated, particularly by the Bretton Woods Institutions, as panacea for Africa's economic problems and development lag in the 1980s and the tool for restoring economic equilibrium and growth. To Adedeji and his associates, the short-term policy concerns should not be divorced from long-term development objectives and perspectives of the country or group of countries concerned. Countries should naturally adjust to changing circumstances, but if they neglect long-term transformation they risk remaining prisoners to a permanent state of disequilibria and stunted growth. For adjustment policies to be effective they should also not neglect the regional dimension and should be human-centered.

AAF-SAP draws its substantive thrust from the Lagos Plan of

Action and the Final Act of Lagos (Organization of African Unity, 1981), adopted as long-term development strategy by African Heads of State and Government in Lagos, Nigeria, in April 1980.The direct relationship emanates from the Plan's emphasis on alleviation of mass poverty through broadening the production base, self-reliance and self-sustained development within a regional integration context and correcting the continent's standing in the global order.

The traditional Structural Adjustment Programs, primarily conceived within the neoclassical framework, are by nature short-term oriented. They have a built-in contradiction with transformation, no matter what their name suggests. At best, they are poorly linked to growth and development theories. Indeed, even the latter policies are equally deficient; the developments in the new growth theories notwithstanding (see Ros, 2001). Over thirty African countries had had structural adjustment programs by the mid-1990s, without serving their declared objectives, and leaving in their wake serious deterioration in human welfare. To perceptive economists, such a result is inevitable as conditions in developing countries are structurally different from those in developed countries to which economics, as practiced, relates. Writing well before the structural adjustment programs were minted, Dudley Seers took great exception to the behavior of unaccomplished economists lecturing developing countries on the virtues of development, totally ignoring the unique circumstances of less-developed countries (Seers, 1963).

Expressing similar sentiments, and within the context of understanding the nature and remedies for mass poverty in developing countries, Galbraith lamented that "Advice in economic development in the last thirty years came extensively from economists and technicians of the rich world. They have seen what has worked well in these lands and, not surprisingly, have advised the same for the poor countries" (Galbraith, 1979: 20–21). More recently, in a penetrating analysis of the specific difficulties facing developing countries, entitled *Why Developing Countries Fail to Develop*, Mathur submitted that neoclassical assumptions are tyrannically restrictive in understanding how these economies work and that, indeed, a new theory of development was necessary – for which he laid down primary foundations (Mathur, 1991). Dependency perspectives (for example, Dos Santos, 1970) and the lesser known but influential Drain Theory – developed by the Indian economist Naoroji, (1888, cited by Mathur, 1991), and used by Gandhi's

Freedom Movement – are signposts to alternative approaches to those anchored on mainstream neoclassical economics. AAF-SAP is the African chapter in this persuasion. Its legacy arises not only from its analytical and intellectual insights, but equally from its inspiration for further research in a similar vein. The United Nations Children's Fund's *Adjustment with a Human Face* (Cornia et al., 1987), was a substantive contribution to the adjustment debate. However, while the Bretton Woods Institutions initially ignored AAF-SAP – never seeking to discuss it with UNECA or to invite its technical advisors, even when some countries requested their participation in the formulation of the programs – their subsequent contributions and policy recommendations progressively took on board some important orientations of AAF-SAP.

Popular participation is at the center of effective policy-making, as people are its main players and beneficiaries. When people are involved their interests are incorporated and commitment ensured – be that nationally or regionally. Citizens have a fundamental right to be included and to participate in government and express their views on issues affecting their lives. To this effect, Adedeji and his colleagues in UNECA made that right a principal tenet of the Arusha Charter, formally referred to as *The African Charter for Popular Participation in Development and Transformation*, adopted in February 1990 by a broad-based international conference representing African and non-African NGOs, trade unionists, women, youth, African governments and international figures (UNECA, 1990). The participants stated that "…there must be an opening up of political process to accommodate freedom of opinions, tolerate differences, accept consensus on issues as well as the effective participation of the people and their organizations and associations". They further insisted that "…the political system [should] evolve to allow for democracy and full participation by all sections of our societies" (UNECA, 1990: 19). The Charter foregrounds these provisions by stipulating: (i) an environment of peace and stability by establishing strong democratic foundations; (ii) making a cardinal virtue of the culture of self-denial (as opposed to the culture of "me first"); and (iii) balancing entitlement with accountability. The Charter went a long way in premising real development on people's participation. To Adedeji this represented a pair of scissors – both blades (development and participation) are necessary for effectiveness. The overhauling of the social order through civil society had been started.

Africans were invited to draw on their tremendous reservoir of traditional values and cultures to catalyze the development process. A realist, however, may still have wondered what it would take to address the pervasive social and institutional rigidities normally associated with societies in a state of flux (akin to those portrayed in Myrdal's celebrated *Asian Drama: An Enquiry into the Poverty of Nations,* 1968).

Regional integration provides a widened economic space and constituency for advancing African development. For Africa and Adedeji, it constitutes the first line of defense for Africa's survival and progress. The global phenomenon of growing regionalism in recent years – with its spill-over effects – and the fast pace of globalization can only be matched by promoting African integration. For Adedeji, regional integration is the overriding African doctrine. In adopting the Lagos Plan of Action and the Final Act of Lagos, African leaders underscored the strategic necessity of regional integration. When the economic fortunes of the continent faltered during the subsequent decade of the 1980s, particularly under the weight of the unfavorable international economic environment, African leaders insisted that the framework of future continental development should be anchored on regional integration. A blueprint for an African Economic Community and eventually an Economic Union by the year 2027 was adopted in Abuja, Nigeria, in June 1991, barely one month ahead of Adedeji's resignation from the service of the United Nations as the Executive Secretary of UNECA. In his farewell address to the Commission's conference a few months earlier he had laid out a nine-point agenda for the 1990s to prepare the continent well for the twenty-first century (UNECA, 1990). One of these points was to make regional and sub-regional integration an integral part of domestic national policy. For Adedeji, the market is important and should be catalyzed and trade should be facilitated; but it is only when there is a surplus and a wider range of products to trade that internal or external competition can take place. Again, structural solutions were envisaged.

The integration process was perceived as consisting of five interdependent dimensions:

- the integration of the physical, institutional and social infrastructures;
- the integration of the production structures;
- the integration of African markets;

- the creation of an enabling environment through the encouragement of private initiative and enterprise and factor movement across borders; and,
- the adoption of a common approach to policy.

The separate and combined progress in these areas measures the health of the process.

Adedeji addressed the Third Africa Development Forum, organized by UNECA in March 2002, on the theme "Defining Priorities for Regional Integration". Drawing on history and experience, he called for dedicated efforts to further invigorate the integration process and called for the placing of special emphasis on non-economic dimensions alongside economic concerns in the journey towards African integration. According to Adedeji (2002), "The pursuit of economic integration must go hand in hand with the pursuit of political stability at the national, sub-regional and regional levels". A prerequisite is that "The people in the region must have shared visions, shared values and shared social economy." The constituency for integration should also extend beyond governments to citizens. "Economism of regional cooperation is particularly responsible for the slow progress made during the past forty years", he contended.

Enhancing human capacities is a necessary policy dimension of the development schemata. Combined with political commitment, it provides concrete to the architecture. An important component of capacity development is institution building and knowledge generation to inform policies and decisions and to enable effective monitoring. This is an area where Adedeji, particularly through the authority of UNECA, made tangible contributions in support of regional integration. The important actions in this regard are:

1. Establishment of Regional Economic Communities:

    - formation and subsequent strengthening of Economic Community of West African States (ECOWAS)
    - establishment of the (Preferential Trade Area for Eastern and Southern Africa) PTA, now common market for Eastern and Southern Africa (COMESA)
    - Establishment of Economic Community of Central African States (ECCAS).

2. Establishment of thirty UNECA-sponsored institutions, covering such important development and integration areas as development planning, cartography, solar energy, social development, demography, aerospace surveys, engineering design and manufacturing, standardization and finance.
3. The forging of an alliance for regional integration consisting of the three premier African organizations – Organization of African Unity (OAU; now African Union or AU), UNECA and the African Development Bank – designated by African leaders as the joint secretariat entrusted with the implementation of the Abuja Treaty Establishing the African Economic Community.
4. The strengthening of UNECA to serve Africa better. Adedeji was the prime mover of such major transformational and infrastructural programs as the United Nation's Transport and Communication and Industrial decades. He effectively used the convening power of UNECA to develop ideas and common African positions on various development issues and concerns.
5. The focus on Africa's learning and research institutions, notably universities and training institutions that underpin sub-regional or continental development and integration.[1]

Regional integration links the various threads of Adedeji's ideas; it is the pinnacle of his development architecture and the greatest challenge for African development. How far has Africa travelled along the road of integration?

Goals and record of regional integration

Africa pursues regional integration to open up its economic space and achieve economies of scale, as a means of creating a united front to tackle its own domestic development challenges as well as the challenges of globalization. The envisaged environment is one of political and social harmony. Regional integration reduces the risk of conflict and helps build trust among members. It is also a means of addressing the problem of balkanization of the generally small

---

1 Of course, there are other integration and capacity building institutions and related intergovernmental organizations in various parts of the continent, including River Basin Organizations, some of which date back to the pre-independence era. However, to create institutions is one good thing, but to sustain and recognize them is another. Sadly, most of the UNECA-sponsored institutions, and indeed the greater number of African universities and research centers, are in financial distress.

African economies and establishing an enabling framework for greater wealth creation. Public goods such as the environment, peace and security and trans-boundary water resources as well as pandemic diseases such as malaria and HIV/ AIDS are more effectively addressed within a cooperation arrangement.

African integration is ultimately aimed at achieving African unity. With unity of purpose, the harmonized approaches and the discipline provided by common strategies will galvanize political will and facilitate major sub-regional and continent-wide transformational projects such as those for energy and transport and communications.

Within this framework, 14 Regional Economic Communities (RECs) were established, with some of them dating back to the colonial times (for example SACU – 1910, original EAC – 1919).[2] The goals of the majority of them are to achieve economic union (CEMAC, CEPGL, EAC, ECCAS, ECOWAS, IGAD, SADC, UEMOA and UMA). Others target custom unions (COMESA, SACU); free trade areas and integration in some sectors (CENSAD); multi-sectoral integration (MRU); and sustainable development through common diplomacy and cooperation on environment and trade (IOC). All RECs were required to converge in an African Common Market and Economic Union by 2027.

Table 5.1 below maps the overall objectives and current status of the Regional Economic Communities (RECs). Overlapping remains a serious problem even after the African Union (AU) recognized only eight RECs.

Table 5.2 gives a compressed summary of sectoral areas targeted by RECs' treaties.

---

[2] A full list of acronyms and abbreviations that appear in this chapter is provided at the front of this book.

Table 5.1 RECs' objectives, status and overlaps

RECs	No. of Countries	No. of Overlapping RECs	RECs overlapping	Ultimate objective	Current stage
I. AU RECs					
CENSAD	28	8	ECCAS, CEPGL, EAC, UEMOA, ECOWAS, MRU, CEMAC, UMA	Free trade area and integration in some sectors.	Not yet free trade area.
COMESA	19	4	IGAD, CEPGL, EAC, CENSAD	Common market.	Customs union. Common external tariff under discussion.
EAC	5	3	IGAD, COMESA, SADC, CENSAD	Full economic union.	Common market.
ECCAS	10	3	CEMAC, CEPGL, CENSAD	Full economic union.	Semi-free trade area.
ECOWAS	15	3	UEMOA, MRU, CENSAD	Full economic union.	Semi-customs union.
IGAD	7	4	EAC, COMESA, SADC,	Full economic union.	Not yet free trade area.

AFRICAN INTEGRATION AND DEVELOPMENT

			CENSAD		
SADC	14	6	IGAD, EAC, CEPGL, COMESA, SACU, IOC	Full economic union.	Free trade area.
UMA	5	2	IGAD, CENSAD	Full economic union.	Free trade area not achieved. But conventions on investment, payments, transport exist.
II. Other RECs					
CEMAC	6	2	ECCAS, CEPGL	Full economic union.	Customs union. Common external tariff. Monetary zone.
CEPGL	3	3	EAC, ECCAS, SADC	Full economic union.	Preferential trade arrangements signed.
IOC	4	2	COMESA, SADC	Sustainable development through cooperation on diplomacy, trade and environment.	Multilateral programs elaborated in priority areas.
MRU	3	2	ECOWAS, CENSAD	Multi-sectoral integration.	Conflict stalled progress.
SACU	5	4	CEPGL, ECCAS, SADC, EAC	Customs union.	Customs union.

UEMOA	8	2	**ECOWAS, CENSAD**	Full economic union.	Customs union: Monetary zone

Source: Compiled from UNECA sources and RECs websites and documents.

Table 5.2: Sectoral goals of RECs

AU RECs	Agriculture/ food & security	Trade	Money & finance	Industry	Transport/ communication & energy	Natural resources & utilisation	Human resources & labour mobility	Cross-cutting issues
CEN-SAD	xx	xx	x	Xx	xx	x	X	xx
COMESA	xx	xx	xx	Xx	xx	xx	Xx	x
EAC	xx	xx	xx	Xx	xx	xx	Xx	x
ECCAS	xx	xx	xx	Xx	xx	xx	X	xx
ECOWAS	xx	xx	xx	Xx	xx	xx	xx	x
IGAD	xx	xx	x	X	xx	xx	X	xx
SADC	xx	xx	xx	xx	xx	xx	X	xx
UMA	xx	xx	x	xx	x	x	xx	x
Other RECs								
CEMAC	xx	xx	xx	xx	xx	xx	xx	x
CEPGL	x	x	x	X	xx	x	X	xx
IOC	x	x	x	X	x	xx	X	x
MRU	x	x	x	X	x	x	X	xx
SACU	x	xx	x	X	x	x	X	x
UEMOA	xx	xx	xx	xx	xx	x	xx	x

Source: Compiled from various UNECA reports on assessing regional integration (2004–2009) and RECs' websites.

Notes
Trade = trade and market integration, trade facilitation
Money and finance = monetary and financial integration, macro-economic policy convergence etc.
Cross-cutting issues = culture, health, peace and security, gender, etc.
xx = Elaborate sectoral intervention for the RECs
x = Less sectoral emphasis

The data shows that not only do the RECs overlap geographically, but also in the areas of their focus. The eight groups recognized by the AU as the building blocks of the Union show more sectoral intensity than the remaining six RECs, except in the case of CEMAC and UEMOA. The sectoral overlap, however, conceals the complexities of the individual REC's projects. The rationalization exercise may have to be deepened, with a view to selecting only those projects that could ultimately help achieve continental integration. This will be the acid test for the demonstration of political will.

The progress is mixed: for example, take trade, which is the common factor to all integration arrangements. Overall intra-African trade averaged about 11 per cent, compared to 73 per cent for Europe and 50 per cent for each of the Americas and Asia. While other regions trade overwhelmingly within their regions, Africa directs close to 90 per cent of its trade to other parts of the world. Only EAC, SADC, UEMOA, IGAD and ECOWAS surpassed or were closer to the average ratio. Markets are not sufficiently integrated horizontally and vertically.

Most RECs have infrastructural programs. Moreover, Africa has had two Transport and Communications Decades – for the 1980s and 1990s. Major African initiatives include the Trans-African Highway, the Oil and Gas Pipelines, the Yamoussoukro Decision to liberalize the African air space and NEPAD. Infrastructure was also supported by major finance institutions like the World Bank and the African Development Bank. There are also joint initiatives by donors and African countries, such as the Sub-Saharan Transport Policy Program.

The road network is still thin compared to other regions – 5 kilometers per 1000 inhabitants compared to 12 kilometers and 18 kilometers per 1000 inhabitants for Latin America and Asia respectively. Missing links in the Trans-African Highway (21 per cent), border delays and poor quality of roads constitute the greatest challenge to regional integration. The railway network is disconnected, with only three out of the nine operating gauges conforming to international standards.

There are serious efforts to initiate and/or expand the oil and gas pipelines; however large hydro-electric projects such as the Inga Dam, which could double electricity generation on the continent, remain lofty dreams. Currently, only 20 per cent of the hydro-electrical power potential of the continent is utilized. There are also efforts to expand and modernize the information and communications network, yet the gap between Africa and the rest of the world is still very wide. For example, internet use per 1000 inhabitants is only 6.8, compared to 27.7 for the world average. The mobile telephones subscribers are higher, at 27.5, compared to the global average of 59.6 in 2009.

The recent improvements in infrastructure notwithstanding, Africa is still saddled with comparatively high costs of doing business. Out of 183 countries covered by the *World Bank Index of Doing Business* published in 2010, between 34 and 43 African countries are among the 62 worst performers.

The effective exploitation and harnessing of the continent's ample natural resources could best be done through cooperation arrangements. In this regard, there are numerous water development initiatives. But only SADC, CEPGL, MRU and ECOWAS have significant activities. Historically, cooperation on water issues has occurred through river and lake basin organizations. Water sharing arrangements are currently facing trying tests. Many RECs have targeted food security and sufficiency and have programs for harmonizing polices, developing regional markets for agricultural products and setting up of common research institutions. However, the gaps between plans and actual performance have been quite significant. The continent is yet to witness decisive efforts in investment in irrigation and the improvement of rural infrastructure.

In the area of labor mobility, and given that many RECs made provisions in their protocols for free movement of people and right of residence and establishment, only ECOWAS has abolished entry visas.

Macroeconomic convergence and monetary stability are main anchorages for regional integration. In this regard, many RECs have pertinent objectives and are making efforts to deregulate their financial systems. Performance is encouraging, albeit inadequate.

Regional capital markets remain under-capitalized.

While the integration process is still largely shallow, there appears to be a race among RECs to proclaim more advanced stages of integration. Integration institutions continued to proliferate and their programs expand. However, the means at their disposal are limited. The adjustment time for countries may not be adequate for the tasks at hand. The limited technical or administrative capabilities of the RECs are often overstretched. The RECs have also seriously overlapped, so that most countries belong to more than one community. In fact, the intensity of overlapping has increased over the years. Between 2000 and 2009, the number of countries which were members of one REC fell from six to three, and those which were members of four REC groupings increased from one to three. The majority maintain membership in two or three RECs.

The overall picture is one of inadequate and uncertain progress, although the growth rate of integration, as computed by UNECA for the five-year period following the ratification of the African Economic Community in 1994, has kept pace with that of gross domestic product (See UNECA, 2004). However, the integration speed may not be enough to significantly propel the integration process.

Why is progress so limited and slow despite the numerous protocols and meetings to foster integration? Have the policies or actions deviated from the original schemes? Do the approaches followed fully appreciate the nature of the challenge of integration on the continent? Or are the efforts wholly inadequate? What are the most plausible explanations and indeed the corrective measures?

The explanations for this lackluster performance are numerous and complex, but the following nine factors stand out:

- limited productive capacity, supply-side constraints and poor market integration and information
- formidable barriers to trade
- infrastructure networks are alarmingly inadequate and disjointed
- limited interface between RECs and national structures and rivalry between national and regional priorities
- poor integration of natural resources in internal production and resource sharing nexus
- poor constituency for regional integration among government bodies as well as the people

- overlapping of membership and programs overstretched RECs' capacities, which are further constrained by inadequate links between integration constituencies, i.e. the governments, civil society, development partners and the World Trade Organization
- inadequate financing for integration projects
- inadequate political will.

While these factors are critical, it is, however, uncertain that efforts to make advances in them separately will make a decisive difference to the integration process. Recognition of the underlying factors is one thing and effective action in a concerted and cohesive manner is another. Reflections on the appropriateness of the current African integration model – which is not actually Vinerian and market-based (Viner, 1950), nor is it fully development-based and structurally oriented – may be in order. Hence the need for a search for a new paradigm or, alternatively, a serious overhaul of the current approach, taking on board the new and emerging factors in the continent's internal and external environment. Re-engineering will, however, be met with the inadequacy of the current theoretical models: with their emphasis on geography (Krugman, 1991) and cooperation on macroeconomic coordination (Fine and Yeo,1996) or their primary focus on infrastructure and natural resources development (Robinson,1996). These variants will face some political objections as they constitute selective departure from the original African integration scheme. After all, political commitment is the most decisive factor in the success or failure of the integration process. A revisiting of the structure and modalities of operation may be warranted. This is a demanding and complex exercise that, for the sake of consistency and continuity, the three African premier organizations (AU, UNECA and African Development Bank) should task themselves with. The challenge is to make integration more effective, inclusive, fair and sustainable.

Developmental integration: Agenda for a willed future

Some more enduring orientations are needed, to effectively deliver integration within a developmental context. Commitment to continental integration is pivotal, but it needs more substance and action rather than rhetorical statements. Primarily, countries in Africa should take full advantage of the momentum generated by recent growth to consolidate the unity project. Integration should be rebuilt around priorities to face the internal and external challenges in African countries and, in the process, ensure that the leadership is a compact involving all citizens and their governments.

Major steps are needed to re-launch regional integration. As priority African countries should:

(i) Take charge of their development destiny. A fitting starting point would be to rebase development primarily on own efforts, away from development through aid (loans). Breaking the vicious circle of poverty could best be served through developing and mobilizing local resources. Imported equipment is more expensive because of insurance and interest costs and therefore local products can only compete through keeping wages very low; thereby negating the objective that development should result in an increase in real incomes. Failure to pay debts will result in the familiar donor conditionalities. Donor priorities are often inconsistent with the core African objectives of self-reliance and self-sustained development: indeed, the current aid doctrine is crafted to support only the policies that donors consider prudent.

When the strategy is to use loans to create capacity to increase commodity exports to earn foreign exchange, producing countries receiving similar encouragement from donors or acting separately often fall prey to the fallacy of composition trap and thereby have to contend with lower long-term prices which will act as restraints to real wage increases. Vexed by this development-through-loans dilemma, many African leaders are increasingly calling for regaining the initiative through their own efforts and taking charge of their own development instead of leaving this to donors and aid groups to dictate. But ownership of development programs will need to be matched by serious efforts to mobilize local resources as the primary means of funding them. Partnerships should be built around the priorities. Aid would then have a context.

(ii) Build educational, innovation and knowledge capacities in a regional integration context. Regional integration should be knowledge-intensive. Competitiveness and efficiency in general require better skills and improved organization as well as new ways and means of production and service delivery. Education is key for the accumulation of quality human capital; hence the importance of creating an enabling environment and capacity for science and technology and innovation. Creating regional and sub-regional innovation systems, aligning educational and training syllabuses and establishing regional accreditation systems will contribute to the reciprocal recognition of professional qualifications and ultimately labor mobility. Foreign investors would thus have a pool of qualified and regionally recognized labor force to draw on.

(iii) **Significantly expand regional – and reorient sub-regional – infrastructural networks to facilitate regional trade and primarily link members and reduce transaction costs.** Physical infrastructure needs to be redirected towards providing more support for integration. There should be significant upgrading of the transport and communication sector. Information and communication technology services should also be reoriented to help build the knowledge economies and facilitate trade. The ample energy potential, particularly the hydro-based, should be effectively tapped and regionally deployed.

(iv) **Modernize and expand production sectors for more availability, diversity and competitiveness.** Agricultural and industrial capacities should be substantially expanded, diversified and modernized. The low level of intra-African trade mentioned earlier on is a reflection of the weaknesses of current setups. The requisite capital demands are obviously huge, given the initial conditions. But real transformation will not take place unless and until these capital resources, both physical and human, are sunk. Changing production patterns, building quality infrastructure and changing production culture to bring it more in line with production chains are strategic pre-conditions.

(v) **Create material conditions for flow and retention of cross-border and foreign investment and acknowledge and facilitate the role of the private sector in enhancing regional integration.** African countries should go beyond enacting attractive investment codes. They need to take practical steps for building regional networks for firms and businesses. Common standards for governing the private sector behavior are necessary – such as those targeted at achieving sub-regional consistency, harmonization of company laws, codes of conduct, rules and regulations governing commercial and professional practices and processes, etc. Such steps will permit the development of sub-regional industry associations and chambers of commerce to facilitate sub-regional private sector integration. They will also catalyze the development of partnerships, including those with transnational companies.

(vi) Manage regional integration inclusively and create a constituency for people committed to regional integration. The people and the private sector should be the engines of integration since they are the investors, producers, distributors and ultimately the beneficiaries. Integration should no longer be essentially driven by the state. While the role of the private sector is recognized, it remains limited. Ideally, there should be a symbiotic relationship between the private sector and the public sector and an enhanced role for private enterprises and initiative in promoting regional integration. People's commitment cannot be guaranteed without sufficient information on the goals and objectives and indeed visible rewards of integration. An effective communication strategy is sorely missing.

(vii) Rationalize the RECs, build their capacities and interfaces with each other, as well as with the AU and national structures. The institutional architecture for regional integration is generally weak. The RECs have limited capacities and no real authority to enforce decisions. Their technical and financial resources, already limited, are further overstretched due to overlapping of memberships. Besides, duplication of programs and multiplicity of RECs confuse national integration structures and sap their energies. Rationalization of the groupings will no doubt enable them to focus and become more efficient. There are different possible scenarios (Suliman, 2009). But the AU had already resolved to recognize only eight of the fourteen RECs as its building blocks. The AU Commission has developed a Minimum Integration Program to streamline the sectoral objectives in an attempt to speed up the realization of the Common Market and Economic Union by the stipulated date of 2027. The exercise may help streamline sectoral interventions, but has not remarkably reduced the overlapping problem. Further studies to outline feasibility trajectories are needed to graduate RECs for full convergence on the target date of 2027.

(viii) Design innovative approaches to finance regional integrations, institutions and integrative sub-regional and continent-wide infrastructural programs and the establishment of development funds for lagging regions. The integration institutions are invited to think and act out of the box to overcome the financing constraint. So far, assessed contributions augmented by grants have proved inadequate and unsustainable. For the continent as a whole the problem seems more binding, given the low rates of savings. Foreign aid is inadequate, inflexible and uncertain. Foreign direct investment is also highly concentrated in a few countries and in natural resources. Capital markets are yet to gain currency at the sub-regional and regional levels. Innovative mechanisms, including those which help attract foreign investment, should therefore be explored. Given the large amounts needed by, in particular, infrastructural investments, priority should be given to strengthening capital markets as they can agglomerate capital, pool and diversify risks and mobilize cross-border and international finance. Diaspora bonds and remittances could also be explored. RECs which have not tapped the possibilities of self-financing mechanisms – such as import tax levies – should do so. But all these measures would require an enabling regional policy environment and convergence to establish investor confidence. African countries may also consider establishing development funds to integrate lagging regions.

(ix) Translate political commitment into positive actions and give RECs supranational authority to enforce common community decisions. The integration project is essentially a political and economic undertaking. Without absolute political commitment to implementing integration decisions, programs and policies at the national level there would hardly be progress at the sub-regional and continental levels. Countries should honor their commitments and overcome their apparent reluctance to subordinate their national authority to that of the groupings to which they belong.

Conclusion

The challenge that Africa faces today, as in the past, is how to increase the development impact of regional integration, given the political, cultural and economic realities, including globalization. Therefore, the content and pace of integration greatly matter. For one thing, Africa will not survive and compete unless it achieves significant progress in these two interdependent areas. There needs to be a qualitative shift in its development paradigm and economic structure away from low value-added or primary production towards higher technology content for domestic as well as for regional and global trade. Regional trade would then have more range and quality of products to exchange, while external trade could compete. But development and integration processes have to be democratic, people-centered and equitable to be owned by society. To this effect,

Adedeji's development and regional integration architecture and vision remain relevant and enduring. If so, why then has progress in both development and regional integration been so modest? The lacunas seem to have more to do with modalities, the range and quality of the efforts to deepen integration and externalities, such as Africa's external environment, than with the underlying philosophy. Adedeji's frustration with the "economism" of regional integration is probably that, in his view, it crowded out the popular participation dimension and as such may have not exerted enough pressure to secure good governance in the continent and unleash peoples' participation in development and supporting regional integration. Be that as it may, the stalling of development is the fundamental cause and effect. It is gratifying, however, that Adedeji has already been there – ahead with ideas when regional integration groupings are formed or development perspectives are to be outlined – and remains engaged as the twin processes face the harsh realities of Africa and the world. He was not lacking in courage to fault African leaders, development partners and even the African people when deemed necessary. Yet he gained their respect. They all saw in him the attributes of a genuine and worthy son of Africa – the Africa he struggled to reshape.

References

Adedeji, A. 1990. *Structural Adjustment for Socio-economic Recovery and Transformation: The African Alternative.* Addis Ababa, UNECA.

Adedeji, A. 1991. *Preparing Africa for the Twenty-First Century: Agenda for the 1990's.* Addis Ababa, UNECA.

Adedeji, A. 2002. "History and prospects of regional integration in Africa." Presentation at the Third Meeting of the UNECA's African Development Forum, on the theme of "Defining Priorities for Regional Integration", mimeograph, Addis Ababa, 5 March.

Cornia, GA, Jolly, R and Stewart, F. (eds) 1987. *Adjustment with a Human Face, Protecting the Vulnerable and Promoting Growth.* UNICEF, Volume I. Oxford: Oxford University Press.

Dos Santos, T (1970) 1981 "The Structure of Dependence", *American Economic Review* (1970), reprinted in I. Livingstone (ed.) *Development Economics and Policy: Readings.* London: George Allen and Unwin.

Fine, J and Yeo, S. 1996. "Regional integration in sub-Saharan Africa:

Dead end or a fresh start?" in: P Collier, B Ndulu and A Oyejide (eds) *Trade Liberalization and Regional Integration.* London: Macmillan.
Galbraith, J. 1979. *The Nature of Mass Poverty.* New York: Penguin Books.
Krugman, P. 1991. *Geography and Trade.* Cambridge. MA: MIT Press.
Mathur, P. 1991. *Why Developing Countries Fail to Develop.* Houndmills, Basingstoke, Hampshire RG21 2XS and London: Macmillan Academic and Professional Ltd. Michigan Press.
Mistry, P. 1998. "Regional dimensions of structural adjustment in Africa" in: J. Teunissen (ed.) *Regionalism and the Global Economy: The Case of Africa.* The Hague: FONDAD.
Myrdal, G. 1968. *Asian Drama: An Enquiry into the Poverty of Nations*, New York: Twentieth Century Fund.
Naoroji, D. 1888. *Poverty of India: Papers and Statistics.* London: W. Foulger and Co.
Organization of African Unity. 1981. *Lagos Plan of Action for the Economic Development of Africa, 1980 – 2000.* Addis Ababa: OAU.
Robinson, P. 1996. "Potential gains from infrastructural and natural resources investment coordination in Africa" in J. Teunissen (ed.) *Regionalism and the Global Economy: The Case of Africa.* The Hague: FONDAD.
Ros, J. 2001. *Development Theory and the Economics of Growth,* Michigan: University of
Seers, D. 1963. "The limitations of the special case", *Oxford University Institute of Economic and Statistics Bulletin* 25(2).
Suliman, Y. 2009. "African integration and the challenge of rationalization" in *Laintegracion y el desarrollo en Africa.* Los Libros de la Catarata. Barcelona. (Results of the seminar on "Regional Integration in Africa: Achievements and Prospects", held in Barcelona on 29 June 2009).
UNECA (United Nations Economic Commission for Africa). 1989. *African Alternative Framework to Structural Adjustment Programmes for Socio-Economic Recovery and Transformation (AAF-SAP).* Addis Ababa: UNECA.
UNECA and AU. 2006. *Assessing Regional Integration in Africa II: Rationalizing Regional Economic Communities.* Addis Ababa: UNECA.
UNECA. 1990. *African Charter for Popular Participation in Development.*

Addis Ababa: UNECA.
UNECA. 2004. *Assessing Regional Integration in Africa*, UNECA Policy Research Report. Addis Ababa: UNECA.
UNECA. 2007. *Status of Regional Integration in Central Africa.* 2007. Yaoundé: UNECA.
UNECA. 2009. *Economic Report on Africa 2009*. Addis Ababa: UNECA.
Viner, J. 1950. *The Customs Union Issue.* New York: Carnegie Endowment for International Peace.

PART 3.
BUILDING INSTITUTIONS AND FINANCES TOWARDS THE DEVELOPMENT OF AFRICA

CHAPTER 6. AFRICAN COUNTRIES: THREE DEFICITS AND THREE FUTURES

Ejeviome Eloho Otobo

Introduction

In 1983, the United Nations Economic Commission for Africa (UNECA), under the leadership of Adebayo Adedeji, published a little noticed but highly significant report. Entitled *ECA and Africa's Development 1983–2008: A Preliminary Perspective Study*, the report charted two scenarios for Africa's development prospects over a twenty-five-year horizon. It referred to these scenarios as the historical trends scenario or a horrendous future (pessimistic) and the normative development scenario or a "willed future" (optimistic).
We can gauge the significance of the *Perspective Study* by excerpting the summary of the pessimistic scenario from the introduction to that study, which was signed by Adedeji. In it, *UNECA* foresaw

> *that the region as whole would require more food imports and perhaps would have to depend on more food aid. Over 90 per cent of all capital goods required for development would still have to be imported from outside the region after nearly half a century of independence. Critical intermediate goods like fertilizers and cement would still have to be bought from outside Africa. On the social side, all services would deteriorate in terms of quantity and quality. A smaller portion of the population would be able to have access to education, health or water. Cities would become overpopulated shantytowns*

as housing would become less available. As a result of such socio-economic difficulties, the political situation would worsen. Then, riots, crimes and misery would be the order of 2008 if present trends continue without conscious change. With the weak and fragile socio-political systems, the sovereignty of African States will, then, be at stake. As such, self-reliance and independence will, to the generation of 2008, sound slogans of the past. (1983: 2)

The underlying premises in the pessimistic scenario were twofold: First was that African countries would witness growing dependency on foreign imports and support; and second, they would experience a possible deterioration in their political, economic and social conditions. Was this prognosis proven right? The answer to the question comes in three parts: (i) by examining some important events that occurred immediately after the publication; (ii) by identifying the key trends that emerged much later; (iii) by highlighting other developments that took place towards the end of the period covered by the *Perspective Study*.

Even UNECA's pessimistic forecast could not have anticipated what was to come about a year after the *Perspective Study* was issued. A huge swathe of the Horn of Africa and Sahel countries was hit by severe drought and famine in 1984–1985. This pattern was repeated in 1994–1995 and in 2006, albeit with lesser intensity.

Moreover, on the twenty-fifth anniversary of the *Perspective Study*, several African countries experienced food riots in early 2008. The story that most dramatically confirmed aspects of UNECA's dire prediction was published on page 6 of the *Financial Times* edition of 4 April 2008 under the headline, "Fear of unrest mounts as hunger spreads in Africa" and datelined, ironically, in Addis Ababa, the headquarters of UNECA. In it, the *Financial Times* reported that "rising food prices could spread social unrest across Africa after triggering riots in Niger, Senegal, Cameroon and Burkina Faso ... the cereal imports bill for the continent's poor countries is forecast to surge to US\$15.2 billion, up 49 per cent from last year and more than double the US\$6.5 billion of five years ago". Riots subsequently erupted in more countries in the course of that year.

On the economic front, Africa experienced dismal economic performance throughout the 1980s, leading to that period being labeled as a "lost decade" to Africa's development. More significantly, the political developments in the later part of the 1980s and much of the 1990s, as will be explained in detail later, turned out to be particularly turbulent. However, beginning around 1995, African countries began experiencing a gradual economic upturn. The period from 2000 through 2008, the last eight years covered by the *Perspective Study,* confounded parts of the prediction, as the continent witnessed respectable economic growth.

Although African countries witnessed improvements in economic growth, especially in the past decade, this has not translated into much improvement in social conditions. The evidence of continuing poor social conditions has been manifested not so much in overpopulated cities becoming shantytowns that were predicted – although there is some of that. Instead, it has been reflected in a set of mainly social indicators in the Human Development Index that was developed in 1990 and in the social-oriented components of the Millennium Development Goals adopted in 2000. African countries rank very low on the Human Development Index and are lagging behind in many of the Millennium Development Goals.

Moreover, as will be shown later, many countries in the continent have become very dependent on official development assistance, which includes international food aid. Thus, many aspects of the dire predictions have been proved right. Given that economic and social projections are particularly fraught with errors this was not a bad record. With the benefit of hindsight, it has turned prophetic. The question persists as to why Africa did not fare much better. This critically turns on the issue of the structural constraints that have prevented African countries from realizing their full potentials.

Diversity in performance and in deficits

In attempting an explanation for diversity in performance, it helps to remember that Africa is not a monolithic entity. The *Perspective Study* itself recognized that all African countries could have differentiated economic performance. This should not be surprising. Africa is a continent of considerable diversity, consisting of 54 countries, each with its own idiosyncratic circumstances reflected in contrasting economic, historical and political experiences and with different levels of natural, human and economic endowments. A year before the release of the *Perspective Study*, for example, the degree of ideological divergence among African countries was well captured by the American political scientist Crawford Young in his 1982 book entitled *Ideology and Development in Africa*. In it, he classified African countries into three categories by the then prevailing regime types: "Afro-Marxists", "Popular Socialists" and "African Capitalists".

Africa is a continent that is also currently witnessing significant divergent political experiences. "Today, the 53 African countries[1] can be classified into four categories according to where they lie on the peace and development spectrum: those still in conflict; those emerging from conflict; those where democratic stability is racked by disruptive political tensions and undermined by weak institutions and governance practices; and those where democratic consolidation is buttressed by stable economic growth" (Otobo, 2006: 8).

In the past decade, Africa has witnessed considerable progress on many fronts. The economic growth rate has held steady at an annual average of about 5 per cent in the first eight years of the last decade. There is a growing trend of democratic consolidation and of greater political commitment and public support to improved governance, signaled by the increasing number of countries signing on to the African Peer Review Mechanism of the African Union – a process for monitoring policies, standards and practices in economic and political governance of the subscribing member states. Civil conflicts have fallen sharply. All these are having a salutary effect on investment in the continent. As Mo Ibrahim has put it, "Given Africa's rich natural resources, financiers are finally waking up to investment potential of the continent…yet the concern about how well African countries are governed is real and remains" (Ibrahim, 2010: 8).

Accentuating this positive outlook for the continent are the findings of three reports released in June 2010. The first of these reports (Boston Consulting Group, 2010) notes that Africa's top forty companies – referred to as the African Challengers – are now doing well in terms of profitability and growing international presence. It also identifies as "African Lions" a group of fast-growing nations in the continent, namely: Algeria, Botswana, Egypt, Libya, Mauritius, Morocco, South Africa and Tunisia. The overall thrust of the second of these reports (McKinsey Global Institute, 2010) is that the continent is experiencing an economic vibrancy reflected in economic growth of about 5 per cent from 2000 through 2008 –

---

1 This was written before independence of South Sudan in July 2011.

which is twice more than the pace of the 1980s and the 1990s; that economic growth has come from the natural resources sector (a third of the growth) but also from the agriculture, banking, construction, transport and telecommunications sectors; and that today the rate of return on foreign investment in Africa is higher than in any other developing region. The third report, *"Africa wealth cheque report"*, by *Africa-Investor* "identified US$1.671 trillion of potential wealth in six key sectors – agriculture, water, fisheries, forestry, tourism and human capital. This represents a combined market size today of the US$909 billion and US$762.4 billion of additional production" (*Africa-Investor*, 2010: 50–51).

In his book entitled, *Emerging Africa: How 17 Countries Are Leading the Way*, Steven Radelet (2010), classifies sub-Saharan African countries into the following four categories: emerging countries, threshold countries, other countries and oil exporters. He argues that the 17 countries which he classifies as emerging economies on the basis of their steady economic growth from 1996–2008 have great economic prospects. Nine years earlier, in its *Economic Report on Africa 2002*, UNECA had heralded the evolving upsurge in African economic performance.

Yet, it is important to recognize that there are some structural constraints which have impeded Africa's development in the past and still cast shadows over its long-term prospects: These can be referred to as deficits. Indeed, a distinguishing common feature is that individual African countries suffer in varying degrees from three main deficits: stability deficit, organizational deficit and scientific deficit. The present and prospective divergence in political stability and economic growth and development among African countries is essentially the by-product of how individual countries cope with these deficits. This also explains why their path of progress will be different. To paint a more accurate portrait, several African countries suffer from stability deficit; many suffer from organizational deficit and most from scientific deficit. There are many mutually reinforcing linkages among these deficits. The stability deficit leads to organizational deficit and the combination of the two deficits leads to neglect of and lack of investment in science and technological capacity; further deepening the stability and organizational deficits. The combination of these three structural deficits has had critically constraining effects on Africa's development. Whether individual African countries are able to overcome the three deficits will determine what the future holds for each of them. The remainder of this chapter examines the manifestations of the triple deficits, their consequences on Africa's development and their implications for Africa's future.

Africa's three deficits

Stability deficit

Africa's stability deficit is profound and has been persistent. It has manifested itself in several ways, most notably in conflicts, serial coups, and weak rule of law as well as poor democratic governance practices. The degree to which conflicts have contributed to the stability deficit is reflected in conflict trend analysis. When UNECA made its forecast twenty-eight years ago, there were four countries in the throes of conflict in the continent, all of them associated with struggle for independence. As the United Nations Secretary-General, Kofi Annan, stated in his report, "By 1996, 14 of the 53 countries of Africa were afflicted by armed conflict, accounting for more than half of all war-related deaths worldwide" (1998: 3). Today, there are only five countries experiencing civil conflicts in the continent. While these numbers reflect a progressive trend in the winding down of violent civil conflicts, their consequences have been corrosive. Conflicts not only lead to significant loss of lives but also wreak havoc on the economy and society in other ways: by destroying infrastructure, degrading institutions, fraying political consensus, breaking social trust and reducing economic output.

Regarding the last point, Paul Collier has noted that "civil war tends to reduce [economic] growth by around 2.3 per cent per year, so the typical seven-year war leaves a country around 15 per cent poorer than it would have been" (2007: 27). Indeed, the central thesis of that book is that African countries which form the bulk of the 58 countries in the "Bottom Billion" that account for the one billion poorest people in the world are caught in one or another of the four traps that have stymied their development efforts: in addition to the conflict trap, the other three are the natural resources trap, "landlocked with bad neighbor" trap and "bad governance in a small country" trap.[2]

---

2 Although he did not present the complete list, Paul Collier has subsequently disclosed the list of 58 countries in the Bottom Billion: 39

Coup d'états have also been a significant contributory factor to the stability deficit in the continent. There is, of course, another perspective which views coups not so much as a source of instability but both as a possible source of progress – insofar as progressive-minded coup leaders become agents of development – and as something to be harnessed to guarantee democracy. The experience in Africa has mostly not borne this out. Though coups wreak less havoc than civil wars, coups do have corrosive effects on democracy and good governance. There have been a total of 92 successful coups, 128 attempted coups, 37 plotted coups and 54 alleged coups in Africa between 1960 and 2010 (Marshall, 2006). Since 2000, when African countries under the auspices of the Organization of African Unity – now African Union – adopted the *Lome Declaration on Framework for Response to Unconstitutional Changes of Government,*[3] there have been eleven coups in eight African countries: Madagascar (2002 and 2009); Central African Republic (2003); Guinea-Bissau (2003 and 2012); Sao Tome and Principe (2003); Mali (2012) Mauritania (2005 and 2008); Guinea (2008); and Niger (2010).

Coups can both be a response to conflict and instability and can increase the possibility of conflict – they have, indeed, triggered civil wars in several African countries. In particular, coups and violent civil conflicts are often the manifestation of deep-seated ethnic differences which existing political institutions and processes have failed to address. Civil wars and coups are a manifestation of state breakdown, which is an important example of anti-growth policy syndrome (Fosu and Naude, 2009). The combination of persistent conflicts and frequent coups has had many deleterious consequences: it has decimated government capacities, degraded political institutions and has led to state fragility that is a characteristic feature of many of the countries in the continent. State fragility refers to the inability or unwillingness of a state to deliver basic safety and security and provide basic social services and to lack of monopoly in the use of force in its territory. A study undertaken by the Department for International Department (DFID, 2005) listed 26 African countries among the 46 fragile states globally.

---

of the 58 countries caught in one or more of the four traps are from Africa (Collier 2009: 239–240).
3   This provision has now been codified as article 30 of the Constitutive Act of the African Union.

Coups and conflicts are not only extreme manifestations of fragility but also major sources of derogation from and weakening of rule of law and democratic governance. As Nobel Peace Laureate Wangari Maathai has argued, "good governance and development rest on three legs: democracy principles, sustainable and accountable management of natural resources and a strong culture of peace" (2009: 56). She adds that "a number of countries are trying to balance on two of the stool's three legs. Some are teetering on only one leg; a few have none whatsoever and have collapsed". That collapse is particularly evident in the lack of transparency and accountability that has bedeviled natural resources management in most of the countries that are a treasure trove of an array of minerals and energy resource wealth. The Organization for Economic Cooperation and Development (2007) has noted that "natural resource wealth has not induced growth and has been associated with corruption and violent conflict in several [African] countries". Natural resources are like elections in one important respect. Just as natural resources can be drivers of growth, so elections are a key vehicle for democratic consolidation. But if either is badly managed, they can become either a trigger or driver of conflict, as the experience in several African countries has shown. The violence and instability from poor natural resource management and elections has further deepened the stability deficit in various African countries.

Stability deficit shows up in other ways, notably in high incidences of crime and lack of public security. This is quite often a reflection of the inability of law enforcement agencies to ensure public safety. A pervasive sense of lack of public security and personal safety can be a major disincentive to investment, which is a critical factor in low economic growth.

The importance of stability as a critical factor in development was well articulated by Adam Smith, in *The Wealth of Nations*. He said, "Little is required to carry a state to the highest opulence but peace, easy taxes and a tolerable administration of justice". Prolonged periods of coups, conflict and weak democracy mean that not only have many African countries not known peace and been unable to collect taxes but they have a remarkable lack of tolerable administration of justice.

As former Commonwealth Secretary-General, Emeka Anyaoku, has noted, prosperity rests on two foundations: institutional and technical. In his words: "The institutional foundations consist of respect for private property; rule of law, often expressed in an effective legal and regulatory framework and a sound financial system; while the technical foundations include high literacy rate, critical mass of technical expertise (in particular in sciences, engineering, medicine and management) and entrepreneurial risk-taking and innovation" (Anyaoku, 2009: 68–69). The next two sections examine the deficits in these areas.

Organizational deficit

The term "organizational deficit" encapsulates both institutional weakness and serious capacity deficiencies, both of which have characterized many African countries. There are various notions of the term "institutions". One is the idea that institutions are rules of the game, viewed either as rules that set constraints or as behavior following a set of rules. Another is that institutions are organizations or governance structures: these also encompass firms and markets that are subject to norms and rules. The term "institutional weakness" is also used to refer to a paucity of or a weak institutional infrastructure. The concept of institutional infrastructure covers informal but also formal mechanisms that set and enforce standards concerning accountability, transparency, predictability, rule of law and quality of policy. Capacity, on the other hand, refers to the ability to undertake a wide range of development tasks. In its report, the Commission for Africa[4] stated "Africa's history over the last fifty years has been blighted by two areas of weakness. These have been lack of capacity – the ability to design and deliver policies; and accountability – how well a state answers to its people" (2005: 14).

Organizational deficits extend beyond issues of lack of capacity and lack of institutional infrastructure and encompass issues of leadership as well as such intangibles as poor work ethic, low motivation to increase performance and the negative impact of socio-cultural factors on organizational productivity. Organizational deficit has several adverse consequences, the most notable being the marked weaknesses of the institutions of economic management and political governance to effectively perform their functions. This shows up in

---

4 The Commission for Africa was appointed by Prime Minister of the United Kingdom, Tony Blair in 2004, to prepare a report examining Africa's development challenges ahead of the July 2005 Gleneagles G8 Summit.

part in persistent lack of effectiveness in undertaking such critical functions as articulating, planning, financing, implementing, monitoring and evaluating the countries' development programs. It also shows up in the lack of political will to undertake needed changes or reforms. In either case, this can lead to loss of public confidence in the competence and commitment of government to serve its people; often the trigger of violent protests or agitations. At its core, organizational deficit is the lack of a critical mass of managerial and scientific and technological cadre to run either private sector operations or public sector institutions. The focus of this chapter is on the capacity and institutional infrastructure needed to deliver on development policies. Capacities can be managerial and scientific. This section focuses on managerial capacities, leaving issues of scientific and technological capacity for the next section.

A well-functioning economy and society rests on the fulcrum of an effective public sector and a vibrant private sector. The public sector is needed to deliver on the basic social contract between government and its people. The elements of such a contract include the ability of the state to provide safety and security, to deliver basic social services, to help protect the physical environment and to manage the economy, in particular by enforcing property and contract rights and ensuring effective regulation of markets and policing of competition. These are the minimum functions of state. There are intermediate and activist functions of the state that include offering a vision for society, fostering market initiatives, providing disaster relief, resolving conflicts on economic distribution and brokering public-private partnerships. Thus, the private sector plays a complementary role to the state by producing the goods and services needed by society in an efficient and socially responsible manner.

While the government department or agency is the basic unit of public sector service delivery – whether that service is policy-making, regulation of safety or social service delivery – in the private sector, the firm is the basic unit of production. The rather sub-optimal performance of the public and private sectors in the continent are attributable to several factors. Notably, these include the political and policy instabilities that have marked many African countries, the limited adaptation of technology in these organizations and the lack of critical mass of managerial and technical capacity to run these organizations.

Technical assistance has both substituted for and helped to redress the dearth of local capacity in many instances. The scale, if not the scope of technical assistance, is reflected in the approximately US$5 billion allocated annually from official development assistance to technical cooperation in the continent. Part of the explanation for the limited role of aid in creating national capacity in recipient countries is that the share of country programmable aid continues to fall: it has declined over the years. Yet, this trend coincides with the growing dependence of many African countries on aid. Country programmable aid refers to what remains after deducting debt relief, food aid, humanitarian aid, technical cooperation, financial support for non-governmental organizations, administrative costs and cost of promotion of development awareness and research in donor countries. Although the typical poor, low-income country depends on aid for about one-third of its budget, a recent analyses on aid trends in Africa showed that about twenty countries in Africa have crossed this threshold; with most conflict-affected or post-conflict countries' aid share of national budget ranging from 90 per cent to over 700 per cent.[5]

The interplay between the public and private sectors is critical to how an economy produces goods and services. Typically, there are a host of institutional infrastructures built around supporting or monitoring this interface. These include regulatory agencies that set or enforce standards on financial, environmental, health and labor matters. But there are other institutions created to promote, facilitate or leverage public support for private enterprise development, for example, trade and investment promotion agencies as well as agricultural extension services. But most of these institutions tend to be either inchoate or inadequately staffed.

In a real and important sense, the debates on structural adjustment policies in Africa that raged in the 1980s were focused in part on the relative role of internal versus external factors in Africa's dismal economic performance in that decade, in part on individual countries' abilities to implement sound macroeconomic policies, and in part on the appropriate role of the state, with a particular focus on its role in the productive sector of the economy. Those who argued

---

[5] See "Africa's dependence on aid: Net official aid as a percentage of government expenditures, 2008" on page 4 of *Financial Times*, 2 June 2010.

for moving away from the so-called state-dominated model, typically organized around the then ubiquitous state-owned enterprises, took the view that these had become dysfunctional as a unit of production. One of the outcomes of that debate is the degree to which there is less reliance, in Africa today, on state-owned enterprises and more on private firms or some form of public-private partnership arrangements. The progress in that transition is reflected in the strides that the private sector firms have made in such sectors of the economy as banking, telecommunications and tourism. Yet, there can be no room for complacency. Even the McKinsey report acknowledged that "although African growth is due to more than [natural] resources, the continent will continue to profit from rising global demand for oil, natural gas, minerals, food arable land and other natural resources" (McKinsey Global Institute, 2010: 14).

Thus, it should be noted that the frequently encountered observation that Africa is rich in natural resources but rife with poverty stems mainly from the combination of organizational deficit and scientific and technological deficit. This has some echo of Paul Romer's observation that "a poor developing economy typically suffers both from a large technology gap and a reduced absorptive capacity" (1993: 555).

Scientific and technological deficit

Science is the engine of economic growth. Science stimulates growth through inventions, innovation and imitation (adaptation). Scientific knowledge leads to technological inventions and innovations, which get converted into new goods and services; the creation of such products in turn increases economic output and wealth. The key to wealth creation is economic growth, which is critically dependent on increased productivity, which itself depends on organizational competence and scientific and technological skills. As Ngozi Okonjo-Iweala has observed, "cognitive skills – measured by reading, mathematics and science tests – have a substantial, robust effect on economic growth ... as cognitive skills could foster innovation and promote technology diffusion by equipping the workforce with the ability to absorb, process and integrate new ideas into production and service delivery" (2010: 9).

Throughout history, advances in science and technology have been the key sources of growth, and they also defined historical eras. Thus, we speak of the era of the agricultural revolution, the industrial era and the post-industrial era; with each era organized around a particular factor of production, propelled by specific drivers of growth and creating its economic and political order (see Table 6.1). This is a schematic representation of a more complex reality. Yet, it presents a graphic illustration of the historical evolution of the role of various factors of production as sources of economic growth in historical perspective. In thinking about this, it helps to note that fixed factors such as land and capital experience diminishing returns over time; while dynamic factors such as knowledge are marked by increasing returns. Thus it has been noted that "at the dawn of the 21st century, however,…African economies continue to be dominated by the production of agricultural and mineral goods for export…yet the global trend is toward developing an economy based on producing manufactured goods and services, both for the domestic market and for export" (Alioune, 2003: 25–26). The implication of this observation is that to the extent that African economies are still heavily reliant on primary commodities – minerals, mines and agriculture – they are on the opposite end of a knowledge-driven economy.

Table 6.1: Factors of production as sources of economic growth in historical perspective

Dominant factor(s) of production	Drivers of growth	Dominant economic order	Dominant political order	Era/Age
Knowledge	knowledge-base: in particular greater application and use of information technology, synthetic products, nano-technology, biotechnology, etc.	market economy (globalization)	democracy	Information Age and Green Economy Age (Post-Industrial)

labor	management (tools of analysis and decision-making)	capitalism vs. significant state ownership	democracy vs. socialism	Industrial Age
capital	physical capital (factories, rail, electric light, telephone, telegraphy, etc.)	capitalism	liberalism	Industrial Age
land	natural resources (mines, agriculture, minerals, etc.)	trade imperialism (mercantilism)	colonialism	Agricultural Age (pre-industrial)

Note: This table represents considerable simplification of the complex evolutionary trends in science, economy and society.

African countries need a critical mass of scientific and technological expertise to adapt to and solve the continent's pressing public policy issues, ranging from building and maintenance of infrastructure to industrial development, from environmental to natural resource management, from agriculture to aviation, and from health to housing needs. Yet, most countries suffer severe shortages of skilled scientists, especially in the fields of science, technology, engineering and medicine. The link between mastery of science and technology and economic development is enduring and strong. Economic power is directly correlated with scientific power. No nation can emerge as an economic power or even a military power without first being a leading nation in science and technology. The most successful and dynamic economies share certain key attributes, such as high levels of investment in research and development, good educational system, high number of inventions and an economic structure with a significant share of manufacturing and export structure marked by a high share technology products. On the other hand, as the Nigerian political sociologist Uwazurike (2006: 33) has warned, "technological laggards are history's orphans". International measurements or comparisons of advances in science and technology activities among countries usually focus on a composite of indicators: expenditure and human resources devoted to science and technology, innovations and production and exports of high-technology products. African countries have pronounced deficits in each of these areas.

This chapter examines four manifestations of such deficits in Africa, namely: the low expenditure in research and development; growing size of African science and technology expertise in the diaspora, as proxy for loss of capacity in the home countries; low ranking of African universities among the world universities, as a proxy for sound educational system; and the share of manufacturing and high technology products in exports.

The most severe of Africa's scientific deficits is in investment in research and development, indicated by research and development expenditure. Expenditure in research and development includes the total expenditures by key actors in the country, namely: industry, government agencies and public laboratories, universities, and equivalent higher educational institutions and private institutions. At present, Africa's share of world research and development is less than 1 per cent and Africa's research and development expenditure is less than 1 per cent of their gross domestic product and much of that is concentrated in South Africa and Egypt.

Closely linked to the declining quality – or indeed intensifying the deterioration in institutions in higher learning in the continent – is the high level of top expertise in form of brain drain from the continent. According to Obasi, Achike and Obasi (2006), estimates by the UNECA and the International Organization for Migration show that: the number of African professionals leaving the continent was 27,000 between 1960 and 1974, rising to 40,000 between 1975 and 1984 and to 60,000 between 1985 and 1989; since 1990, an estimated 20,000 professionals have left the continent annually; over 300,000 professionals reside outside Africa; and 30,000 of them have doctorate degrees. These figures not only highlight the magnitude of the problem of brain drain but also illustrate the extent to which the continent is being denuded of scientific expertise. Indeed, some African leaders lament that there are more doctors from their countries residing abroad than in their countries of origin. Yet, brain drain can become "brain gain" if governments can creatively tap into the expertise of their citizens in the diaspora.

Universities are the citadels of higher learning and, quite often, the centers of research in science and technology. The link between science and technology, universities, education and economic growth in Africa was well highlighted by Juma (2007:27) when he said that

"Africa faces two major challenges: recognizing the importance of [scientific] knowledge in economic growth and reforming [African] universities so they contribute to development". Yet, there is growing evidence of quality problems in universities in Africa. One measure of this is the placement of African universities in *The Times Higher Education World University Rankings* for 2012–2013. These rankings assess universities across all of their core missions: teaching, research, knowledge transfer and international outlook. In the 2012–2013 survey, there was no African university among the top hundred universities worldwide and there was only one among the top two hundred and four among the top four hundred universities were all from South Africa. The role of scientific and technological knowledge in transforming primary commodities into semi-manufactured and manufactured goods is well recognized. The more science and technology capability a country has, the more likely that its exports will embody high value addition in form of processed products which command higher prices. The continuing high dependence of many African countries on a single or a few primary commodities for exports reflects the lack of progress in diversification (see Table 6.2 for a selection of major African economies). The high share of primary commodity as a percentage of merchandise in various countries shows that the route of industrialization through trade continues to elude Africa. Diversification of an economy away from dependence on primary commodities to high value-added sectors is in many important respects a measure of both organizational competence and scientific and technological prowess of a country. It is an indication that the country has the managerial capacity to launch on a path of creating niches in dynamic sectors of the economy and it imbues the economy with flexibility in terms of adjusting rapidly to changing economic trends. Most important, in this era of globalization, it is evidence that a country has the technical expertise to penetrate and participate in the production and supply chains of global competitive technology sectors. The inability of African countries to participate in the production and supply chains of globally competitive sectors or move up the economic value chain is mostly linked to the lack of scientific and technological skills.

Table 6.2: Commodity dependency and diversification of selected African economies, 2011-2012

Country	Commodity** as % total merchandise exports	Manufactured exports as % total merchandise exports	High technology as % total merchandise exports	High technology as % total manufactured product exports	Primary commodity as % gross domestic product
Algeria *b*	99.1%	0.9%	0.7%	76.2%	35.3%
Angola*	99.8%	0.2%	0.1%	34.0%	62.8%
Botswana *b*	93.0%	6.9%	1.5%	21.3%	31.2%
Democratic Republic of Congo *s*	89.0%	4.1%	2.9%	69.9%	33.8%
Egypt *b, n, m, s*	59.9%	39.7%	14.0%	35.3%	7.5%
Kenya *s*	64.7%	35.3%	10.6%	30.0%	10.2%
Libya *b*	97.4%	2.5%	1.6%	63.9%	71.7%
Mauritius *b*	34.6%	51.9%	6.0%	11.6%	7.9%
Morocco *b, m*	37.8%	62.2%	24.5%	39.3%	8.2%
Nigeria* *n, s*	98.1%	1.9%	0.5%	26.9%	47.1%
South Africa *b, m, s*	58.8%	35.5%	8.4%	23.7%	13.2%
Togo*	68.5%	31.5%	6.6%	21.0	19.6%
Tunisia *b, m*	27.9%	72.1%	16.4%	22.8%	10.6%

Source: All data on commodity dependence was retrieved from United Nations Conference on Trade and Development (UNCTAD) global statistical data base, as of 20 May, 2013.

Notes:

** Definition on UNCTAD commodity groupings can be obtained from http://unctadstat.unctad.org/UnctadStatMetadata/Classifications/Methodology&Classifications.html#Distribution%20of%20products

* The other three African countries in the Boston Consulting Group list from where five of the forty "African Challengers" firms were drawn.

b Among eight African countries classified as "African Lions" in Boston Consulting Group report (2010).

m Among the four African countries classified as diversified economies in the McKinsey Global Institute report (2010).

n Among the 11 large population countries worldwide that could rival the original G7 countries by 2050, listed in Goldman Sachs report "The N-11: More Than Acronym" released in March 2007.

s The five countries in each of Africa's five sub-regions viewed as the growth pole/hub in their sub-regions (the concept was made popular by ex-President FW de Klerk of South Africa).

Africa's three futures

Although the problems of conflict, coups and humanitarian crises dominate and distort international perceptions of the continent, Africa has witnessed remarkable progress in the past decade. Conventional analyses of progress or lack of it in Africa has focused either on the political factors or economic trends. Seldom are the two brought together and even much rarer is the case when the political, organizational and the scientific and technological dimensions are combined to offer a comprehensive view.

By integrating the stability, organizational and scientific and technological perspectives, it is possible to gain considerable insights into the factors that will shape the futures of African countries. The picture that emerges from that composite portrait is clear: all African countries do not face the same futures. Instead, African countries face three distinct futures, which can be referred to as those of *competitiveness, cooperation* and *conflict*. One question that naturally arises is why individual countries will end up with one future rather than another. The future that each country faces will critically depend on the nature and magnitude of the deficits in their individual country-contexts. This will, in turn, be a result of the combination of initial conditions – at independence – and the path that a country has followed since; in particular the efforts that have been made to address or overcome the deficits. The scale and scope of efforts required to overcome the deficits will vary considerably across countries – the more the deficits, the greater the effort; and conversely, the fewer the deficits the less the effort required for a particular deficit.

To understand how those futures will evolve is to understand the points of intersections among stability, organizational competence and scientific and technological capacity. The group of countries that combine political stability, organizational competence and scientific and technological prowess will emerge as the most competitive. This combination of attributes means that the governments of these countries will exert significant continental or even extra-continental influence. Their companies will extend their presence beyond national and continental boundaries into other continents driven by growing organizational competence and mastery of science and technology. More than these countries need political stability to buttress their economic growth, they need strong scientific and technological skills to climb up the product value chain at competitive cost structure. This group of countries will be few indeed. To draw on the metaphor of lions that suffuses the reports by the Boston Consulting Group (2010), McKinsey Global Institute (2010) and before that Alioune (2003), this category of countries can be referred to as the "roaring lions".[6]

The next category of countries will be those that have a modicum of political stability and organizational competence but scant mastery of scientific and technological knowhow. To the limited extent that their firms will compete, it will mainly be in a sub-regional context and in very limited sectors. One of the reasons for this is that the labor force of these countries might not offer better technical skills relative to the wages (cost of labor) found elsewhere in the continent or around the world. Similarly, their governments might hold some sway only in a sub-regional context and, to some extent, in the continental context. They will be in a mode of regional cooperation not competitiveness. This group can be referred to as the "shackled lions".

The third category of countries are those plagued by continuing political instability or the ever-present danger of lapsing or relapsing into conflict in the context of weak institutions and very limited managerial capacity. Countries in this category will manifest the traits

---

6   This categorization of countries broadly corresponds to those proposed in my 27 December 2006 article in the *Financial Times*, cited earlier in this paper.

that can be referred to as ""bruised" or "wounded lions". These countries have high political risk with limited upside potentials with regard to investment opportunities, given weak infrastructure and negligible scientific and technological knowhow.

Enhanced regional integration can make a major contribution to the continent's economic dynamism by creating a large market for production and exchange. Yet, as has been argued elsewhere, "The African experience is replete with instances [in which] regional economic groups have been weakened or stalled by prevalence of conflicts in one or more countries within the same group"; another example of how stability deficit undercuts foundations of development (Otobo, 2004: 124).

There are four political risk trends in Africa that bear close watching: (i) how the countries experiencing or that have experienced popular uprisings, especially in North Africa, will navigate the transition to a stable democratic order; (ii) how and when the few remaining conflicts will wind down; (iii) whether the cycle of coups that began in 2000 – the so-called "new generation of coups" – will flare up; and (iv) how the upcoming elections in several countries will be managed. Each of these trends contains the seeds of potential turbulence ahead. However, there is no inevitability to these four trends degenerating into conflict or chaos.

Africa has witnessed significant political, economic and social changes since UNECA issued the *Preliminary Perspective Study* in 1983. A notable positive development is the degree to which there is growing divergence in the economic prospects and political outlook of the countries in the continent. This is very good news because that will comprehensively undermine the uniformly bleak portrayal of the continent that frequently dominate some analyses and commentaries. The prospects for individual countries will mostly divide along the three futures that have been sketched. Looking ahead, if considerable progress can be made in addressing the three deficits, a very large number of countries in the continent will emerge politically stable, socially cohesive and economically vibrant.

References

Africa-Investor. 2010. "Africa wealth cheque report", *Africa Investor Magazine* 8(4): 50–51.

Alioune, S. (ed.) 2003. *Africa 2025: What Possible Futures for Sub-Saharan Africa?* Pretoria: University of South Africa Press.

Anyaoku, E. 2009. "Can responsible capitalism help Africa's prosperity?" in P Cormack and R Goodman (eds) *Responsible Capitalism: Essays in Morality, Ethics and Business*. London: First Magazine.

Boston Consulting Group. 2010. *The African Challengers: Global Competitors Emerge from the Overlooked Continent.* Boston Consulting Group.

Collier, P. 2007. *The Bottom Billion: Why the Poorest Countries Are Failing and What Can Be Done About It.* Oxford: Oxford University Press.

Collier, P. 2009. *Wars, Guns and Votes: Democracy in Dangerous Places.* New York: Harper Collins.

DFID (Department for International Development). 2005. *Why We Need to Work More Effectively in Fragile States.* London: DFID.

Fosu, A and Naude, W. 2009. "The global economic crisis: Towards syndrome-free recovery for Africa". Discussion Paper 2009/03. Helsinki: United Nations University-World Institute for Development Economic Research.

Ibrahim, M. 2010. "Prizing leadership in a hopeful Africa", *The Financial Times* 15 June 2010.

Juma, C. 2007. "A modern Africa: Universities can spur development", *John F. Kennedy School of Government Bulletin*, Winter 2007: 27.

Maathai, W. 2009. *The Challenge for Africa.* New York: Pantheon Books.

Marshall, M. 2006. *Conflict Trends in Africa, 1946–2004: A Macro-Perspective.* London: Department for International Development, Ministry of Defense and Foreign and Commonwealth Office (joint publication).

McKinsey Global Institute. 2010. *Lions on the Move: The Progress and Potential of African Economies.* McKinsey Global Institute.

Obasi IN, Achike AI and Obasi SN. 2006. "Arresting the tide of potential brain drain among academics in African universities: A case study in failure from a Nigerian experience". Proceedings of the 2006 Conference of the International Academy of Management and Business. Las Vegas, Nevada, USA, 22-25 January.

Okonjo-Iweala, N. 2010. "What's the big idea? To reposition Africa as the fifth BRIC: A destination for investment, not just aid". Address at Harvard Kennedy School, Cambridge, MA, 14

May 2010.
Organization for Economic Cooperation and Development. 2007. "Ensuring Fragile States are not left behind". Fact Sheet December 2007. Available at www.oecd/dac/fragile-sates/resource.
Otobo, EE. 2004. "Regionalism and trade: Glimpse of Africa's experience". *The New School Economic Review* 1(1): 124.
Otobo, EE. 2006. "Recognize efforts to strengthen democracy in Africa". *The Financial Times* 27 December, 2006.
Radelet, S. 2010. *Emerging Africa: How 17 Countries are leading the Way*. Washington D.C: Centre for Global Development.
Romer, P. 1993. "Ideas, gaps and object gaps in economic development", *Journal of Monetary Economics* 32: 555.
UK Commission for Africa, 2005. *Our Common Interest*. London: UNECA.
UNECA. 1983. *ECA and Africa's Development 1983–2008: A Preliminary Perspective Study*. Addis Ababa: UNECA.
United Nations Secretary-General. 1998. "The causes of conflict and the promotion of durable peace and sustainable development in Africa" (A/52/871-S/1998/318). New York: United Nations.
United Nations Secretary-General. 2010. "Progress report on the causes of conflict and the promotion of durable peace and sustainable development in Africa" (A/65/152). New York: United Nations.
Uwazurike, PC. 2006. *Instrumental Pan-Africanism: Good Governance, HiTech, the Diaspora and Africa's Fate in the Age of Hyper Globalisation*. New York: Chaneta Publishers and Times Square.
Young, C. 1982. *Ideology and Development in Africa*. New Haven: Yale University Press.

CHAPTER 7. INSTITUTION BUILDING FOR DEVELOPMENT IN AFRICA

Hesphina Rukato

Introduction

Recent years have seen a revival of interest in the study of institutions. In part because of the prevalence and dominance of neoclassical economics in the last three decades and its emphasis on a frictionless world where there is no uncertainty, the accent on institutions in development as it emerged in the 1960s was to experience some decline during the 1980s. It was, however, given a new boost, that was also accompanied by a much more nuanced and sophisticated frame of analyses, following the renewed visibility which institutional economics enjoyed in the wake of the Nobel Prize awarded to Douglas North in 1993. The works of Douglas North has inspired a resurgence of interest and a host of other studies, mostly set within the broader context of the development debate that sought to assess: the nature, role, and importance of institutions – understood in terms of rules, norms and values – in successful socio-economic transformation; the sources of institutional differences across countries; the channels through which institutions may affect economic performance; and the quantitative importance of these links.

Building and strengthening of the capacity of African institutions to achieve accelerated development has been central to Adebayo

Adedeji's work. This is evidenced by his groundbreaking leadership in the development of the Lagos Plan of Action, Chapter VIII of which focused on "Measures to build up and strengthen economic and technical co-operation including creation of new institutions and strengthening of existing ones" (Organization of African Unity, 1980: 73), and his chairing of the High Level Panel of the audit of the African Union (AU) in 2007.

It is important to note that in spite of the many efforts, African institutions have remained weak for a period of thirty years, between when the Lagos Plan of Action was adopted, and when the AU Audit was undertaken. In 1980, the Lagos Plan of Action stressed the importance of Member States taking responsibility for the success and effectiveness of institutions they create. As chairperson of the High Level Panel on the audit of the AU, Adedeji had contributed a foreword to the ensuing AU publication in which he noted that: "The idea that somehow Africa's deliverance from political fragmentation, socio-economic underdevelopment, poverty and disease, etc. will come from outside the continent has become so ingrained in official and public discourse that the decision that this review should be undertaken has come as a surprise to many, in and outside Africa" (African Union, 2007: iii). What did not surprise many, however, is the fact that the recommendations of the Audit were never seriously considered, nor implemented.

The purpose of this chapter is to review and analyze the current approaches in institution building for development in Africa, with a view to making a case for new approaches that will make institutions more responsive to the development agenda of the continent, and the needs of the people, thereby making them more relevant. At the global level, Africa remains one of the poorest continents in the world, in spite of its rich natural resource endowments. Many institutions have been established to deal with the challenges of underdevelopment and rampant poverty at the continental, regional, and national levels. The chapter analyses the rationale that led to the development of some of the key institutions that are leading the continent's development agenda today. The chapter also analyses the initial motivation for the setting up of the institutions and whether they are still relevant and responsive to current needs and future targets. In cases where the rationales and objectives for the institutions continue to be relevant, the chapter analyses the capacities, resources, and effective work processes to deliver on their mandates. It also looks at the structural and policy frameworks of these institutions, with a view to assessing their effectiveness for service delivery. Included in the review are the continental institutions, namely, the AU and regional institutions, and the Regional Economic Communities (RECs).

The Millennium Development Goals (MDGs) Review Summit in New York (20–22 September 2010) concluded with the United Nations General Assembly reiterating its "deep concern at the multiple and interrelated crises, including the financial and economic crises, the volatile energy and food prices and ongoing concerns over food security as well as the increasing challenges posed by climate change and loss of biodiversity which have increased vulnerabilities and inequalities and adversely affected development gains, in particular in developing countries." (United Nations General Assembly, 2010: 2)

In addition, the Review Summit recognized giving more attention to Africa, especially those countries that are significantly off track to meet the MDGs by 2015, and strengthening institutions at all levels (United Nations General Assembly, 2010: 8). The 2010 United Nations General Assembly Report urged African countries to focus on those MDGs that would assist them in achieving their long-term development goals. This assessment comes in the face of many development efforts by African governments, civil society, communities, and private sector in partnering for development. But are these efforts enough? While there are pockets of development success here and there, the larger picture is not positive, as pointed out above. Even though extensive internal and external resources are channeled annually into these institutions, the continent still remains the "object of pity" in the world. Yet by their very nature, these institutions should be a reflection of the people's development aspirations, their national values, and based on their historical experiences and vision for the future. The basis for the establishment of these institutions should be defined by some form of national, regional and continental consensus on where the country, region, and ultimately continent wants to go in relation to the rest of the world. This requires that there be a thread that binds the national vision to that of the region, and of the continent. It also requires that there be sufficient national conversation and mobilization of consensus to determine what constitutes key institutions and the requisite mandates, and what enables them to deliver on the aspirations of the people.

Creating ownership of key institutions needs to take place at all levels: local, national, regional and continental. It is also the only way in which, for example, regional economic communities can become true building blocks in the continent. While the principle of subsidiarity is well acknowledged, it is true that these regional and continental institutions are established by member states, which must commit themselves, financially and politically, to their effective functioning. However, the situation on the ground shows that the political and financial commitment is not always available. As stated in the Lagos Plan of Action:

> ... after pressing for the establishment of an institution, many African governments, even after having approved the legal document setting up the institution concerned, either fail to become members of the institution or, if they do, fail to give it adequate financial and material support. The net result is that the growth of such an institution is stifled, disillusion sets in and the collective self-reliance of African countries is undermined. (Organization of African Unity, 1980: 72)

Institution building at the continental level

The formation of the Organization of African Unity

At the continental level, the first Pan-African institution to examine is the Organization of African Unity (OAU). The political independence of 17 countries in 1960 inspired the leaders of the time to establish the OAU in 1963[1] primarily to bring about the total political independence of the continent. In addition, the OAU sought to:

- promote the unity and solidarity of the African States
- coordinate and intensify their cooperation and efforts to achieve a better life for the people of Africa
- defend their sovereignty, territorial integrity and independence
- eradicate all forms of colonialism from Africa

---

1 Benin; Burkina Faso; Central African Republic; Chad; Côte d'Ivoire; Democratic Republic of Congo; Gabon; Ghana; Madagascar; Mali; Mauritania; Niger; Nigeria; Republic of Congo; Senegal; Somalia and Togo.

- promote international cooperation, with due regard to the Charter of the United Nations and the Universal Declaration of Human Rights.

Given the history and colonial reality of Africa at the time, the focus of the OAU – in collaboration with all the liberation movements – was to fast track the end of colonialism in Africa. To this end a Liberation Committee[2] was established to assist in spearheading these efforts. A second effort was required to translate the dividends of political independence into improving the lives of the people. However, domestic challenges such as the lack of skills and resources and external factors in the form of interference from the former colonial masters, imposition of trade liberalization policies, and the effects of the Cold War hampered progress (Baah, 2003).

As African countries won their independence in the 1960s and 1970s, they were faced with many challenges: The way Africans had governed themselves was distorted by colonial rule. This was not surprising as the new states were artificial creations of Europeans. They had few resources to support them, and few educated Africans had received training in the ways of colonial statecraft, business, and economics. In addition, their economies had been oriented toward trade with their colonial masters, often depending upon a few resources or crop. The desire for political independence was always tied to the desire for economic independence and development. The people of Africa wanted to shape their own economies and create more wealth for the development of their societies. (Badejo, 2008: 18)

Old global alliances were no longer at play, and Africa had an opportunity to form new global partnerships based on the new global and continental dispensation. Clearly, there was a need to re-examine the role of the OAU vis-à-vis the new global order. At the same time, a new leadership, The New Partnership for Africa's Development (NEPAD) was emerging in Africa; ready to take responsibility of the future of the continent, in partnership with its people. While taking cognizance of the way its colonial history had shaped the continent, the leaders resolved that even though Africans could not change their history, they had the responsibility and ability to shape their destiny.

---

2 The Coordinating Committee for the Liberation of Africa (Liberation Committee) organized diplomatic support and channeled financial, military and logistical aid to liberation movements.

It is in this context that African leaders of the time decided to transform the OAU into the AU.

The Formation of the African Union

The AU was launched in 2002 to replace the OAU. While the OAU had five objectives, the AU has 14 objectives (See Figure 7.1). An assessment of these 14 objectives indicates that most of them are not achievable in the short to medium term mainly because it is not possible for a continental institution such as the AU to be the solution to every one of the continent's problems. There is also no clear articulation in the AU processes as to how the 14 objectives are to be attained, given the little capacity that exists in the AU commissions, or guidance on which of the objectives should be attained at the regional level, and which ones at the national level. In addition, much more could be achieved if there was a clear articulation of what role is to be played by strategic partners such as the African Development Bank and the United Nations Economic Commission for Africa in the attainment of the AU Objectives. Furthermore, a review of previous efforts could also assist in the exploration of solutions to some of the challenges that Africa faces today. For example, the Lagos Plan of Action has a very clear roadmap towards industrialization, covering the national, regional and continental levels. These strategies need to be revisited, instead of trying to come up with new inventions.

Figure 7.1: Objectives of the African Union

Article 3 of the AU Constitutive Act spells out the objectives of the AU as follows:
1. Achieve greater unity and solidarity between the African countries and the peoples of Africa;
2. Defend the sovereignty, territorial integrity and independence of its Member States;
3. Accelerate the political and socio-economic integration of the continent;
4. Promote and defend African common positions on issues of interest to the continent and its peoples;
5. Encourage international cooperation, taking due account of the Charter of the United Nations and the Universal Declaration of Human Rights;
6. Promote peace, security, and stability on the continent;

7. Promote democratic principles and institutions, popular participation and good governance;
8. Promote and protect human and peoples' rights in accordance with the African Charter on Human and Peoples' Rights and other relevant human rights instruments;
9. Establish the necessary conditions which enable the continent to play its rightful role in the global economy and in international negotiations;
10. Promote sustainable development at the economic, social and cultural levels as well as the integration of African economies;
11. Promote cooperation in all fields of human activity to raise the living standards of African peoples;
12. Coordinate and harmonize the policies between the existing and future Regional Economic Communities for the gradual attainment of the objectives of the Union;
13. Advance the development of the continent by promoting research in all fields, in particular in science and technology;
14. Work with relevant international partners in the eradication of preventable diseases and the promotion of good health on the continent.

At the structural level, the commissions of the AU are: Peace and Security; Political Affairs; Infrastructure and Energy; Social Affairs; Human Resources, Science and Technology; Trade and Industry; Rural Economy and Agriculture; and Economic Affairs. The AU has been faced with a number of structural and operational challenges. From a sectoral point of view, it is quite clear that there are areas of overlap and duplication in the manner in which the commissions were determined. The "silo" approach to the work processes of the commissions make cohesive delivery on the AU objectives less possible. Other challenges include the fact that all the commissioners are elected by member states, even though functionally they are supposed to report to the chairpersons of the commissions. Practically, therefore, they work in ways that prioritize political loyalties before structural functionality. Inadequate capacity and resources and lack of flexibility in administrative and financial policies and procedures also hampered delivery of services. Furthermore, attracting and retaining the best African experts under these conditions is difficult. This results in a vicious cycle of member states that are unable to pay their contributions for the effective running of the commissions, and who are, at the same time, demanding more delivery from the commissions.

Due to the poor financial contribution from member states, the commissions rely heavily on donor funding to support even the most strategic programs of the AU. This does not demonstrate commitment of African leadership to the objectives of the organization. At the national level, the majority of Africans do not really know much about the AU, let alone its sectoral programs. This is mainly because member states have no national process for integrating into the AU processes, which in many cases are seen as the business of the departments of foreign affairs. Very rarely do member states discuss AU matters at cabinet level. This further explains why most AU decisions remain unimplemented by member states, because AU matters are not seen at the national level. In addition, the AU commissions do not have outreach programs to popularize the AU and its structures and processes.

The disconnect between the member states, their processes, and those of the AU means that the continental structures remain unaccountable to the constituencies that set them up, and report more to those that give them the money. For example, most of the financial support for the RECs' integration programs is derived from development partners such as the United Kingdom's Department for International Development, The United States Agency for International Development, the Japan International Cooperation Agency, the World Bank and the European Centre for Development Policy Management, to name only a few.

In 2013, the AU marked 11 years of its existence, and Africa celebrated fifty years of the Establishment of the Organization for African Unity. This presented a good opportunity for a review of the institution, with a view to determining its structure, work processes, mandates and objectives: to ensure that they are all geared towards delivering on the needs of the people, and that there is a clear delineation of roles and responsibilities among the member states, the RECs, and the AU, all working in unison, rather than in competition or duplication. The 2007 audit of the AU was a significant first step towards this goal, but its recommendations are not being implemented.

Institution building at regional level – Regional Economic Communities

The post-independence era witnessed a growing need by African countries for cooperation and regional integration in advancement of the establishment of the African Economic Community. Some of the RECs, such as the East African Community and the Economic Community of West African States were established in the 1960s and 1970s, and have gone through cycles of transformation to keep pace with emerging needs. For example, the Economic Community of West African States was transformed into a commission (Awareness for Development) in 2007. The number of AU recognized RECs (see Table 7.1 below) has grown to the current eight (United Nations Economic Commission for Africa, 2010). Detailed objectives for each of the RECs are outlined in Table 7.2. While the RECs have endeavored to advance the integration agenda, they also face a number of challenges, which have constrained their effective delivery of economic development and regional integration (African Union, 2007).

Table 7.1: The eight RECs recognized by the AU and the other six integration blocs

The 8 RECs recognized by the AU	The other 6 integration blocs
Arab Maghreb Union	Economic Community of Great Lakes Countries
East African Community	Southern African Customs Union
Economic Community of West African States	Mano River Union
Southern Africa Development Community	West African Economic and Monetary Union
Community of Sahel-Saharan States	Central African Economic and Monetary Community
IGAD - Inter-Governmental Authority on Development	Indian Ocean Commission
COMESA - Common Market for Eastern and Southern Africa	

ECCAS - Economic Community of Central African States	

Table 7.2 RECs and their objectives

	REC	Objectives	Date of establishment
1.	Arab Maghreb Union	• Strengthen all forms of ties among Member States (in order to ensure regional stability and enhance policy coordination); • Promote free circulation of goods, services, and factors of production in the region; • Promote common defense and non-interference in the domestic affairs of the partners; • Promote the development of agriculture, industry, commerce, food security, and the setting up of joint projects and general economic cooperation programs.	1986
2.	Community of Sahel-Saharan States	• Establish a comprehensive economic union based on a strategy implemented in accordance with a developmental plan that would be integrated in the national development plans of the member states; • Eliminate all barriers to regional unity; • Coordinate pedagogical and educational systems at the various educational levels, including cultural, scientific and technical fields.	1998

3.	Common Market for Eastern and Southern Africa	• Cooperate in developing natural and human resources for the good of all the people of the region, including promotion of peace and security in the region.	1981
4.	Economic Community of Central African States	• Develop capacities to maintain peace, security and stability as essential prerequisites for economic and social development; • Develop physical, economic, and monetary unity; • Develop a culture of human integration; • Establish an autonomous financing mechanism for Economic Community of Central African States; • Establish a Central Common African Market as an ultimate goal.	1983
5.	East African Community	• Promote sustainable growth and equitable development within partner states; • Strengthen and consolidate long-standing ties between partners; • Strengthen and enhance participation of the private sector and civil society; • Mainstream gender into all its programs and enhance the role of women in development; • Promote good governance; • Promote peace, security, and stability.	1967

6.	Economic Community of West African States	• Promote cooperation and integration, leading to the establishment of an economic union in West Africa in order to raise the living standards of its peoples, and to maintain and enhance economic stability, foster relations among member states and contribute to the progress and development of the African Continent (Economic Community of West African States, 1975: 4).	1975
7.	Inter-Governmental Authority on Development	• Promote joint development strategies and gradually harmonize macro-economic policies and programmes in the social, technological and scientific fields; • Harmonize policies with regard to trade, customs, transport, communications, agriculture, and natural resources, and promote free movement of goods, services, and people within the region. • Create an enabling environment for foreign, cross-border and domestic trade and investment; • Achieve regional food security and encourage and assist efforts of Member States to collectively combat drought and other natural and man-made disasters and their natural consequences; • Initiate and promote programmes and projects to achieve regional food security and sustainable development of natural resources and environment protection, and encourage and assist efforts of Member States to collectively combat drought and other natural and man-made disasters and	1996

		their consequences; • Develop and improve a coordinated and complementary infrastructure in the areas of transport, telecommunications and energy in the region; • Promote peace and stability in the region and create mechanisms within the region for the prevention, management and resolution of inter-State and intra-State conflicts through dialogue; • Mobilize resources for the implementation of emergency, short-term, medium-term and long-term programmes within the framework of regional cooperation; • Promote and realize the objectives of the Common Market for Eastern and Southern Africa and the African Economic Community; • Facilitate, promote and strengthen cooperation in research development and application in science and technology.	
8.	Southern Africa Development Community	• Achieve development and economic growth, alleviate poverty, enhance the standard and quality of life of the people of Southern Africa and support the socially disadvantaged through regional integration; • Evolve common political values, systems and institutions; • Promote and defend peace and security; • Promote self-sustaining development on the basis of collective self-reliance, and the inter-dependence of Member States;	1992

		<ul><li>Achieve complementarity between national and regional strategies and programmes;</li><li>Promote and maximise productive employment and utilisation of resources of the region;</li><li>Achieve sustainable utilisation of natural resources and effective protection of the environment;</li><li>Strengthen and consolidate the long-standing historical, social and cultural affinities and links among the people of the Region.</li></ul>	

The RECs have taken on a complex and demanding agenda due to the varied objectives they seek to fulfill (see Table 7.2). Their mandates range widely; dealing with health, food security, infrastructure, MDGs, education and culture. Yet, in line with the principle of subsidiarity, some issues, such as education and culture, are best addressed at the national level. So, while some RECs have economic and integration agendas with clear implementation strategies, others have political objectives. For instance, the Inter-Governmental Authority on Development have simply bitten off more than they can chew (African Capacity Building Foundation, 2006). Some have economic integration agendas with strategies, while others have political objectives (Mackie et al, 2010).

Given that a number of the RECs such as the East African Community, SADC– even though it has been transformed over the years – and the Economic Community of Central African States were established before the new global and continental order described above, it is imperative to re-engineer them by re-appraising the approaches by which they were set up, their mandates, their capacities, as well as whether or not they are delivering on the current needs of the regions and member states they represent. The irony of the situation is that in a bid to be relevant, the RECs have broadened their mandates to a point of near paralysis. There is so much to be done with few or no resources that they end up not achieving anything beyond preparing for the annual summits of heads of state and government, meetings of ministers of foreign affairs and experts' meetings, and initiating a few missions aimed at mobilizing external resources and partnerships.³ It must be noted, however, that not all the RECs have the technical coordinating committees as in the case of SADC.

The primary supposition in the formation of RECs is that there is strength in regional cooperation and integration so that the RECs will deliver benefits to member states, individually and collectively, in a manner that individual countries cannot do for themselves. However, an assessment of the multiple memberships of the RECs by member states is that they have weakened the RECs, rather than strengthening regional integration and the attainment of the African Economic Community. For example, of the 53 African countries, 27 members belong to two regional groupings, 18 belong to three RECs, and one country is a member of four RECs. Only seven countries have maintained membership in one bloc (Badejo, 2008). Not only do issues of multiple memberships affect member states' abilities to make financial contributions, it also tends to undermine the overall functionality of the RECs. Member states that belong to more than one REC operate in ways that are not mutually reinforcing to the overall continental development objective. For example, the Democratic Republic of Congo belongs simultaneously to the SADC, Central African Monetary and Economic and Community, Economic Community for Central African States, and Economic Community for the Great Lakes Countries.

In addition, while some of the sectoral focus areas of the RECs have become highly technical, the most important decisions at the REC level are made by ministers of foreign affairs, who make recommendations to heads of state and government, who in turn "adopt" those recommendations. Even though sectoral ministers are sometimes brought on board or consulted, the consultations are not deep enough to warrant committing generations of Africans to financial or economic decisions on the basis of foreign affairs experts

---

3   SADC structure includes an annual summit meeting (a meeting of the Council of Ministers, and a number of specialized sectoral co-coordinating offices). The supreme policy-making organ of SADC is the summit held annually, and attended by heads of state and government and/or their representatives. A meeting of representatives from member countries at ministerial level is held at least twice a year. In addition, special meetings are held to co-ordinate and develop regional policies in specific sectors, such as Ministries of Tourism and Ministries of Trade and Industry.

and ministers. For example, in the case of SADC, there is a Standing Committee of Senior Officials, which reports directly to the Council of Ministers (made up of ministers of foreign affairs, defense and security) and ultimately to the summit.

Another assessment of the objectives of the RECs also shows that some of them try to achieve a wide range of activities, some of which are not necessarily relevant to accelerating regional integration. As a result, and also due to a lack of resources and implementation capacity, they end up achieving very little. In some cases, it is not even clear where the responsibilities of the member states end, and where those of the secretariats of the RECs begin. Hence, there is a growing gap between policy objectives and program implementation. It is in this context that the AU Commission initiated a process to develop a Minimum Integration Program, which is aimed at accelerating Africa's integration process through the implementation of agreed projects (African Union Commission, 2010).

Institution building at national level

The institutional set-up at the national levels is also disturbing. Most African countries now hold "elections" every four to five years. In cases where the opposition party comes into power, there is usually a complete overhaul of the institutional set-up, mainly for political expediency. This includes abolishing of certain ministries and a setting up entirely new ones. In cases where the ruling party wins time after time, cabinets are reshuffled and new ministers appointed. In both cases, the affected countries end up with a new national development plan, and/or a new sectoral plan and targets. In either case, during the era of structural adjustment programs the development planning of three to five years was replaced by visions of endless duration. Whereas elections signify that the mandates of newly elected governments have a limited number of years, thus requiring accountability between promise and achievement within the specific years covered by their mandate, visions stretch out indefinitely or for very long durations. This requires that institutions be constructed for the attainment of long-term visions, and not for short-term mandates.

Another challenge that exists at the national level is the tendency to set up new institutions each time a fashionable development agenda or a new fancy comes up. For example, with the adoption of MDGs in 2000, many countries set up national structures to focus on the tracking of the attainment of MDGs. Some countries such as Nigeria actually set up structures to implement projects aimed at achieving MDGs, even though there are other structures that deal with sectoral components of the MDGs.

When NEPAD was adopted as an AU program in 2001, many countries created NEPAD structures, such as ministries, just to focus on the NEPAD issues. While the set-up of ministries and structures was a good demonstration of their commitment to NEPAD, it also faced the challenge of not being able to integrate NEPAD into the national development strategies because of the failure to focus all ministries around the NEPAD agenda, particularly around budgetary issues. Another challenge is that these ministries were set up with specific mandates; hence they have ended up competing with existing line ministries for both influence and resources.

Another challenge that cuts across the national performance of institutions is that there are no organic processes to ensure that the decisions made by member states at the continental and the regional levels are implemented. In addition, there is no mechanism for the regional and continental institutions to report back on their implementation of the decisions which the member states make. This results in the secretariats of the RECs and the AU Commission actually attempting, almost by default, to implement the decisions of the regional organizations, even in areas where it is the responsibility of the member states.

Going forward

Resolving the institutional challenges which the continent faces is far from easy. The existing challenges could actually be symptoms of a bigger challenge relating to the unclear definition of Africa's development paradigm and the lack of a value system that is shared by all. There is a need to have national and regional consensus about people's aspirations for the AU.

Following the definition of Africa's development paradigm, specific questions can be asked regarding the establishment of institutions. These include the purpose of establishing: institutions, drivers for institution building, drivers for the mandates of institutions, to whom these institutions are accountable and how they are accountable. Other questions relate to whether they are achieving their objectives, what the measures of success are, what the responsibilities of governments/member states are and how the institutions are to be capacitated in terms of human, financial and other material requirements. It is very clear that until these questions are answered through in-depth research and articulation of Africa's approach to institution building, it will not be possible to have effective institutions for the continent's development. Such institutions should mirror the values, visions, purposes and targets of the people. These values and targets need to be arrived at through consultations that truly reflect the needs and aspirations of the people on the ground.

Conclusion

Africa has a plethora of institutions, with more or less overlapping mandates, starting at the continental level with the AU Commission. These institutions are poorly capacitated, in terms of human and financial resources. The over-reliance on external support makes the ownership of these institutions by Africans and/or African governments questionable. This leads to further perceptions that, indeed, if the resources are not from the continent, the agendas that drive these institutions cannot possibly be from within the continent. If this is the case, how then can these institutions deliver on the objectives and mandates which are derived from the African people? Africans should, therefore, seek to strike a balance between what can be funded by development partners, and what should be funded by themselves.

Moreover, there is a need to review the ways key institutions driving Africa's development are established, structured and operate. Also needful of a review is the ways Africa's development is resourced from within, both financially and in human terms, including the intellectual drive of the development agenda. Member states need to do more to fund the development work of the RECs. This is the only way to achieve the regional integration agenda. It is inconceivable that such a fundamental agenda to Africa's transformation be left to dictates of external funders. Africans need to demonstrate their commitment to the regional integration agenda by resourcing the secretariats of the RECs. Another critical challenge that needs to be looked at is that of prioritizing and focusing the mandated and work programs of the RECs. Many of the RECs are mandated to do a wide range of things, which undermine effectiveness and impact. It is instructive for each REC to do a regional scan of critical issues as a basis for reviewing their mandates so as to focus on those programs that add value to the regional integration agenda and leave the rest to member states and other development players to work on. If the RECs are to be the building blocks for the attainment of the African Economic Community by 2028, then there is a clear need to review some of their mandates, priority programs, capacities, delivery mechanisms and resourcing for them to be more focused and efficient. The review would then clearly outline mandates, priority programs, capacities and other strategies that are needed to meet the set objectives.

The creation of institutions should be a means to an end, and not an end in itself. There is a need to streamline the continent's development objectives, as defined at the national, regional, and continental levels. The mandates of these institutions obviously have to be rooted in the value system and development approach of the continent. Once this is done, the next step is to align the work of the RECs so that they work in unison, rather than in competition. The competition is in terms of member states, resources from the same member states, and resources from the same partners (including RECs competing with member states for the same donors' attention/money).

Going forward, there is a need to innovate and sacrifice in order to bring dynamism to Africa's development. This includes looking inward for African –led intellectual solutions, rather than external resources and "expert advice" that come with it as a panacea to Africa's development challenges. Africa's future lies in the hands of Africans. A successful review of Africa's development institutions will go a long way in determining Africa's destiny.

References

African Capacity Building Foundation. 2006. *Challenges Facing Africa's Regional Economic Communities in Capacity Building*. Occasional Paper No 5. The African Capacity Building Foundation.

African Union Commission. 2010. *Minimum Integration Programme*. Accessed February 2012 at www.africa-union.org/root/ar/index/MIP%20Big%20Doc%20English%20Version%20Web.pdf

African Union. 2007. *Audit of the African Union: Towards a People-Centred Political and Socio-economic Integration and Transformation of Africa*. Addis Ababa: African Union.

Baah, A. 2003. "History of African development initiatives." Paper presented at the Africa Labour Research Network Workshop in Johannesburg, 22–23 May 2003. Accessed February 2012 at http://www.sarpn.org.za/documents/d0000407/index.php.

Badejo, DL. 2008. *Global Organisation: The African Union*. New York: Infobase Publishing.

Economic Community of West African States. 1975. *Treaty of the Economic Community of West African States (ECOWAS)*, concluded at Lagos on 28 May 1975, ECOWAS Secretariat.

Mackie, J, Bilal, S, Ramdoo I, Hohmeister, H and Luckho, T. 2010. *Joining up Africa Support to Regional Integration*. Discussion Paper No 99, July 2010. Brussels: European Centre for Development Policy Management.

Organization of African Unity. 1980. *Lagos Plan of Action for the Economic Development of Africa 1980–2000*. Addis Ababa: OAU.

United Nations Economic Commission for Africa. 2010. *Assessing Regional Integration in Africa IV: Enhancing Intra-Africa Trade*. Addis Ababa: UNECA.

United Nations General Assembly. 2010. *Keeping the promise: United to achieve the Millennium Development Goals: Draft Resolution: Integrated and coordinated follow up to the outcomes of the United Nations conferences and summits in the economic, social and related fields*. Follow up to the outcome of the Millennium Summit (A/65/L.1). United Nations.

CHAPTER 8. AFRICA'S DEVELOPMENT AGENDA AFTER THE GLOBAL ECONOMIC AND FINANCIAL CRISIS OF 2008-2009

Afeikhena Jerome, Oluyele Akinkugbe and Francis Chigunta

Introduction

The two-year period from 2008 to 2009 was extremely challenging for the global economy as it endured the worst recession since the Second World War. What began as a bursting of the United States housing market and a rise in foreclosures ballooned into a global financial and economic crisis. The crisis quickly spread to Europe through the drying up of inter-bank liquidity and reverberated in emerging markets and developing economies. Five years into the crisis, global financial stability is still in a period of significant uncertainty as a result of heightened concerns about sovereign debt sustainability in many advanced economies, despite bouts of "quantitative easing" and the deepening economic crisis in the Eurozone. Worrying signs are proliferating along with the contrived optimism about a supposed rebound in global economic growth.

The impact on Africa of the global economic and financial crisis became evident in 2009, with the unfolding of the second-round effects of the shock. The effects took the form of weakened demand and lower prices for export commodities, decreased remittances and reduced private capital inflows to much of the continent. As a result, gross domestic product (GDP) expanded by a mere 1.6 per cent in

2009 compared to 4.9 per cent in 2008, breaking six consecutive years of economic growth of 5 per cent or more (African Development Bank, 2009). As economic activity weakened, so did employment in the majority of African countries. Estimates provided by the World Bank indicate that the crises threw between seven and ten million more Africans into poverty and might have led to the deaths of thirty to fifty thousand additional infants before their first birthdays (World Bank, 2010a). The implication of these developments is that the prospects of meeting the Millennium Development Goals (MDGs), including the goal of halving poverty by 2015 and achieving meaningful progress in social development, have become even more daunting for most African countries, especially those in sub-Saharan Africa.

The crisis and the weak recovery that followed raise fundamental questions concerning convectional economic policy. The impact of the global financial crisis is changing the landscape of development for all countries, and in this context policy discussions in developing countries are increasingly focusing on optimizing policy responses. In fact, many countries are rethinking their approaches in light of the impact of the financial crisis, and are seeking to clarify the range of policy options which can intensify employment outcomes as well as reduce poverty. It is in this regard that "post-crisis Africa" has to re-examine its development agenda.

This chapter examines the global economic and financial crisis from Africa's perspective and proffers an agenda for the continent's long-term development and structural transformation. It was inspired largely by Adebayo Adedeji's key documents and contributions to the debate on Africa's growth and development. Significantly, the global financial crisis was also Adedeji's focus at the Aboyade Annual Memorial Lecture and the Golden Jubilee Anniversary of the Department of Economics, University of Ibadan on 26 November 2008. In the lecture, he forewarned Africa, once again, on the dangers of reliance on unfettered markets and identified liberalization, privatization, financialization and speculation as the four horsemen of the apocalypse. He also argued strongly for an African regional monetary institution which would facilitate the move towards inter-currency convertibility, monetary integration and improved monetary management (Adedeji, 2008).

Africa and the global financial crisis

Economic and financial crises are not new to developing countries. It has been observed that the majority of these crises during the past five decades took place in developing countries and the major trigger was excessive dependence of emerging countries on capital flows from developed countries and from loose domestic monetary and fiscal policies (Claessens et al, 2010). In contrast, the global financial crisis of 2008–2009 had its roots in the sub-prime mortgage sector in the United States. The sustained rise in asset prices, particularly for houses, on the back of excessively accommodative monetary policy and lax lending standards during 2002–2006, coupled with financial innovations and complex financial products, resulted in a large rise in mortgage credit among American households, particularly the low credit quality households (Taylor, 2009). At a fundamental level, however, the crisis could be ascribed to the persistence of large global imbalances which, in turn, were the outcome of long periods of excessively loose monetary policy in the major advanced economies during the first decade of the new millennium (Mohan, 2008; Taylor, 2009).

While Africa was not responsible for the global financial crisis, it has become the innocent victim. Financial markets in Africa remain largely underdeveloped, and, until recently, this was perceived as a major weakness as it implied weak financial integration with the rest of the world. Virtually no banks or other financial institutions in Africa outside of South Africa held United States or European subprime mortgage-backed securities or other risky derivative securities. Even South Africa, which is by far Africa's largest economy and the most integrated into the global financial system, had an exposure risk that was quite limited, given the continuing existence of somewhat pervasive capital and foreign exchange controls.

It is also important to note that, prior to the crisis, several African countries did many things right, such as adopting prudent macroeconomic policies and building up foreign exchange reserves. At the same time, the external environment was quite favorable, as reflected in high commodity prices, booming international and regional trade and the prioritization of aid and debt relief by the international community.

The impact of the global financial crisis on Africa has attracted intense scrutiny and the focus of several engagements on Africa in recent years (see, for example, African Development Bank, 2009 and Jerome and Akinkugbe, 2010). At the onset of the crisis, the widely held view was that the impact on African countries would be minimal because of aforementioned limited integration of African economies into the global financial system. But this turned out to be untrue, as the continent was hard hit by the crisis.

However, the biggest threat to the African economy was not the credit crisis itself but its secondary effects which were felt through loss of export earnings (both manufactured exports and commodities), net outward flow of capital, loss of earnings from tourism and migrants' remittances, and reduced aid and other development assistance inflows. Consequently, the global financial crisis prompted an economic slowdown in Africa, a continent where most countries were already hit by the rise in the prices of food and energy (Jerome and Akinkugbe, 2010). Hence, the decade-long sustained and accelerating growth that Africa witnessed between 1995 and 2007 came to a grinding halt as a result of the global crisis of 2008–2009. Per capita income fell by nearly 1 per cent in 2009 – the first such contraction in a decade (World Bank, 2010a).[1]

However, given the heterogeneity of African countries, the crisis has affected some countries much more than others. The region's middle-income and resource-rich countries, which are more integrated into global markets, were the hardest hit, with growth slipping by about 4.5 per cent in 2009. Slumping energy prices depressed earnings of oil-exporting countries, contributing to the weak economic performance of these economies. South Africa, which is Africa's biggest economy, went into recession in May 2009, its first in 17 years, due to a sharp decline in the key manufacturing and mining sectors. The economy contracted at an annualized rate of 6.4 per cent between January and March 2009, compared with the same period a year earlier. In the first three quarters of 2009, the economy shed a staggering 959,000 jobs (Assubuji, Luckscheiter and Ben-Zeev, 2009). In Botswana, GDP dropped by 10.3 per cent, the strongest decline in

---

1 While performance varied across countries, Africa, as a whole, had average annual real GDP growth rates of around 5 per cent between 1995 and 2007, or annual increases in per capita GDP of over 2 per cent, as a result of improved macroeconomic policies, favourable commodity prices, and significant increases in aid, capital flows and remittances. These growth rates brought Africa in line with the trends for other developing countries (World Bank, 2010a).

economic activity in Africa in 2009, owing to lower production and the diamond price. Between January and August 2009, export of Kenyan horticultural products fell by 35 per cent in volume terms compared with the same period in 2008. Tourist revenues in Tanzania fell to US$302.1 million between January and April 2009 compared with US$388.2 million for the same period in 2008 (UNECA and African Union, 2010).

The financial crisis also had discernible impacts on the social sectors and the MDGs in many countries. Even though prior to the crisis, sub-Sahara Africa lagged behind other regions on all the MDGs – including poverty reduction – because of what has been acknowledged as lower initial starting conditions, practically all the MDG trend lines for sub-Sahara Africa have been headed in the right direction for more than ten years. Although the effects will not be apparent for many more years, the crisis interrupted this progress (World Bank, 2010b). A few years from the target date for attainment of the MDGs, available statistics and projections from international development partners suggest that Africa is not on track to meet most of these goals; more so, as the continent continues to grapple with the previously discussed negative impacts and the resource cutbacks that characterized the global financial crisis. Before the crisis in 2008–2009, Africa made encouraging progress on some of the MDG targets, particularly poverty reduction. The proportion of Africans living on less than US$1.25 a day fell from 58 per cent in 1990 to 51 per cent in 2005. But the absolute number of poor people rose from 296 million to 388 million in the corresponding period (World Bank, 2010b).

The crisis attacked two critical drivers of progress toward the MDGs: faster growth and better service delivery. The World Bank *Global Monitoring Report 2010* estimates that, with slower growth rates, drastic cutbacks in aid and other development assistance flows consequent upon the crisis, the delivery of aid-financed social services in many African countries continues to suffer (World Bank, 2010b). Current projections show that the poverty rate for sub-Saharan Africa will be 38 per cent by 2015, rather than the 36 per cent it would have been without the crisis. The continent will, therefore, fall short of MDG 1: halving the year 2000 poverty rate by 2015. This suggests that the crisis will leave an additional twenty million people in extreme poverty by 2015 (World Bank 2010b: 6).

The crisis also affected progress on Africa's other human

development indicators. Prior to the crisis, the World Bank estimated that Africa was the region with the fastest progress in primary school completion (the average primary completion rate increased from 53 per cent to 65 per cent between 2000 and 2008.) In particular, there was noticeable progress in several low-income countries, including Mozambique, Rwanda, Ethiopia, and Burundi that had 50 per cent or higher improvement in completion rates, even though starting from a low base. African countries also made substantial progress in closing the gender gap in primary school enrolment ratios. More and more girls have been enrolling in primary schools across the continent. However, improvement varied between 5 to 40 per cent increase for low income countries in Africa. Benin, Burkina Faso, Ethiopia, Guinea, and Liberia saw a 20 per cent increase in their gender parity index between 2000 and 2008 but changes were less for Zambia and Rwanda, which had much higher initial values in 2000 (World Bank, 2010b). The crisis may have halted this progress as many African countries resorted to cutting spending, rather than risk a new debt crisis. For example, Zambia slashed its health spending by a third in 2010, while Mali, Benin, and Niger reduced their schools budget (Kyrili and Martin, 2010).

But Africa rebounded rather quickly from the global economic and financial crisis. Sub-Saharan Africa attained a growth of 4.6 per cent in 2012, just shy of Africa's pre-crisis average of 5 per cent recorded between 2000 and 2008 (World Bank, 2013), making Africa one of the fastest growing regions in the world – as has been the case in recent years. A third of the countries grew at 6 per cent or more. An analysis by *The Economist*[2] also found that, over the ten years leading to 2010, six of the world's ten fastest-growing economies were in sub-Saharan Africa. Angola, in fact, grew more than any other country in the world.

The growth surge could be attributable to government action to end armed conflicts, improved macroeconomic conditions and microeconomic reforms undertaken to create a better business climate. Growth has also been supported by strong demand from other developing countries, particularly China, which has relatively high resource intensity in production and a fast growth rate. Though high-income countries are the destination for some 57 per cent of

---

2   See *The Economist*, 6 January 2011, p. 14. The identified countries are Angola, Nigeria, Ethiopia, Chad, Mozambique and Rwanda.

the exports originating from sub-Saharan Africa, weak growth means that their contribution to the total growth of the sub-continent's exports is much smaller. As a result, the share of high-income countries in total sub-Saharan Africa exports is falling. For instance in 2002, the European Union accounted for some 40 per cent of all exports from sub-Saharan Africa, but by 2010 that share had fallen to about 25 per cent – while China's share increased from about 5 per cent to 19 per cent over the same period (World Bank, 2012).

The remarkable growth performance notwithstanding, Africa still faces a number of challenges. The continent is the only region of the world that has experienced an increase in poverty over the last three decades, in stark contrast to the dramatic gains in the fight against poverty that were achieved particularly in Asia. Africa's recent growth has not been inclusive as it fails to provide remunerative employment opportunities; hence the majority of the people are still enmeshed in poverty and rising inequality. Thus, Africa is still home to a disproportionate 30 per cent of the world's poor, despite comprising merely 10 per cent of the world population. Worse still, the number of African people in extreme poverty has doubled to some 300 million since the mid-1980s and is expected to reach 400 million by 2015. Achievements in the area of human development have remained dismal. The 2013 MDGs progress report indicates that Africa is clearly off track in meeting five out of the eight MDGs by 2015 (African Union Commission, UNECA, United Nations Development Programme, and African Development Bank, 2013).

Most countries in the region are also grappling with the problems of climate change, high disease burden, poor infrastructure, brain drain, violent conflicts and lack of development of productive capacity. Moreover, in the last few years, African countries have had to deal with the effects of rising food and energy prices and the complications emanating from the global financial and economic crisis, especially the financial turmoil generated by the intensification of the fiscal crisis in Europe. These multiple crises are reversing progress made by the region in economic performance and jeopardizing efforts by African countries to achieve the MDGs.

African development experience and strategies

Africa's development experience has been extremely varied, cyclical and sporadic, while lagging behind the rest of the world until recently, as shown in Figure 8.1. After a spurt of post-independence economic growth and nascent structural and social transformation, external shocks, poor policy responses and ineffective development strategies resulted in economic stagnation in the 1980s as the gains of the first two decades of independence were wiped out and poverty intensified. This contrasts sharply with the rest of the developing world, where per capita incomes more than doubled and even increased by four-fold or more in some of the most successful developing countries (Ajakaiye and Jerome, forthcoming).

Similarly, while the successful developing countries witnessed economic transformation from primary production to more diversified industrial production and subsequently to more sophisticated service industries with considerable progress towards becoming knowledge economies, virtually all African countries have remained primary producers – the only exceptions being Mauritius and South Africa. In addition, while the successful developing countries have witnessed remarkable progress in human development, especially in the areas of health and education, virtually all African countries remain at the lower end of the Human Development Index. Correspondingly, while successful developing countries were able to pull the majority of their people out of poverty, most Africans continue to wallow in poverty (Ajakaiye and Jerome, forthcoming).

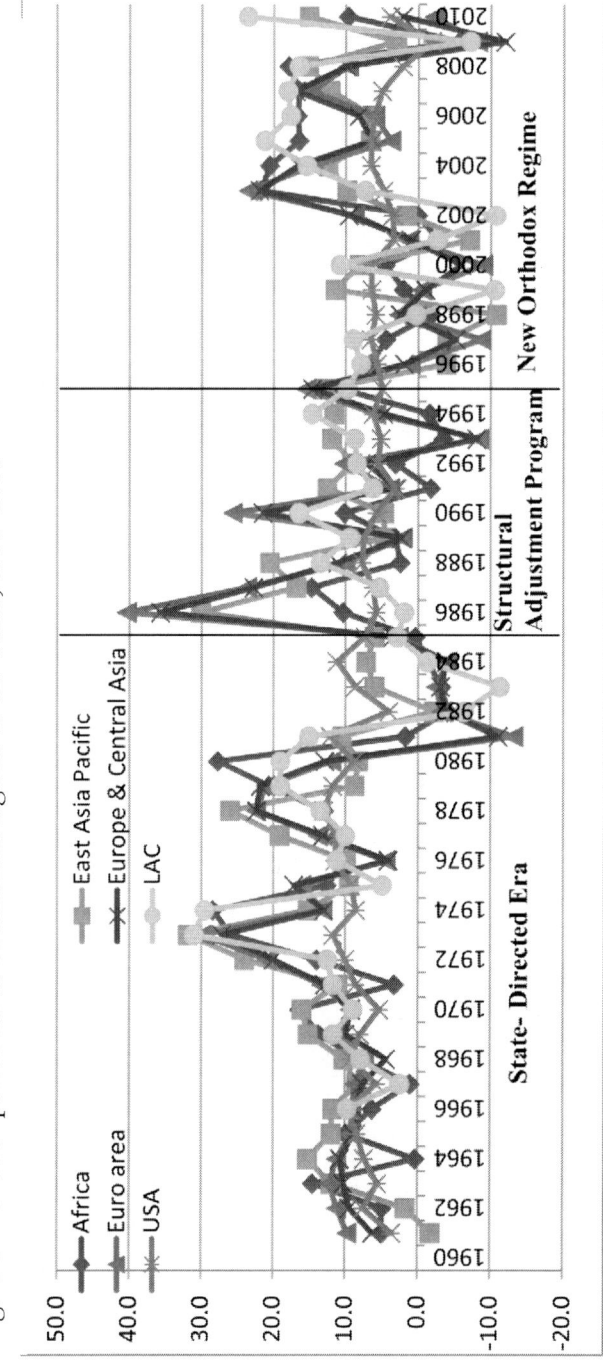

Figure 8.1: Growth performance of different regions of the world, 1960–2010

Source: UNECA, 2012.
Note: Not all the countries have information available throughout the whole period

Although recent years have brought some respite to obviate this picture of gloom for Africa, as annual growth soared to some 6 per cent during 2006 and 2007, yet this period of optimism appears fragile and built on soaring commodity prices as much as anything else. Consequently, recent growth in Africa has not been accompanied by significant structural transformation. Indeed, the economic structures of several African countries, especially the resource-rich countries, became more concentrated, thus making them more vulnerable to external shocks. United Nations Industrial Development Organization (UNIDO) data indicated that Africa's share of world manufacturing output was a paltry 1.49 per cent in 2012, corresponding to 10 per cent of China's market value added. Manufacturing as a share of GDP for Africa was only 10 per cent in 2012, compared to 23 per cent in Asia and Pacific and 15 per cent in Latin America (Jerome, 2013). This is the backdrop to the continued efforts to articulate development strategies that launch Africa on a path of economic diversification and long-term development. The next section reviews some of those efforts.

Initiatives by African leaders: Structural adjustment programs and poverty reduction strategies

African leaders have not been bereft of ideas on how to solve the problem of underdevelopment on the continent, and these have, indeed, led to several turf battles. When the African development predicament emerged at the end of the seventies and the beginning of the eighties, African governments responded with the economic blueprint – the *Lagos Plan of Action for the Economic Development of Africa, 1980–2000*.[3] The Lagos Plan of Action (LPA) was crafted by Africans working through two major institutions – the United Nations Economic Commission for Africa (UNECA), led by Adedeji, and the Conference of Ministers of Finance and Economic Planning and the Secretariat of the then Organization of African

---

3 The African Plan of Action had been adopted by the UNECA Council of Ministers of Economic Development, Planning and Finance before it was submitted for approval and endorsement to African Heads of State and Government, whose meetings were held under the umbrella of the Organization of African Unity in Lagos Nigeria, where the distinguished Heads of State gave it the title of African Plan of Action (APA) in 1987.

Unity. It was later endorsed by the African Heads of State and Government in Lagos in 1980.

The LPA enunciated the goals of collective self-reliance. It sought to adopt a new development strategy of an inward-looking pattern rather than the inherited externally oriented pattern. The LPA emphasized, among other things, the development of domestic markets in Africa rather than reliance on external markets, the control of natural resources by the respective countries, the role and importance of domestic factor inputs in development, the imperative of self-sufficiency in food production, the development of human capital and the provision of social infrastructure for the African people. Clearly, by concentrating on sectoral programs, the LPA – like the previous import substitution industrialization strategy – envisaged structural transformation of African economies. The LPA repudiates the whole logic of the ragging neo-liberal development thinking of the time. Not surprisingly, it did not elicit necessary support from the international financial institutions and the international community. In spite of its clear vision of sustainable, equitable and poverty reducing growth accompanied by structural transformation, the LPA achieved very little as the World Bank used its leverage on many African countries to persuade them to jettison it.

Within a year after the LPA was adopted, the World Bank launched a report entitled, *Accelerated Development in sub-Saharan Africa: An Agenda for Action* (World Bank, 1981), otherwise known as the Berg Report, having been named after its principal author, Elliot Berg. The report was a scathing criticism of the LPA, eulogizing the role of the market and external trade in economic development, with a spirited attack on the state in Africa. The path to economic development in Africa – the report concluded – was for the continent to liberalize its economy, cut back on the role of the state and privatize public enterprises. It is now firmly established in the specialized literature that the Berg Report provided the theoretical justification and formed the crucible on which the structural adjustment programs that were to be imposed on Africa, and especially Sub-Sahara Africa, from the mid-1980s up to the end of the 1990s was construed.[4]

---

4   For an interesting account of the events in the World Bank and other institution that eventually led to the introduction of structural adjustment programs, see, for example, Stein (2008).

Based on the World Bank's Berg Report, the international financial institutions initiated a policy-based lending strategy and tied development assistance to structural adjustment policies with a focus on macroeconomic policies. Ignoring underlying structural defects, the Berg Report blamed Africa's economic weaknesses on domestic "policy inadequacies and administrative constraints" and advocated substantial currency devaluation and trade liberalization, along with the dismantlement of industrial protection measures (World Bank, 1981). These recommendations formed the basis of structural adjustment programs – market-oriented policy packages that became conditional to International Monetary Fund and World Bank loans made to African countries desperate for convertible currency needed to service external debts.

It should be noted that, while the International Monetary Fund was initially responsible for short-term, typically anti-inflationary macroeconomic stabilization programs and the World Bank for more medium-term, market-liberalizing structural adjustment programs, their policies converged around what was subsequently dubbed the "Washington Consensus". This consensus is generally seen as spearheading the global trend towards greater economic liberalization since the 1980s. While its policy priorities have changed over time (responding, in part, to poorer-than-expected economic performances in implementing countries), it has remained the "conventional wisdom" at the core of economic policy-making across most of the African continent (see, for example, Stiglitz, 1998 and Stein, 2008).

Another World Bank Report in 1989 – *From Crisis to Sustainable Growth* – emphasized "wider issues of state failure" in Africa, stressing governance issues and policy reforms (World Bank, 1989). In 1994 there was yet another World Bank report – *Adjustment in Africa: Reforms, Results and the Road Ahead* – which emphasized sound macroeconomic management as prerequisites for growth and poverty reduction. Not surprisingly, these reports and the associated policies conveniently ignored the issue of structural transformation, as this would have been inconsistent with the dogmatic aversion to government intervention in economic matters, especially in industrial development, local value addition and creation of remunerative jobs, all of which are necessary for inclusive growth and development.

Throughout the adjustment years, the Bretton Woods Institutions seized much of the initiative, and foreclosed the debate by literally insisting that it was either their way or nothing, with African scholars and policy-makers largely relegated to reactive protest. With the shift of emphasis from human development to macroeconomic stability (as recommended by numerous International Monetary Fund and World Bank reports), the ministries in charge of local government, rural development, education, health and employment and infrastructural development were downgraded. Instead, the ministries of finance and central banks were promoted since they were dealing directly with the World Bank and the International Monetary Fund. In several African countries, the Ministry of Finance and Economic Planning was stripped of its economic planning functions in order to focus all its attention on financial issues – mainly inflation and exchange rate management.

While the LPA could not be achieved, Africa, especially under an excruciating adjustment regime, continued to tinker with alternative development strategies separate from the neo-liberal doctrine of structural adjustment. These strategies, among others, included Africa's Priority Program for Economic Recovery (1986–1990), which was presented to the United Nations (UN) General Assembly as a blueprint for Africa's development, and subsequently modified and adopted by the UN General Assembly as the UN Program of Action for Africa Economic Recovery and Development (1986–1990). Also, UNECA developed a counter-proposal to structural adjustment programs, titled *Alternative Framework to Structural Adjustment Programmes for Socio-Economic Recovery and Transformation* (AAF-SAP) in 1989.

Under the leadership of Adedeji, UNECA proposed AAF-SAP in response to the challenge of the General Assembly of the United Nations that Africans should not content themselves with criticizing structural adjustment programs, but should come up with an alternative to structural adjustment programs — if they dared. The response to this challenge by the UNECA Secretariat came in 1989, when it unveiled AAF-SAP – prepared by Adedeji and his team and approved by the UNECA Council of Ministers and by the Organization of African Unity in 1989.

For the productive sectors, policies advocated in AAF-SAP include:

- land reforms for better access and entitlement to land for productive use

- enhancement of the role of women as agents of change
- modernization of the food production sector
- allocation of an increasing share of foreign exchange for imports of vital inputs
- sectoral allocation of credit using credit guidelines that would favor the food sub-sector and the manufacture of essential goods
- use of selective nominal interest rates in such a way that interest on loans for speculative activities would be greater than the rates on loans for productive activities
- rehabilitation and rationalization of installed productive and infrastructural capacities
- removal of subventions to parastatals other than those in the social sector and nationally important strategic basic industries
- use of limited, realistic and decreasing deficit financing for productive and infrastructural investments that have little import content.

From the above, it is evident that Adedeji used AAF-SAP as the basis for challenging the neo-liberal paradigm (Onimode, 2004; Cline-Cole, 2006). The thrust of AAF-SAP is that adjustment should be an integral process of socio-economic transformation, based on the principles of self-reliance and self-sustainment advocated in the LPA.

However, all these economic proposals for Africa's development remained mere statements of intent as the dominant forces in the global economy were either opposed to or gave cold reception to them. The tendency was to deploy political and economic leverage on African countries to sway them away from such blueprints. Nonetheless, the recognition that the neo-liberal policies of the 1980s and 1990s ensnared many African countries in a cycle of debt, inequality and entrenched poverty led to widespread calls for a scrapping of structural adjustment policies and the cancellation of the debt burden. The World Bank and International Monetary Fund have attempted to shake off the negative image of structural adjustment programs through the introduction of "new" strategies aimed specifically at poverty reduction along with "sustainable" debt relief for Heavily Indebted Poor Countries.

Heavily Indebted Poor Countries and poverty reduction strategy papers

The fight against poverty took center stage in the preoccupation of public authorities in Africa and the international community from the mid-1990s. Based on a 1996 World Bank report, *A Continent in Transition*, and under intense and sustained pressure from the international civil society organizations as the problems of implementing liberal reforms contained in the structural adjustment programs of the 1980s and early 1990s became evident, the World Bank and other international actors began to lay out a new approach to development that placed greater emphasis on poverty reduction and the participation of civil society organizations. Thus, poverty reduction strategies became the framework for economic policies and development choices in most African countries.

This reorientation of economic policies was reinforced by the adoption of the Heavily Indebted Poor Countries initiative for debt reduction, with the adoption of a poverty reduction strategy as a precondition for accessing support. Most African countries committed to the poverty reduction path from the mid-1990s and a great number of them have reached the Heavily Indebted Poor Countries completion point that allows them to benefit from significant external debt reduction and increase social sector spending in order to combat poverty and assist vulnerable populations. Despite these initiatives, growth remained weak and fragile, and far from the levels required to achieve the MDGs and reduce poverty by half by 2015. Like the underlying development thinking of the period, issues of structural transformation and the role of the state did not receive any serious attention.

The New Partnership for Africa's Development

In the last decade or so, a renewed urge to reclaim the setting of development agendas in Africa by African leaders was galvanized with the establishment of the New Partnership for Africa's Development (NEPAD) in October 2001.[5] NEPAD is the second

---

5 In all, four African leaders, namely, Thabo Mbeki of South Africa, Abdoulaye Wade of Senegal, Olusegun Obasanjo of Nigeria and Abdelaziz Bouteflika of Algeria, were critical to the establishment of NEPAD.

major attempt by African leaders, after the aborted Lagos Plan of Action, to muster a collective will to engineer economic development in Africa. It represents a pledge by African leaders, based on a common vision and a firm and shared conviction that they have a pressing duty to eradicate poverty and to place their countries, both individually and collectively, on a path of sustainable growth and development, and, at the same time, to prepare them to participate actively in the world economy and in global politics.

NEPAD has seven priority areas of intervention:

- strengthening mechanisms for conflict prevention, management and resolution
- promoting and protecting democracy and human rights
- restoring and maintaining macroeconomic stability
- revitalizing and extending the provision of education, technical training and health services, with high priority accorded to HIV/AIDS, malaria, and other communicable diseases
- promoting the role of women in social and economic development
- building the capacity of the states in Africa
- promoting the development of infrastructure, agriculture and its diversification.

To achieve the above, NEPAD calls for policy reforms and increased investments in the priority areas of agriculture and food security, science and technology, environment, trade and market access, governance, infrastructure (energy, transport and water sanitation, and information and communication technologies), gender, and capacity development. NEPAD, in conjunction with the African Development Bank and UNECA, also continues to emphasize the participation of the private sector, civil society organizations and the African diaspora in fostering development on the continent. Unlike previous initiatives by African leaders and their institutions, which challenged the orthodoxy and/or emphasized structural transformation and government intervention, NEPAD does not do so. Accordingly, the developed world typified by the G8 has given tacit approval and overwhelming support to the NEPAD initiative, as it is perceived to be in tune with the prevailing new orthodoxy of development thinking.[6]

---

6 As part of the process to integrate NEPAD into the African Union structures and processes, the 14th African Union Summit, held in Addis

Adedeji has, however, cautioned that pursuing NEPAD's goals should not be done at the expense of the LPA's principles of structural transformation and socio-economic transformation (Cline-Cole, 2006). He suggests that NEPAD should not just be preoccupied with the inflow of resources; it needs to engage more with the policies and operational strategies of international partners in Africa.

The developmental state and economic transformation in Africa

In recent years, especially following the global economic and financial crisis, there seems to be a convergence of ideas, at least within the African Union Commission and UNECA, on the imperatives of a democratic developmental state in Africa as a panacea for the achievement of rapid economic development in the region. This is given impetus by two reports: The UNECA *Economic Report on Africa: Governing Development in Africa: Role of the State in Economic Transformation*, 2011, and *Good Growth and Governance in Africa: Rethinking Development Strategies* edited by Noman, Botchwey, Stein, and Stiglitz (2011).

The two reports suggest that the state has a crucial role to play in facing the current and emerging development challenges in Africa. In particular, the UNECA *Economic Report on Africa* (2011) advocates that Africa's developmental states should undertake three major tasks to achieve economic transformation: planning the process, formulating appropriate policies, and implementing the plans and policies. The report, therefore recommends that the developmental state approach should be operationalized through disciplined planning while avoiding the pitfalls of state intervention, such as capture, through a competent and autonomous bureaucracy responsible for planning and implementation as well as constructing a development-oriented coalition between committed political leadership, the bureaucracy, the private sector employers and employee associations and civil society.

Ababa, Ethiopia, from 25 January to 2 February 2010, decided to strengthen the NEPAD program by transforming the NEPAD Secretariat into an implementation agency – the NEPAD Planning and Coordinating Agency.

Setting the agenda for Africa's long-term growth

There are several compelling reasons why Africa needs to reclaim the debate on its development and take responsibility for its actions. As the depth, duration, and world-wide responses to the crisis showed, the dominant neo-liberal Washington Consensus economic paradigm has fallen into great disrepute. What was hitherto hailed as the only road to growth and prosperity has now come under fierce attack by the same countries and institutions that promoted it for several years.[7] It is, therefore, not surprising that the World Bank's *World Development Report* (2008) makes a few guarded references to the mistakes made under structural adjustment programs. An evaluation of the World Bank's research output from 1988 to 2005, chaired by Angus Deaton, challenged the institution's reputation as the world's "knowledge bank", referring to its habit of taking "new and untested results" as hard evidence that its preferred policies work, singling out the flagship World Development Reports published annually as a medium through which advocacy of the World Bank's favored policy recommendations sometimes takes precedence over over-balanced analysis.[8]

Paradoxically, Justin Yifu Lin, former World Bank Chief Economist, in response to the global economic and financial crisis, unveiled a new framework for rethinking development in 2009, anchored on new structural economics. This proposed framework, which is essentially neo-classical in orientation, recommended that, in

---

[7] The generation-long critiques of the Washington Consensus by eminent persons, such as Muhammad Yunis, Amatya Sen, Joseph Stiglitz, etc. readily come to mind in this regard. Similarly, in terms of promoting, at the local level, an alternative and inclusive development, experiences in Latin America (Mexico and Guatemala in particular) – which have since formed the basis for directional and conceptual change of the United Nations Development Program human development-centered approach and the Human Development Indices – continue to put to task the long-standing referral to the Washington Consensus.

[8] The evaluation was carried out by a panel consisting of Angus Deaton (Chair), Princeton University; Kenneth Rogoff, Harvard University; Abhijit Banerjee, Massachusetts Institute of Technology; and Nora Lustig, Director of the Poverty Group at United Nations Development Program. The panel, in turn, selected thematic evaluators and asked them to review a random sample of 186 research projects.

addition to an effective market mechanism, the government should play an active role in facilitating industrial upgrading and infrastructure improvements (Lin, 2011). It notes the structural differences between developed and developing countries, and acknowledges the active role of the state in facilitating the movement of the economy from a lower to a higher stage of development.

In the aftermath of the recent global financial crisis from which Asia has emerged rather quickly and relatively unscathed, there are important lessons for Africa. The spectacular growth of many economies in East Asia, especially Hong Kong, South Korea, Singapore, and Taiwan – collectively known as the "four tigers" – over the past four decades has amazed the economics profession and provoked a torrent of books and articles attempting to explain the phenomenon. From 1973 to 1993, income per capita in all the rapidly growing economies of East and Southeast Asia – China, Hong Kong, Indonesia, Malaysia, Singapore, South Korea, Taiwan and Thailand – grew by 4 to 9 per cent a year, doubling or even, as in Korea, quintupling over those twenty years (Roemer, 1996). In addition to the "four tigers", spectacular growth performances were also recorded by Malaysia, Thailand and Indonesia over the same period and by China since 1978 – which recently emerged as the second biggest economy in the world and the largest exporter. Together, these eight countries grew at about twice the rate of what was witnessed in the rest of East Asia and the industrial economies. They grew about three times as fast as those in Latin America and South Asia and about five times as fast as those in sub-Saharan Africa. And they were all countries that did not have structural adjustment programs.

Growth rates in the transition economies of China and Vietnam in the last three decades further reinforce the argument as to how important it could be for Africa to take a cue from the East Asian experiences in terms of understanding the underlying factors that promote sustainable growth and development. Remarkably, none of the countries in East Asia followed the orthodox policies of the Washington Consensus to the letter, and most of them were predominantly state dominated.

With the global economic and financial crisis, the move to greater Asian dominance in the global economy has now been accelerated. In general, the underlying characteristics of the growth trajectories of the Asian "tigers" could be pinned down to the following closely integrated and mutually reinforcing factors:

- agrarian reforms and a dynamic agricultural sector
- rapid growth of exports which were not 100 per cent in their raw state but have gone through a process of value added before being exported
- rapid demographic transition
- high investment and saving rates
- high investments in human capital.

Export orientation and export growth created a demand for skilled workers and this justifies the value of investments in education and human development. The dynamic agricultural sector allowed labor to shift into export industries. The rapid demographic transition also heightened the need for more investment in education as sustainable avenues were being created for the growing pool of savings and resources were being invested in the development of needed physical and social capital. All of these are indications of the benefits of fostering interactions between growth drivers in an economy for the accelerated development of key sectors.

On the other hand, governance in Africa has been catastrophic, combining, to a large extent, limited capacity for forward-looking and growth-promoting policy choices, with continuing reliance on externally imposed programs that served only the strategic interests of the development partners. This contrasted rather sharply with experiences of the East Asian economies whose "benevolent dictators" displayed a very high degree of economic pragmatism. African leaders, even in the rare instances where they were not plunderers, tended to be ideologically driven and deficient in their ability to harness growth potentials that are abound domestically.[9] The academe in Africa stood apart and aloof in contrast to their Asian colleagues.

The need for inclusive growth

Despite positive trends achieved in Africa for close to a decade before the onset of the global crisis, economic growth did not raise

---

9   The "benevolent dictators" in Africa, unfortunately, did and still do sit tight in office "till death do us part".

incomes high enough to sufficiently trigger any notable progress in meeting the MDGs and other anti-poverty benchmarks. A number of structural factors, including high ratio of foreign debt to national income, lack of far-reaching investment in agriculture and upstream agribusiness, poor communication and transportation infrastructure, high population growth and the high burden of disease, continue to constrain growth and development prospects. As a result, many countries still rely on external aid to balance their budgets and to provide basic social services. Political instability continues in many parts of the continent, and few states constitute a transparent and representative democratic governance system.

In going forward, there is no doubt that inclusive growth should assume more prominence in the years ahead. This is heightened by the Arab Spring, youth unemployment and growing inequalities which have brought forward the urgent relevance of the inclusive growth agenda.

The need to review Africa's development strategies

The foregoing can only point in one direction: it is time for Africa to review its development strategies and to make them more resilient against future external shocks, and to focus on the delivery of social and economic services more broadly, effectively and inclusively. African countries need to lead the debate on the continent's development and take bold and decisive actions when the need arises. Genuine development needs should be viewed more as endogenous processes rather than as initiatives that can be "imported" from abroad. In this respect, it is imperative that Africans restore their self-confidence, trust African expertise, and promote the use of African endogenous knowledge and technology.

The aftermath of the crisis is, therefore, a pointer to the ever present concerns that if Africa is to reclaim the debate on its development, it has to take responsibility for its actions, and has to harness all available resources – human and natural – as well as implement appropriate recommendations from the pile of previously crafted documents and strategies. This is the development philosophy that Adedeji has espoused all through his career. Adedeji's thinking on African development stresses the importance of "indigenization" of national and continental economic development in order to forge an Africa which, having inherited or borrowed development policy would subsequently be able to revive its own economic assumptions and design its own policies. It is this vision, driven in part by a firm belief that economic growth was merely a means to the more desirable end of structural transformation for increased self-reliance that informed his insistence on an Africa-formulated alternative development strategy.

An Africa-determined development agenda necessarily requires an elaborate review of existing development frameworks to take into account more recent developments in the global environment. The integration of contributions by academics, the private sector, and civil society organizations in the areas of gender equality, trade, finance, food sovereignty, and human and social rights should all be harnessed to ensure the development of a framework for Africa's new growth and development paradigm. Within this framework, the role of the state and the market in promoting economic growth and development needs to be properly redefined.

What is emerging from the existing development frameworks is that the laissez-faire prescriptions – less activist and more enabling – assigned to the role of governments in the past three to four decades are to be replaced by active interventions of governments in economic activities (especially in the social service sectors), and through mitigating measures as the economic stimulus packages. There is need for a review and rebalancing of the roles of the state and that of the market within development, growth and poverty-reduction strategies. Needless to say, too, records of achievements in the Southeast Asian countries have shown that the state just cannot be the only player. It has to work with the private sector and the civil society in the drive for inclusive development.

It is also important to revisit export-oriented strategies. Without necessarily advocating a swing towards inward-looking strategies, it is important that domestic demand be significantly strengthened. At the same time, measures for active and competitive participation in the global value chains need to be accelerated. Further redirection efforts lie in the treatment of environmental issues (including measures to address climate change and biodiversity loss) as part of the solution to the crisis, by fostering a more sustainable development policy.

With less than 7 per cent of the world's total emissions of greenhouse gases, Africa has contributed the least of any world region to the global accumulation of greenhouse gas emissions.

However, the continent is particularly vulnerable to climate change effects due to its overdependence on rain-fed agriculture, compounded by factors such as widespread poverty and overall weak institutions, intervention and implementation capacity. The impacts range from energy shortages, reduced agricultural production, worsening food security and growing malnutrition, to spreading disease, more humanitarian emergencies, growing migratory pressures and increased risk of conflict over scarce land and water resources (Africa Partnership Forum, 2008).

As part of deepening the sustainable development agenda, the concept of green economy is also receiving significant international attention. The adoption of green economy in the context of sustainable development and poverty eradication was one of the two themes of the 2012 United Nations Conference on Sustainable Development (Rio+20). The green economy agenda aims at reconciling low-carbon and sustainable development with other valued outcomes, such as, job creation, poverty alleviation, and high economic growth. In this regard, Africa needs to plan for "green growth" that emphasizes environmentally sustainable economic progress to foster a low-carbon and socially inclusive development strategy.

Above all, there is a need to reform the global financial architecture, including the exchange rate system, in order to underpin macroeconomic stability and to avoid debt traps and speculation. This would involve going "back to the basics" – to the rules invented at the 1944 Bretton Woods Conference – in particular, fixed but adjustable exchange rates reflecting fundamentals such as inflation rates. Keeping real exchange rates stable would prevent major distortions in international trade and currencies. Africa and other developing countries have been unjustifiably left out of mitigation measures. It is imperative that they are included in the quest for solutions and the governance architecture of international financial institutions.

The global economic downturn has also heightened the importance of strengthening intra-African integration and South-South cooperation. African countries need to strengthen efforts aimed at promoting economic integration as a central component for the continent's development in an increasingly globalizing world economy. Regional integration in Africa is currently among the lowest worldwide. As United Nations Conference on Trade and

Development (2009) indicated in its *Economic Development in Africa Report*, intra-regional trade represents only 9 per cent of exports, compared to 71 per cent in Europe and 46 per cent in developing Asia – both regions in which it has clearly served as a stepping stone for economic development. Similarly, intra-African investment accounts for only 13 per cent of all inward foreign direct investment, less than half the figure for Association of Southeast Asian Nation countries. For Africa, strengthening regional integration, especially through trade, investment and movement of labor, could mitigate the adverse effects of the current crisis and make the continent more resilient to future external shocks. In addition, regional integration could support the development of infrastructure in such key sectors as transportation, communications and energy by allowing for economies of scale in their production. South-South cooperation in more recent times is assuming significant discussion, not just because of the increasing aid, trade and foreign direct investment flows from the Big Ten to Africa, but also in terms of the triangular cooperation that it fosters.[10]

Finally, one of the major lessons emerging from the global financial crisis is that African countries need to deepen their policy and regulatory frameworks as well as their structural reform measures in order to attract sufficient private capital inflows, diversify their export basket, and insulate the financial system from complex but unmanageable financial instruments. They will also need to rationalize and strengthen the various institutions they have created to enhance such efforts. In particular, they will need to strengthen their governance systems and processes. Evidently, the launching of NEPAD and the African Peer Review Mechanism, and the aid-trade-investments complementarities inherent in BRICS's (Brazil, Russia, India, China and South Africa) African agenda within the redefined G20, have been acclaimed as important initiatives that have high potential to give a new boost and direction to the development efforts of African countries. It is expected that the smooth and efficient functioning of these institutions and alliances will move

---

10 The Big Ten countries are: Brazil, China, India, Kuwait, Saudi Arabia, South Africa, Republic of Korea, Turkey, United Arab Emirates and Venezuela. These countries, among which the BRICS (Brazil, Russia, India China and South Africa) play a particularly prominent role, are estimated to have in recent times provided bilateral development assistance of more than US$100 million per annum to Africa.

Africa in the desired direction of enhanced South-South and triangular cooperation.

Conclusion

The global economy has witnessed momentous changes since the financial crisis erupted in 2008. Conventional ideas about the workings of the economy are being questioned as they fail to deliver on the development aspirations of the people. Vocal protests from Wall Street to the streets of Athens and Tahrir Square in Egypt are asking for new thinking in policy-making and intellectual circles. It is increasingly recognized that faith has been shaken in the economic policy prescriptions which helped to generate the crisis and that turned a blind eye to its build-up.

Departing from "business as usual" is not confined to developing countries, but has become a pressing need in even the most developed economies. In Europe especially, the global financial and economic crisis which erupted in 2008 exposed the frailty of certain economic policy strategies and the vulnerability of sovereign governments if they are left prey to market sentiment. This trend highlights the urgent need for new economic thinking that puts greater emphasis on inclusive and sustainable growth.

The crisis has – paradoxically – provided a unique opportunity to accelerate growth and poverty reduction in Africa. It has also created opportunities for accelerating progress with implementing structural reforms in the areas of private sector development, financial sectors, labor markets, and social safety nets, the importance of diversification of the economic bases as well as with deepening regional integration. A new development paradigm – which focuses on the structural transformation of Africa and socio-economic diversification and draws largely from a number of past documents inspired by Adebayo Adedeji and by other African writers in the LPA, AAF-SAP, African Charter on Popular Participation and Transformation, and NEPAD – is needed. The LPA is as relevant today as it was three decades ago when it was first developed. In both the LPA and AAF-SAP, Adedeji has provided the necessary framework for academics, the private sector and civil society organizations to build upon and chart out a new path that will ensure Africa's sustainable growth and development.

This is also an opportune time to renew the social contract between the state and citizens and to reconsider the results of finance-led globalization. Internationally and nationally, neglected public institutions need to be rebuilt with popular assent, while avoiding the one-size-fits-all approach to economic development, which has largely failed. Accordingly, careful detailed and contextually relevant country level studies should regularly underpin the articulation of policies and programs necessary to initiate, sustain and advance the goals of inclusive, equitable and poverty reducing growth accompanied by structural transformation in Africa.

References

Adedeji, A. 2008. "Neo-classicalism and all that: The mantra of marketisation, liberalisation, privatisation, globalisation and financialisation". University of Ibadan Department of Economics Golden Jubilee Anniversary and Ojetunji Aboyade Annual Memorial Lecture, 26 November.

Africa Partnership Forum. 2008. *Climate Challenge to Africa: A Call for Action*. 10th meeting of the Africa Partnership Forum. Available at: http://www.africapartnershipforum.org//meetingdocuments/40333574.pdf

African Development Bank. 2009. "Impact of the crisis on African economies: Sustaining growth and poverty reduction: African perspectives and recommendations to the G20", a report from the Committee of African Finance Ministers and Central Bank Governors (C-10) to the British Prime Minister as part of the agenda for the April 2009 G20 Summit in London, African Development Bank, Tunis.

African Union Commission, UNECA, the United Nations Development Programme, and the African Development Bank Group. 2013. *Assessing Progress in Africa toward the Millennium Development Goals: MDG Report 2013: Food Security in Africa: Issues, Challenges and Lessons*. Available at http://www.afdb.org/fileadmin/uploads/afdb/Documents/Publications/Millennium%20Development%20Goals%20(MDGs)%20Report%202013.pdf

Ajakaiye, O and Jerome, A. forthcoming."Economic development: The experience of sub-Saharan Africa" in B Currie-Alder, R. Kanbur, D. Malone and R. Medhora (eds) *International Development: Ideas, Experience, and Prospects*. Oxford: Oxford University Press, forthcoming.

Assubuji, P, Luckscheiter, J and Ben-Zeev, K (eds). 2009. "The global economic crisis and South Africa", *Perspectives* 3/2009. Cape Town: Heinrich Böll Stiftung. Available at: http://www.boell.org.za/downloads/Perspectives_3-09.pdf.

Claessens, S, Ariccia, G, Igan, D and Laeven, L. 2010. "Lessons and policy implications from the global financial crisis", *IMF Working Papers*, WP/10/44.

Cline-Cole, R. 2006. "Adebayo Adedeji" in D. Simon (ed.) *Fifty Key Thinkers on Development*. London: Routledge.

Jerome, A 2013. "Industry in Africa within the post-2015 development agenda", background paper prepared for UNIDO for the 20th Conference of African Ministers of Industry (CAMI 20) 10–14 June 2013, Nairobi, Kenya.

Jerome, A and Akinkugbe, O. 2010. "The global economic crisis, Africa's social sectors and an agenda for long-term growth on the continent". *Africagrowth Agenda:* October–December: 6–11.

Kyrili, K and Martin, M. 2010. "The impact of the global economic crisis on the budgets of low-income countries". Research Report, Development Finance International for Oxfam.

Lin, JY. 2011. "New structural economics: A framework for rethinking development". *World Bank Research Observer*, 26(2): 193–221.

Mohan, R. 2008. "Global financial crisis: Causes, impact, policy responses and lessons". Speech by Dr Rakesh Mohan, Deputy Governor of the Reserve Bank of India, at the 7th Annual India Business Forum Conference, London Business School, London, 23 April.

Noman A, Botchwey K, Stein H and Stiglitz JE (eds). 2011. *Good Growth and Governance in Africa: Rethinking Development Strategies.* Oxford: Oxford University Press.

Onimode, B (ed.). 2004. *African Development and Governance Strategies in the 21st Century: Looking Back to Move Forward: Essays in Honour of Adebayo Adedeji at 70.* London: Zed Books.

Organization of African Unity. 1980. *Lagos Plan of Action for the Economic Development of Africa, 1980–2000.* Republished by UNECA, April 1980. Available at: http://www.uneca.org/itca/ariportal/docs/lagos_plan.pdf.

Roemer, M. 1996. *Could Asian Policies Propel African Growth?* Boston: Harvard Institute for International Development, Harvard University.

Stein, H. 2008. *Beyond the World Bank Agenda: An Institutional Approach to Development.* Chicago: University of Chicago Press.

Stiglitz, J. 1998. "More instruments and broader goals: Moving toward the post-Washington Consensus". UNU/WIDER Lecture. Helsinki: World Institute For Development Economics Research, United Nations University.

Taylor, J. 2009. *The financial crisis and the policy responses: An empirical analysis of what went wrong.* Working Paper 14631. New York: National Bureau of Economic Research.

UNECA and Africa Union. 2010. "Overview of economic and social conditions in Africa in 2009". Meeting of the Committee of Experts of the 3rd Joint Annual Meetings of the AU Conference of Ministers of Economy and Finance and ECA Conference of African Ministers of Finance, Planning and Economic Development, Lilongwe, Malawi 25–28 March.

UNECA. 1989. *African Alternative Framework to Structural Adjustment Programmes for Socio-Economic Recovery and Transformation (AAF-SAP).* Available at: www.uneca.org/publications/ESPD/old/aaf_sap.pdf

UNECA. 1990. *African Charter for Popular Participation in Development.* Adopted at the International Conference on Popular Participation in the Recovery and Development in Africa, Arusha, United Republic of Tanzania, 12–16 February. Addis Ababa: Economic Commission for Africa.

UNECA. 2011. *Economic Report on Africa 2011: Governing Development in Africa – The Role of the State in Economic Transformation.* Addis Ababa: Economic Commission for Africa.

UNECA. 2012. *Economic Report on Africa 2012: Unleashing Africa's Potential as a Pole of Global Growth.* Economic Commission for Africa: Addis Ababa.

United Nations Conference on Trade and Development. 2009. *Economic Development in Africa: Strengthening Regional Economic Integration for Africa's Development.* New York and Geneva: United Nations. Washington, D.C: World Bank.

World Bank. 1981. *Accelerated Development in Sub-Saharan Africa: An Agenda for Action.* Washington, D.C: World Bank.

World Bank. 1989. *From Crisis to Sustainable Growth: A Long Term Perspective Study.*

World Bank. 1994. *Adjustment in Africa: Reforms, Results, and the Road Ahead.* Oxford: Oxford University Press.

World Bank. 2010a. *Africa's Pulse. An Analysis of Trends Shaping Africa's Economic Future*. Washington, D. C: World Bank.

World Bank. 2010b. *Global Monitoring Report 2010: The MDGs after the Crisis*. Washington D. C: The International Bank for Reconstruction and Development/World Bank.

World Bank. 2012. *Global Economic Prospects 2012: Uncertainties and Vulnerabilities*. Washington, D.C: World Bank.

World Bank. 2013. *Global Economic Prospects January 2013: Sub-Saharan Africa Annex*. Washington D.C: World Bank.

PART 4.
CONFLICT, DEMOCRACY AND DEVELOPMENT IN AFRICA

CHAPTER 9. CAUSES OF CONFLICT AND THE DYNAMICS OF CONFLICT ACTIVATION

James Katorobo

Introduction

This chapter focuses on Adebayo Adedeji's contribution to the understanding and management of intra- and inter-state conflicts in Africa. Adedeji's fundamental proposition is that in order to resolve conflicts we need to thoroughly comprehend them so as to master them. This theme resonates with the title of a seminal book Adedeji edited in 1999 that has influenced subsequent African conflict studies since its publication – including a review of African conflicts and governance on which this chapter is based (Katorobo, 2009a).

Advantages of comprehending and mastering African conflicts

Adedeji's analytic assumptions are that without a comprehensive understanding of the roots of conflict in Africa, the conflicts cannot be controlled. There are many interconnected causes of conflict and the entire conflict phenomenon is highly complex: "This means that we must accept as axiomatic the proposition that until the root causes of conflict are fully comprehended and addressed, they cannot be mastered and that the mastery of conflicts is imperative to achieving lasting peace and good governance in a country" (Adedeji,

1999: 7). Adedeji explained this concept further, stating that there must be "full comprehension of the underlying causes and the histories of conflict...understanding the origins of conflict means developing a framework for comprehending (i) how the various causes of conflict fit together and interact; (ii) which among them are the dominant forces at a particular moment in time; and (iii) what policies and strategies should be crafted to address these causes in the short, medium and long term" (10).

Adedeji's study of this problem – and the ensuing edited work – is pan-African in that seven country cases have been selected, representing all sub-Saharan regions: Rwanda and Burundi (Central Africa), Liberia and Sierra Leone (West Africa), Angola (Southern Africa), Sudan (East/North Africa), and Somalia and Somaliland (Horn of Africa). The study was also carried out in five countries in actual conflict.[1] (It was, however, not executed in Somalia and Sudan because of high insecurity.[2])

The overall objective of Adedeji's study was to lay the foundations for a system of good governance in post-conflict societies. According to him "our overarching objective must be to seek a system of governance that unites rather than marginalises; building bridges of confidence and reconciliation rather than pitfalls of alienation; shares power rather than monopolises it; and decentralises rather than centralises, thus yielding space to civil society, with the international community playing the extremely useful role of catalyst, and supporting factor for domestic advocates of governance improvement." (17)

---

[1] The study was successfully carried out in five conflict countries, which the author of this chapter considers a great achievement.

[2] The author (James Katorobo) has experienced working in some of the post-conflict countries covered by Adedeji's study. He spent one and a half years in Rwanda immediately after the genocide and another year working as United Nations Development Program (UNDP) governance expert on Somalia, before moving to Somaliland for another one and half years.

Negative consequences of African conflicts on socio-economic development and good governance

Armed rebellion and civil wars have had severe negative effects on African economies, trapping them in stagnation for decades. The limited growth and economic assets they managed to create are wantonly destroyed during violent conflicts. The agricultural and industrial modernization achieved in Kenya and Zimbabwe was destroyed in this manner during the armed civil strife arising out of political conflicts and failed elections (post-election violence). Adedeji had predicted over a decade previously that civil wars result in economic disaster and retrogression, but many African countries, heedless of the warning, had plunged headlong into disaster. For all who cared to listen the warning was stark: "The opportunity cost of conflict is enormous. Not only do conflict countries forego development, they also invariably retrogress. The more violent and protracted the conflict, the greater and more pervasive the negative development" (Adedeji, 1999: 12). Adedeji further stated that the impact of conflicts on the economy is devastating; that the resulting human deprivation is more excruciating than income poverty and that poverty and conflict feed on each other and go hand-in-hand with poor governance.

As proof that Adedeji's warning had not been heard by parties to conflicts in Africa, eight years later, the devastating effects of conflicts on African political economies and societies had grown very high and become grim. The results of a study published in 2007 of 23 African countries that experienced armed struggle or severe violent crisis between 1990 and 2005 revealed a staggering loss of US$300 billion, representing an average annual economic shrinkage of 15 per cent of GDP. "It is therefore particularly shocking that the cost estimated for those 23 countries is US$284bn (in constant year 2000 $) from 1990 to 2005, representing an average annual loss of 15 per cent of GDP. This amounts to an average of US$18bn per year lost by Africa due to armed conflict" (International Action Network on Small Arms, 2007: 7). This massive loss of resources was equivalent to total international aid to Africa from the major donors. The opportunity cost is enormous; this is money that could have been used to meet Africa's need for education and health and to deal with the HIV and AIDs pandemic. No effort should be spared in finding the causes of African conflicts and preventing them.

The role of conflict activation and mobilization

Social scientists tend to dismiss factors such as ethnicity, religious intolerance or racism/internal colonialism as causes of violence, economic deprivation (poverty) or social marginalization. The analytic error is to try to determine the causal effects of one factor by holding the other factors constant. However, because these factors work in unison (several combinations), it is futile to focus on only one. Secondly, they require activation and mobilization. The principle of activation was proposed and used by Elmer E. Schattschneider in 1975. In most cases, marginal groups such as slum dwellers, laborers, peasants and the powerless accept their lot and may justify it as an act of the gods. They may not define their existence in terms of grievances caused by the rulers or the upper classes. It is these groups that Schattschneider classified as the "semi-sovereign people". The theory (principle of activation) that he advanced is that the semi sovereign people require leaders to sensitize, arouse and mobilize them. Without this activation, the semi-sovereign people will remain dormant.

Figure 9.1 presents the inverse relationship between increasing conflict activation over time and declining peace conditions. This relationship is manifested in four groups of conflict issues in Africa: disputed colonial intra- and inter-state boundaries, economic inequality, political and social exclusion and ethnicity, clannish tendencies and racism. Each of these groups is a summary of many specific factors. Leaders use these differences to incite one group against another and one group may be aroused to confront alleged enemies. If homogeneity exists on any of these factors, antagonists will define conflict at the next level where differences exist. There is religious and tribal homogeneity in Somalia, and so conflicts have been defined at the level of clans and that is the level at which fighting is taking place.

Community differences such as ethnicity, religion, race, poverty and wealth should be considered as potential fault lines in the social structure. People can coexist with these divisions as long as they remain dormant. It is when leaders mobilize competition based on

CAUSES OF CONFLICT

them that conflict is likely to breakout. This is the principle of activation. Without activation, these differences remain latent. When economic inequalities increase, peace conditions decline; when groups and communities are excluded from participating in shaping policies and programs that affect them, then peace conditions decline; and when leadership and access to resources is based on ethnic identity, then peace conditions vanish. In order to prevent conflict activation, conditions for peaceful and harmonious coexistence must be nurtured. Leaders must prevent conflict activation by promoting conflict deactivation through deliberately crafted programs that cut across the fault lines in the social structure. This must be done through politics of inclusion, the economics of fair competition and access and participation and sharing the rewards and the benefits.

Figure9.1 Potential fault lines that result in the breakdown of peace

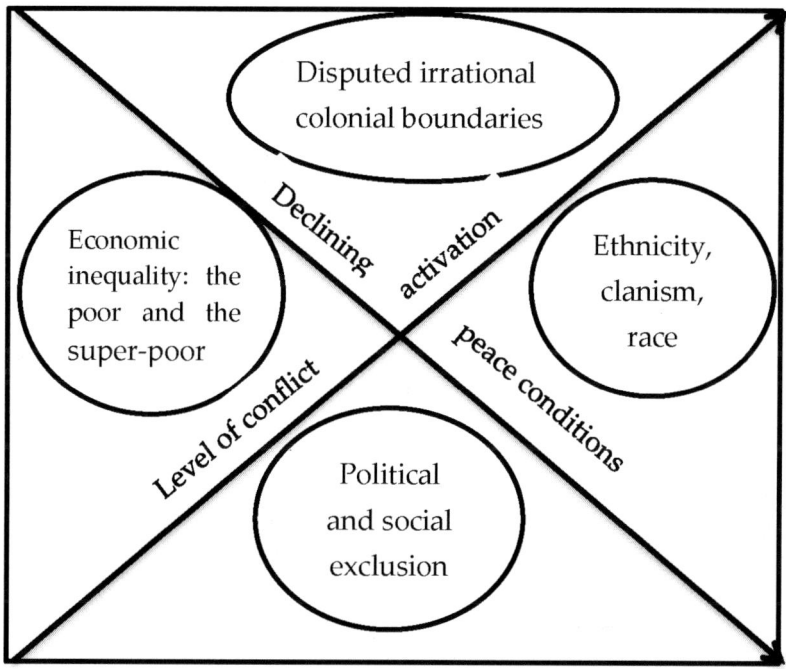

The ten root causes of conflict in Africa

Most conflicts in Africa arise out of: violent elite competition; disputed intra- and inter-state colonial boundaries; struggles over free-floating resources in government and the economy; seeking to change unfairly and unjustly acquired property; and re-enacting unresolved past conflicts. Others include: disputing election results and hanging onto power at whatever cost (wars of succession); a collapsed state fragmenting into warring, unrecognized mini states (Somalia); civil wars fought over extremist ideologies (radical Islam in Somalia); struggles over the existence of a dominant commodity (or mineral), and what has become known as "the resource curse"; and, finally, economic growth without equitable distribution. Each of these is discussed briefly below, in a review of ten major causes of conflict in Africa.

Violent elite competition

The first cause for conflict is elite competition for power that is driven by a winner-take-all mentality. Political power is conceived and practiced as a zero-sum relationship between antagonistic factions that aim at obliterating all perceived enemies: followers are mobilized to wipe out the other side. The violent elite competition is transformed into communal competition mobilized on the basis of communal differences of ethnicity, religion, and modes of production (livestock herders vs. crop producers).

This provides the grounds for subsequent misrule. The winning ruling elite uses political power to reward community-based elites who assisted in the mobilization of followers that led to victory. Society is divided between a ruling group and the ruled groups who experience marginalization and exclusion from the polity and the economy. The excluded leaders and groups demand inclusion and participation. They begin with peaceful means, but when these do not succeed, they resort to violent means. The state then unleashes the army, the police and other state instruments of coercion on them. The opponents are driven underground where they resort to another round of armed rebellion.

These patterns of unequal access to political, economic, and military assets tend to mirror ethnicity, clans, and race. Society comes to be divided between the rich, the super-rich, the poor and the super-poor. The transformation of diversities into armed rebellion depends on the existence of a high probability of one group dominating the others.

Disputed boundaries

In many African countries, colonial boundaries cut across communities, creating problems of ethnic minorities. The majority ethnic groups tend to marginalize and oppress these minorities and exclude them from participation in the polity and economy, resulting in the politics of irredentism in which ethnic groups located at the border identify with their compatriots in a neighboring country (the Banyarwanda of Uganda in Kisoro and those in Rwanda, the Samia of Uganda and those of Kenya at the border between the two countries, the Banyamulenge in Eastern Congo and their kin in Rwanda and Burundi).

Free-floating property

A distinction can be made between resources which are claimed, owned and for which someone is in possession, and resources which are not owned for which no one is in possession. Social scientists refer to this second category of resources as free floating. The existence of free-floating resources tends to generate fierce struggle and competition for them and the conflict so activated is at the heart of national and grassroots conflicts in Africa. For example, after Idi Amin chased the Indians out of Uganda, their commercial properties became free-floating resources available to successive regimes to allocate and reallocate to supporters.

Removal of free-floating properties from the supporters of the ousted regime and reallocating them to the new regime followers becomes the basis of the power of patronage in the hands of the ruling government. In many African countries, a large percentage of land may be owned by the state as public land and may be available as free-floating resources of the government to allocate. As the amount of free-floating resources begins to dwindle, the fight over them also increases, and the competition starts to invade what had been left as protected resources such as forests, wildlife and game parks, which may be degazetted and opened up for reallocation with adverse consequences for the environment.

Many proposed reforms of corporate governance aimed at ensuring that all businesses are registered under up-to-date company laws lead to chaos in the business sector. Similarly, modern comprehensive registration of all land in a country reduces land to a free-floating resource. Real and genuine decentralization of power to local governments reduces the extent to which central governments use resource allocation at the local level for buying grassroots support through patronage. Thus the objective of preventing conflicts at the grassroots level should be promoted through reforms that eliminate free-floating resources that tend to attract ruthless competition and violent struggles to acquire them.

Unfairly and unjustly acquired property

During the colonial period, the British took large extracts of land belonging to the Banyoro and gave them to the Baganda who had formed an alliance with the British and had crushed the Banyoro anti-colonial rebellion. At independence the British left this issue of the "lost counties" unsolved. It was agreed at the London Independence Conference that this issue would be put to a referendum in the "lost counties". The referendum returned two out of eight of the "lost counties" to Banyoro. This caused Uganda's first post-independence crisis that led to the collapse of the Uganda People's Congress and Kabaka Yekka alliance; the flight of the Kabaka of Buganda; the escape of Obote, then prime minister of Uganda, into exile, where he died; the abolition of monarchic institutions in Uganda; and Uganda plunging into several decades of dictatorship and misrule and a succession of armed rebellions.

In Kenya, the Kikuyu lost land to British settlers and armed conflicts in Kenya (fighting in the Rift Valley; fighting in the slums of Nairobi) have their origins in groups that believe that their land was unfairly and unjustly acquired.

Past conflict

"Once a country has experienced a civil war it is much more likely to experience further conflict, so that even though peace is an improvement, risk levels do not return to their pre-conflict level" (Adedeji, 1999: 17). A recurrent conflict is characterized by periods of armed conflict followed by uneasy peace followed again by armed conflict. Collier et al. (2003) have coined the concept of "conflict trap" to describe a recurrent and persistent conflict, stating that once a rebellion has started it appears to develop a momentum of its own. They note that "Getting back to peace is hard, and even when peace is re-established, it is often fragile…The best predictor of whether a country will be in civil war next year is whether it is at civil war now" (79). Further, "the typical country reaching the end of a civil war faces around a 44 per cent risk of returning to conflict within five years (83). The main causes for the return to armed conflict is that the parties to the peace agreements do not meet their commitments for peace and the root causes of the conflict remain unresolved.

Disputed election results and holding onto power

In most of the post-independence African countries, leaders established dictatorships based on the single dominant party or the military. This led to demands for democratic governance and the struggle for power. Where regimes resisted democratic reforms, civil wars raged. During the last two decades democratic electoral reforms have been introduced in many African countries. When genuine multiparty democratic elections have been successfully held, the vote has replaced the gun as the method for access to power and the mode by which one regime can legitimately replace another. However, in several cases, the ruling governments have manipulated and rigged elections in order to hold on power. This has led to violent conflicts arising out of disputed elections. The civil wars in Kenya and Zimbabwe are a result of ruling regimes determined to stay in power at any cost.

A collapsed state

Somalia is the classic example of a collapsed state replaced by ministates based in several regions of the former country: Somaliland in the Northwest, Puntiland in the North and Northeast, Baidoa in the South, and Mogadishu, the former capital. Each of the mini-states is controlled by a warlord with the exception of Mogadishu which is controlled by several warlords. A warlord is supported by pickups (trucks) which are converted and equipped with guns manned by hired gunmen followers (or marauding gangs). The warlord fights other warlords for the control of territory and the population in it. The power of the warlord and the size of territory under control depend on the number of pickups and the armed gangs and armory deployed, as well as fighting skills and leadership. This system is fluid since loss of power will lead to loss of control over the territory. This means that there is constant inter-warlord fighting depending on the balance of terror among them. Attempts to restore the Somali state at the national level has proved futile in spite of external intervention led by Uganda and Burundi armies approved by the United Nations and African union (AU). Several peace agreements have been signed and governments based on them have been formed but none has been able to endure beyond a few months.

A distinction can be made between levels of state collapse and states placed on a continuum of zero to 100 per cent. The Somali case can be taken as baseline of 100 per cent state collapse. The degree of state collapse may also be measured by the extent to which the state effectively controls territory beyond the capital. The Zairian state located in Kinshasa experiences diminished control as one moves from Kinshasa to the countryside. Large swaths of land, especially in the east, are under the control of rebel forces and foreign exiles from Rwanda, the Interahamwe (Hutu paramilitary organization). Vast territories, such the Garamba forests, beyond the control of the Zairian state have become the ideal hideout for rebel forces (Kony's Lord's Resistance Army) escaping from Uganda and the Sudan.

Collapse of the state happens gradually. The manifest events of collapse are a product of years of accumulated decline and decay of state institutions. As the Somali case has demonstrated, recovery from state collapse is very hard and can take a very long time. As the adage goes, prevention is better than cure.

Extremist ideology

The fact that some individuals can be brainwashed to become suicide bombers demonstrates the power of belief systems and motivation; in short the power of extremist ideology. Two powerful rewards may reinforce each other, namely, first, taking action and dying in the process to please the individual and collective perception of "God" and to be rewarded in heaven; and second, reinforcing the first option with large sums of money for the family left behind. The first taps into religious zealotry, and the second, into family preservation. Whereas Somalia is one of the few African countries that enjoy near complete ethnic and religious homogeneity, it has been crippled by recurrent and permanent civil wars pitting armed extreme radical Muslim factions against other Muslims regarded as lukewarm in their beliefs.

Radical Islamic factions in Africa are linked to external and global radical Islamic movements such Al Qaeda and the Taliban. In areas which they capture they set up administrations based on the

CAUSES OF CONFLICT

Sharia or Islamic law. Extremist Islamist ideology has been at the root of and is the basis of civil wars and armed rebellion in the South of Sudan, Darfur and the north of Nigeria.

While the apartheid regime in South Africa was motivated by white monopoly of the economy and the material riches of the country, it was justified by the construction and the propagation of white supremacy, a racial ideology. Considerable effort was put into convincing both whites and blacks to believe this tenet of racial ideology. Those who rejected the ideology had to be suppressed by coercive instruments of the state, causing them to go underground, get armed and fight the state and the apartheid system on which it was based. They, too, had to construct counter-ideology espousing the virtues of being black in the tradition of negritude and black consciousness.

This category also includes conflicts arising out of extremist ethnic ideology. The structures of ethnic diversity determine the extent to which they translate into ethnic civil war and ethnic cleansing. When there is a large diversity of ethnic groups that are proportionately balanced, even if there is a very strong intra-ethnic identity and sense of ethnic superiority, it is unlikely to result in inter-ethnic civil wars. But where there is a dominant ethnicity, such as the Hutu in both Rwanda and Burundi, in which the Hutus are overwhelmingly dominant (over 80 per cent in both countries), there is a tendency for ethnic extremism to translate into actual inter-ethnic civil wars.

A dominant commodity (or mineral)

Collier et al. (2003) advanced a theoretical proposition that poor, underdeveloped societies that are dependent on a single commodity based on a dominant resource are greatly exposed to conflicts around the control and utilization of the resource. For example, the existence of oil in Kabinda encouraged secessionist movements to break away from Angola. Similarly, the national governments were equally determined to maintain control over Kabinda and to stamp out secessionist activities. In Nigeria, the poor and deprived peoples of the Niger delta are fighting the federal government and the oil companies for the control and sharing of the large petroleum revenues generated in the region.

Most African countries with dominant, rich minerals and commodities are enmeshed in civil wars fanned by struggles to gain access to the minerals and the commodity money. Rebel movements finance their armed rebellion from selling the minerals and commodities. The governments also use revenues from the minerals and the commodities to finance the expansion and equipping of national armies to fight and suppress the armed rebellions, instead of using the revenues for developing the state and particularly the regions from which the resources are located. This has come to be known as the "natural resource curse": to describe a situation of deepening abject poverty and corrupt enrichment by the few in the midst of increasing and spiraling mineral resource-derived revenues accruing to the state. Botswana is an isolated case that has escaped the resource curse – showing that it is not inevitable.

Collier et al. (2003: 127) also contrasted the performance of Sierra Leone and Botswana. In 1961 Botswana and Sierra Leone had the same level of per capita income of about US$1,070. They also both had natural resource endowment in the form of diamond deposits. Through effective democratic economic governance, Botswana proceeded to transform the economy through the mining and export of diamonds. Since independence in 1961, there has been no civil war in Botswana and per capita incomes had risen to US$8,800 in 2001. In the case of Sierra Leone, diamond wealth, in combination with poor governance, led to recurrent civil wars and to the collapse of the state. The level of per capita income had plummeted to US$480 in 2001. The Sierra Leone diamond deposits are alluvial and scattered in many parts of the country and easy for rebels to get access to and thus finance their rebellion. What Sierra Leone has lacked until recent years has been effective democratic and economic governance and a strong and capable civil service with excellent mining policies, legal and regulatory frameworks and strong accountable and decentralized institutions. This same problem explains the failure of the Zairian State (now Democratic Republic of Congo) from exploiting its abundant natural resource endowments scattered throughout the vast country. Botswana is fortunate in that its diamond mines were not scattered. Thus, through effective economic and mining policies, under the practice of popular and democratic governance that gave no room for armed rebellions, Botswana exploited its kimberlitic diamond deposits at three large mines.

Successful economic growth without equitable distribution

At independence, both Uganda and Mauritius had the same level of per capita income. Both countries were not endowed with natural resources, such as the mineral wealth of Sierra Leone and Botswana discussed above. What they required was effective economic growth policies, based on a careful and strategic analysis of the available – even if limited – resources. Indeed, Uganda has a greater range of resources to transform its economy, but wasted three decades in civil wars that destroyed the economy and reduced per capita incomes. Uganda's economic policies lacked strategic focus. The country partially emerged from the conflict trap in 1986 and since then has had over twenty years of economic growth at an annual average rate of 6 per cent. Yet, this has not had a noticeable impact on average per capita incomes. There are several important explanatory factors. First, government has had no policies for the equitable distribution of income, resulting in wealth being concentrated in the hands of a small elite or class of millionaires. Second, there has been an absence of policies to control population growth. Uganda has the world's highest population growth of 3.5 per cent. This has had the effect of wiping out gains from economic growth and curtailing the capacity to invest in further growth. The third factor is the absence of genuine popular democracy with a leader (Yoweri Museveni) and his political party (the National Resistance Movement) that has been in power for the last 25 years. Fourth, while the major civil war ended in 1986, minor civil wars have continued in the North (the Lord's Resistance Army), and in the West, (the Allied Defense Forces). This has caused the regime to increase military expenditure, denying the country a peace dividend through increased spending on the social sector.

Events in Uganda are in sharp contrast with what happened in Mauritius. At independence, Mauritius was faced with a situation of limited natural endowments in terms of land and minerals on which to base its growth and development. What the government of Mauritius did was to take whatever limited resources they had and concentrate on a single goal until it was achieved. It then chose another goal and used the same approach. By this approach, Mauritius avoided what most African economies do: pursuing many goals concurrently and thereby spreading limited resources thinly across very ambitious targets with very limited achievement on any of them. It prioritized its needs and postponed many activities until it had the resources to prosecute them. Thus the Mauritius approach to national planning has been characterized by strategic focus and timing. The first focus was training labor for export, and the second was the textile sector – targeting the consumer appetites of the middle and upper classes of Western developed countries. During this period, the economy grew by about 5 per cent each year and per capita increased from US$1,783.83 in 1980 to US$12,017.06 in 2008. Uganda's GDP has been around 6 per cent per annum from 1986 to now. Yet this growth is not reflected in increased per capita average income. The explanation lies in the rate of population growth. Where Mauritius has kept its population has growth at about 1 per cent, Uganda's population growth of 3.5 per cent per annum, has eaten up any economic surplus, and achieved limited positive distributional effects. Mauritius' economic growth rate is an example of a best practice to be emulated by the other African countries.

Conclusion

Comprehending and controlling African conflicts is a work in progress

In honor of Adedeji's contribution to the understanding and control of African conflicts, the current generation of African scholars should revisit his edited work (Adedeji, 1999). While the book built a strong foundation, the agenda, proposed frameworks, and methodology remain a work in progress. It becomes necessary, therefore, to replicate similar studies, taking the same country cases and adding a few more, based on recent developments in the study of African conflicts. This revised study could be guided by Adedeji and the African Centre for Development and Strategic Studies (ACDESS).

Positive consequences of resolution of African conflicts

Some African countries have emerged out of the trap of recurrent conflicts and have had two decades of sustained growth and development. Ready examples include Ghana, Rwanda, Uganda, and South Africa. Liberia and Sierra Leone are following the good examples set by these countries. The lessons of the recent post-election violence in Kenya and Zimbabwe is the need to plan and practice peaceful and democratic leadership succession using the Adedeji framework which requires comprehensive understanding and mastery of the root causes of these conflicts.

The role of conflict activation and deactivation

There can be peaceful coexistence between and among groups and communities that have differences such as religion, ethnicity, race and class as long as these identities are not politically mobilized for inter-group and inter-community antagonisms. Groups, communities, leaders and followers should be made aware of the dangers of such mobilization. Government should put in place deactivation policies and measures to counteract conflict activation. While freedom of expression should be promoted, incitement to hatred must be discouraged and prevented.

The ten root causes of conflict in Africa

Focusing on one root of conflict is likely to be inadequate. In most conflict situations, several factors are in operation. They are often a recurrence of past unresolved conflicts. We should not be fooled by socio-economic homogeneity, where the population of a country is almost 100 per cent one religious or ethnic group. The conflicts will occur at lower levels of such homogeneity. The combination of causes will vary from country to country: in Somalia, it is a combination of unresolved militarized elite competition, extremist Islamic fundamentalism, collapse of the state into mini-states based on six clans, and disputes on intra- and inter-state boundaries; in Nigeria, it is extremist religious groups, regionalism, and the struggles centered on the sharing of oil resources in the Niger Delta, reinforced by ethnicity; in Uganda and Ethiopia the conflicts are driven by one elite alleged to have overstayed in power by allegation of electoral malpractices and post-election violence; in Kenya and Zimbabwe , it is ethnic-driven elite competition, spilling over into activated and militarized followers at the community level and post-election violence fueled by alleged rigging of general elections.

Designing and implementing enduring post-conflict peaceful governance frameworks

The ten roots of conflict outlined in this chapter can be summarized under one overarching cause of conflict and that is misrule arising out of monopoly of political power (undemocratic governance). It is, therefore, vital that the design of post-conflict governance must focus on the promotion of multiparty democracy, adoption of two five-year term limits for the president, enthronement of a system of transparent and democratic elections that guarantee a peaceful succession of leaders and regimes, and the building of a common and integrated national identity that stamps out tribalism and other forms of extremist ideologies.

It is appropriate and fitting to end this chapter with the following quotation from Adedeji (1999: 17)

> In other words, our search for the comprehension and mastery of African conflicts must encompass a serious effort to postulate a framework of an African model of peacemaking and peace-building that will, inter alia, put together a post-conflict governance system that will ensure that peace prevails and becomes sustainable; a governance system that will draw its inspiration from Africa's ancient values of solidarity, cooperative spirit, self-help, development and humanism.

References

Adedeji, A (ed.).1999. *Comprehending and Mastering African Conflicts*. London: Zed Books.
Collier P, Elliott VL, Hegre H, Hoeffler A, Reynal-Queral M and Sambanis N. 2003. *Breaking the Conflict Trap: Civil War and Development Policy*. Washington, D.C: IMF and World Bank.
International Action Network on Small Arms (IANSA). 2007. *Africa's Missing Billions: International Arms Flows and the Cost of Conflict*. London: Oxfam, Saferworld, IANSA.
Katorobo J. 2009. Harnessing the local governance and development processes for peace building conflict and post-conflict countries in Africa. Unpublished research paper commissioned by UNDESA.
Schattschneider, EE. 1975. *The Semi-Sovereign People: A Realist's View of Democracy in America*, New York: Harcourt Brace College Publisher.

CONTRIBUTORS

Adekeye Adebajo has been Executive Director of the Centre for Conflict Resolution, Cape Town, South Africa, since 2003. He is the author of *Building Peace in West Africa; Liberia's Civil War* and *The Curse of Berlin: Africa after the Cold War*.

Oluyele Akinkugbe is Dean, Faculty of Economics and Management Sciences, University of Namibia, Windhoek.

Ali Abdel Gadir Ali is the Deputy Director-General of the Arab Planning Institute (API), based in Kuwait.

Ademola Ariyo, is a Professor of Economics at the University of Ibadan, Nigeria and is also the Director, Centre for Public-Private Cooperation, Ibadan.

Francis Chigunta is a lecturer in the Department of Development Studies at the University of Zambia.

Babajide Fowowe is a lecturer in the Department of Economics, University of Ibadan, Nigeria.

James Katorobo is a retired Professor of Political Science and Public Administration. He taught in several African universities, including Makerere (Uganda), Botswana, and Lesotho.

Afeikhena Jerome is National Coordinator for the State Peer Review Mechanism anchored at the Secretariat of the Nigeria Governors' Forum (NGF), Abuja, Nigeria.

Richard Jolly is Honorary Professor and Research Associate of the Institute of Development Studies at the University of Sussex. He co-directed the United Nations Intellectual History Project, the final volume of which was published as *UN Ideas Which Changed the World*.

Ejeviome Eloho Otobo is Director and Deputy Head of the Peacebuilding Support Office at the United Nations headquarters in New York.

Hesphina Rukato is founding director of the Centre for African Development Solutions, a non-governmental organization working on sustainable development in Africa. She is the author of *Future Africa: Prospects for Democracy and Development under NEPAD* (Africa World Press, 2010).

Amos Claudius Sawyer is Head, Governance Reform Commission of Liberia., He served as interim President of Liberia from 1990 to 1994 and until recently a research scholar and Coordinator of the Workshop in Political Theory and Policy Analysis, Indiana University, Bloomington, United States of America.

Yousif A. Suliman is Director of the Regional Cooperation and Integration Division, United Nations Economic Commission for Africa.

INDEX

A

Accelerated Development in sub-Saharan Africa
An Agenda for Action · 4, 13, 169

Adedeji, Adebayo · xi, xv, xvi, xvii, 1, 2, 3, 4, 5, 6, 7, 8, 9, 10, 12, 17, 18, 19, 20, 21, 22, 24, 27, 29, 31, 32, 33, 35, 37, 43, 48, 50, 54, 69, 70, 71, 72, 73, 77, 81, 82, 83, 84, 85, 86, 87, 88, 89, 90, 92, 93, 95, 96, 97, 98, 111, 117, 140, 160, 168, 171, 172, 175,179, 183, 184, 185, 191, 192, 193, 198, 204, 205, 206

adjustment · xvi, 2, 4, 8, 18, 19, 20, 21, 22, 23, 24, 26, 31, 32, 33, 34, 35, 38, 39, 48, 54, 55, 56, 57, 60, 72, 83, 91, 93, 94, 95, 105, 112, 127, 154, 168, 169, 170, 171, 172, 173, 176, 177

Adjustment with a Human Face · 95, 111

Africa wealth cheque report · 121, 136

Africa's development agenda · 11

Africa-Investor · 121, 136

African Alternative Framework to Structural Adjustment Programme (AAF-SAP) · xvi

African Alternative Framework to Structural Adjustment Programmes for Socio-Economic Recovery and Transformation (AAF-SAP) · 4, 7, 13, 31, 52, 74, 93, 112, 186

African Capacity Building Foundation · 152, 157

African Capitalists · 120

African Challengers · 120, 134, 137

African Charter for popular participation in development and transformation · 5

African Common Market · 87, 99

African Economic Community · xiii, 87, 96, 98, 105, 147, 150, 153, 157

African Heads of State · 94, 168, 169
African Lions · 120, 134
African Peer Review Mechanism (APRM) · xiii, 5, 84, 85, 89, 120, 182
African Regime types
Afro-Marxists · 120
African Union · x, xiii, xv, 11, 29, 77, 84, 86, 87, 89, 90, 98, 99, 120, 123, 140, 144, 147, 154, 157, 158, 163, 165, 174, 175, 184
African-American Institute · 5
Africa's Priority Program for Economic Recovery · 171
Africa's Regional Economic Communities · 87, 157
Aid
humanitarian · 127, 134, 181
technical · 3, 34, 41, 47, 95, 105, 109, 124, 125, 126, 127, 132, 135, 140, 148, 153, 174
Algeria · 120, 133, 173
Allied Defense Forces · 203
Angola · 12, 17, 133, 164, 192, 201
Annan, Kofi · 122
anti-colonial struggles · 1
Anyaoku, Emeka · 124, 125, 137
APRM Review Panel · 5
Arab Maghreb Union · 147, 148
Arab-OPEC meeting · 19
Arthur Houghton Star Crystal Award · 5
Arusha, Tanzania · 5, 95, 186
AU commissions · 144, 146

B

Berg Report · 19, 20, 22, 26, 30, 169, 170
Berg, Elliot · 19, 20, 22, 26, 30, 31, 169, 170
Boston Consulting Group · 120, 134, 135, 137
Botswana · 40, 42, 120, 133, 162, 202, 203, 207
Bottom Billion · 122, 137
Bretton Woods · 2, 3, 4, 7, 8, 17, 18, 22, 25, 53, 54, 55, 56, 66, 67, 68, 69, 70, 71, 72, 73, 74, 83, 87, 93, 95, 170, 181
Bretton Woods Institutions · 3, 5, 9, 54, 67, 68, 70, 72, 73
BRICS · 182
British Commonwealth · 2
Burkina Faso · 42, 58, 59, 118, 142, 164

C

Cameroon · 59, 118
capital accumulation · 30, 71
Central African Economic and Monetary Community · 147
Central African Republic · 42, 123, 142
Charter of the United Nations · 143, 144
circle of poverty · 30, 31, 107
Civil conflicts · 120
civil wars · 1, 9, 79, 123, 193, 196, 199, 200, 201, 202, 203
Cline-Cole · 12, 83, 88, 90, 172, 175, 185

Cold War · 70, 89, 143, 207
Collier, Paul · 112, 122, 123, 137, 198, 201, 202, 206
colonialism in Africa · 143
Commissariat du Plan · 79
Common Market for Eastern and Southern Africa (COMESA) · xiii, 3, 9, 147, 149, 150
Community of Sahel-Saharan States · xiii, 147
Comprehensive Development Framework (CDF) · xiii, 37, 50
Conable, Barber · 4, 21
Council for the Development of Social Science Research in Africa (CODESRIA) · xiii, 29, 33
Coup d'états · 123
credit squeeze · 31

D

Deaton, Angus · 176
debt relief · 37, 127, 161, 172
de-industrialization · 1
democracies · 36, 49
democratic governance · 5, 122, 124, 179, 199, 202
democratisation · 48
Department for International Department · 123
development assistance · 11, 119, 127, 162, 163, 170, 182
Development Assistance Committee · 19
dismal economic performance · 1, 2, 118, 127
diversification · ix, 7, 10, 19, 57, 132, 133, 168, 174, 183
Dominant economic order · 129

dynamics of conflict · 12

E

East African Community · xiii, 147, 152
Economic Commission for Africa · xiv, 1, 4, 5, 17, 27, 29, 53, 83, 84, 86, 89, 92, 112, 117, 144, 147, 158, 168, 186, 208
Economic Community of Central African States (ECCAS) · xiii, xvi, 3, 9, 83, 97, 148, 149, 152
Economic Community of Great Lakes Countries · 147
Economic Community of West African States (ECOWAS) · xiii, xvi, 2, 82, 97, 147, 150, 158
economic crisis · 1, 20, 137, 159, 165, 183, 185
economic paradigm · 11, 12, 176
Economic Report on Africa 2002 · 121
Egypt · 78, 120, 131, 133, 183
Emmerji, Louis · 5, 12
Era
  Agricultural Age · 130
Ethiopia · 42, 52, 164, 175, 205
European Centre for Development Policy Management · 146, 158
European Coal and Steel Community (ECSC) · xiii, 79
European Economic Community · 3, 19, 79, 80
Eurozone · 159
Executive Secretary · xvi, 2, 3, 7, 17, 29, 92, 96

F

financial sector reforms · 34
Financial Times · 1, 118, 127, 135, 137, 138
First World War · 78
fiscal and external balances · 32, 56

G

Global Monitoring Report · 163, 187
Gordon Draper Award · 5
Gowon, Yakubu · 82, 88
Guinea · 123, 164
Guinea-Bissau · 123

H

Harvard University · 2, 176, 185
High Authority of the European Coal and Steel Community (ECSC) · 3
Horn of Africa · 118, 192
Hutu paramilitary organization · 200

I

Ijebu-Ode · 2, 81, 85
import substitution · 30, 169
Indian Ocean Commission · xiii, 147
industrialisation · 30, 33, 34, 36
industrialization experience · 34
Institute of Administration · 2, 82

institution building · 11, 97, 140, 155
Inter-Allied Maritime Commission · 78
Inter-Governmental Authority on Development · 147, 152
International Action Network on Small Arms · 193, 206
International Conference on Popular Participation in the Recovery and Transformation Process in Africa · 5
International Development Goals · 41
International Gold Mercury Award · 5
International Labor Organization (ILO) · 5
International Monetary Fund · xiii, 2, 18, 27, 37, 46, 48, 50, 51, 65, 74, 83, 84, 86, 170, 171, 172

J

Japan International Cooperation Agency · 146
Jaycox, Edward · 21
Jolly, Richard · 5, 7, 17, 207

K

Kaunda, Kenneth · 88
Kenya · 42, 58, 59, 73, 84, 133, 185, 193, 197, 198, 199, 204, 205

L

Lagos Plan of Action (LPA) · xiii, xvi, 3, 4, 7, 12, 19, 27, 29, 50, 71, 73, 84, 94, 96, 112, 140, 142, 144, 158, 168, 174, 185
Lagos Plan of Action for the Economic Development of Africa · 3, 7, 12, 19, 27, 112, 158, 168, 185
League of Nations · 78, 80
Lewis, Arthur · 20, 23, 26, 27, 30, 51, 69
Liberation Committee · 143
Libya · 120, 133
Lin, Justin Y. · 40, 176
Lome Declaration on Framework for Response to Unconstitutional Changes of Government · 123
London Independence Conference · 198
Lord's Resistance Army · 200, 203

M

Madagascar · 42, 123, 142
Malawi · 8, 42, 47, 48, 50, 58, 59, 186
Mali · 42, 59, 123, 142, 164
Mano River Union · xiv, 147
Mauritania · 42, 123, 142
Mauritius · 120, 133, 166, 203
McKinsey Global Institute · 120, 128, 134, 135, 137
Millennium Development Goals (MDGs) · xiii, 11, 41, 119, 141, 158, 160, 184
Minister of Economic Planning · 9
Ministry of Finance and Economic Planning · 171
Monnet, Jean · 3, 9, 77, 78, 79, 80, 81, 85, 88, 90
Monrovia Strategy for the Economic, Social and Cultural Development of Africa · 3
Morocco · 120, 133
Mozambique · xvii, 17, 42, 164
Museveni, Yoweri · 203

N

Namibia · 17, 42, 207
National Resistance Movement · 203
New International Economic Order (NIEO) · xiv, 7, 18, 19
New Partnership for Africa's Development (NEPAD) · xiv, 84, 143, 173
Niger · 42, 118, 123, 142, 164, 201, 205
Nigeria · 2, 9, 12, 42, 59, 73, 77, 82, 86, 87, 88, 89, 94, 96, 133, 142, 155, 164, 168, 173, 201, 205, 207
Nigerian Civil War · 9, 77
North, Douglas · 139

O

Ogun State · 2
Okonjo-Iweala, Ngozi · 128, 137
Onimode, Bade · 83, 90, 172, 185
Organization for Economic Cooperation and Development · 41, 124, 138

213

Organization internationale de la Francophonie · 2
Organization of African Unity · xiv, xv, 3, 4, 12, 27, 29, 83, 84, 94, 98, 112, 123, 140, 142, 158, 168, 169, 171, 185
Organization of Economic Cooperation and Development · 65
Organization of Petroleum Exporting Countries (OPEC) · xiv, 18
organizational deficit · 10, 121, 125, 126, 128

P

Pan-African · 33, 83, 142
Peace and Security Council · 87
Popular Socialists · 120
Poverty Reduction Strategy Paper (PRSP) · 37
Prebisch, Raul · 4

R

Regional Development Banks · 25
Regional Economic Communities · xiv, 9, 10, 11, 87, 97, 99, 112, 141, 144, 147
Romer, Paul · 128, 138

S

Sao Tome and Principe · 123
Second World War · 9, 77, 78, 159
Seers, Dudley · 94, 112

Senegal · 33, 42, 59, 88, 118, 142, 173
Simon, David · 6, 12, 90, 185
Smith, Adam · 124
South Africa · 2, 18, 42, 85, 86, 89, 120, 131, 132, 133, 134, 136, 161, 162, 166, 173, 182, 185, 201, 204, 207
Southern Africa Development Community · 147
Southern African Customs Union · xiv, 147
state-dominated model · 128
state-owned enterprises · 31, 55, 128
Structural Adjustment Program (SAP) · 53
Sub-Saharan Africa – From Crisis to Economic Growth A Long-Term Perspective Study · 7
Sub-Saharan Transport Policy Program · 103

T

The African Charter for Popular Participation in Development and Transformation · 95
The Economist · 1, 164
The Growth Report Strategies for Sustainable Growth and Inclusive Development · 39
The Power of UN Ideas Lessons from the First 60 Years (2005) · 5, 12
The Society of Cognac Vine-growers · 78

INDEX

The Wealth of Nations. · 124
Third Africa Development Forum · 97
Tunisia · 120, 133
Turkey · 67, 74, 182
Two Scenarios for Africa's Development
   optimistic (willed future) · 10, 81, 117
Two Scenarios for Africa's Development
   pessimistic (horrendous) · 10, 117, 118

U

UN Program of Action for African Economic Recovery and Development (UNPAAERD). · 20
UNICEF · 5, 17, 20, 22, 111
United Nations Children's Fund · 20, 95
United Nations Conference on Trade and Development (UNCTAD) · 133, 182, 186
United Nations Development Program · 20, 65, 66, 74, 176, 192
United Nations Economic Commission for Latin America and Caribbean · 4
United Nations General Assembly · 56, 141, 158
United Nations Industrial Development Organization (UNIDO) · 168
United Nations Program of Action for African Economic Recovery and Development (UNPAAERD) · xiv, 56
United States · 5, 17, 78, 80, 88, 146, 159, 161, 208
United States Agency for International Development · 146
Universal Declaration of Human Rights · 143, 144
University College, Leicester · 2
University of Ife (now Obafemi Awolowo University) · 2
University of Johannesburg · 2
University of London · 2
Uwazurike, Chudi · 130, 138

W

wa Mutharika, Bingu · 47, 50
Walter Hallstein · 80
Washington Consensus · 3, 11, 18, 20, 22, 170, 176, 177, 186
Weiss, Tomas · 5, 12, 25, 27
West African Economic and Monetary Union · xiv, 147
Wolfensohn, James · 37
World Bank · 2, 3, 4, 7, 8, 13, 18, 19, 20, 21, 22, 23, 24, 25, 26, 27, 30, 31, 37, 38, 39, 40, 41, 42, 43, 44, 45, 46, 47, 48, 50, 51, 52, 59, 60, 61, 63, 65, 69, 74, 83, 84, 86, 103, 104, 146, 160, 162, 163, 164, 165, 169, 170, 171, 172, 173, 176, 185, 186, 187, 206

Y

Yar'Adua, Umaru · 86
Young, Crawford · 120

Z

Zimbabwe · 17, 42, 84, 193, 199, 204, 205

051114-200-1-60W